EDUCATION IN A COMPETITIVE AND GLOBALIZING WORLD

TEACHER QUALITY AND STUDENT ACHIEVEMENT

EDUCATION IN A COMPETITIVE AND GLOBALIZING WORLD

Additional books in this series can be found on Nova's website under the Series tab.

Additional E-books in this series can be found on Nova's website under the E-book tab.

EDUCATION IN A COMPETITIVE AND GLOBALIZING WORLD

TEACHER QUALITY AND STUDENT ACHIEVEMENT

KATHERINE E. WESTLEY
EDITOR

Nova Science Publishers, Inc.
New York

Copyright © 2010 by Nova Science Publishers, Inc.

All rights reserved. No part of this book may be reproduced, stored in a retrieval system or transmitted in any form or by any means: electronic, electrostatic, magnetic, tape, mechanical photocopying, recording or otherwise without the written permission of the Publisher.

For permission to use material from this book please contact us:
Telephone 631-231-7269; Fax 631-231-8175
Web Site: http://www.novapublishers.com

NOTICE TO THE READER

The Publisher has taken reasonable care in the preparation of this book, but makes no expressed or implied warranty of any kind and assumes no responsibility for any errors or omissions. No liability is assumed for incidental or consequential damages in connection with or arising out of information contained in this book. The Publisher shall not be liable for any special, consequential, or exemplary damages resulting, in whole or in part, from the readers' use of, or reliance upon, this material. Any parts of this book based on government reports are so indicated and copyright is claimed for those parts to the extent applicable to compilations of such works.

Independent verification should be sought for any data, advice or recommendations contained in this book. In addition, no responsibility is assumed by the publisher for any injury and/or damage to persons or property arising from any methods, products, instructions, ideas or otherwise contained in this publication.

This publication is designed to provide accurate and authoritative information with regard to the subject matter covered herein. It is sold with the clear understanding that the Publisher is not engaged in rendering legal or any other professional services. If legal or any other expert assistance is required, the services of a competent person should be sought. FROM A DECLARATION OF PARTICIPANTS JOINTLY ADOPTED BY A COMMITTEE OF THE AMERICAN BAR ASSOCIATION AND A COMMITTEE OF PUBLISHERS.

LIBRARY OF CONGRESS CATALOGING-IN-PUBLICATION DATA

Teacher quality and student achievement / editor, Katherine E. Westley.
   p. cm.
 Includes index.
 ISBN 978-1-61728-274-4 (hardcover)
 1. Effective teaching. 2. School improvement programs. 3. Learning,
Psychology of. 4. Educational innovations. I. Westley, Katherine E.
 LB2822.8.T44 2010
 379.1'58--dc22
                        2010016729

Published by Nova Science Publishers, Inc. ✚ New York

CONTENTS

Preface		**vii**
Chapter 1	Assessment in Elementary and Secondary Education: A Primer *Erin D. Caffrey*	**1**
Chapter 2	A Highly Qualified Teacher in Every Classroom: Implementation of the No Child Left Behind Act and Reauthorization Issues for the 111th Congress *Jeffrey J. Juenzi*	**43**
Chapter 3	Value-Added Modeling for Teacher Effectiveness *Erin D. Caffrey and Jeffrey J. Kuenzi*	**57**
Chapter 4	Teacher Quality: Sustained Coordination among Key Federal Education Programs Could Enhance State Efforts to Improve Teacher Quality *United States Government Accountability Office*	**77**
Chapter 5	Student Achievement: Schools Use Multiple Strategies to Help Students Meet Academic Standards, Especially Schools with High Proportions of Low-Income and Minority Students *United States Government Accountability Office*	**135**
Chapter 6	Statement of Chairman Ruben Hinojosa, Chairman of the House Subcommittee on Higher Education, Lifelong Learning and Competitiveness – "Preparing Teachers for the Classroom: The Role of the Higher Education Act and No Child Left Behind" *Ruben Hinojosa*	**163**
Chapter 7	Teacher Quality: Approaches, Implementation, and Evaluation of Key Federal Efforts *George A. Scott*	**165**

Chapter 8	Testimony of Sharon P. Robinson, EdD., President and CEO, before the Subcommittee on Higher Education, Lifelong Learning, and Competitiveness, "Preparing Teachers for the Classroom: The Role of the High Education Act and the No Child Left Behind Act" *Sharon P. Robinson*	**177**
Chapter 9	Testimony of Janice Wiley, Deputy Director for Instructional Support Services of the Region One Education Service Center, before the Subcommittee on Higher Education, Lifelong Learning, and Competitiveness – "Preparing Teachers for the Classroom: The Role of the Higher Education Act and No Child Left Behind Act" *Janice Wiley*	**183**
Chapter 10	Testimony of Daniel Fallon, Director, Program in Higher Education, Carnegie Corporation of New York, before the Subcommittee on Higher Education, Lifelong Learning and Competitiveness – "Preparing Teachers for the Classroom: The Role of the Higher Education Act and No Child Left Behind" *Daniel Fallon*	**187**
Chapter 11	Testimony of Emily Feistritzer, President, National Center for Alternative Certification and the National Center for Education Information, before the Subcommittee on Higher Education, Lifelong Learning and Competitiveness – "Preparing Teachers for the Classroom: The Role of the Higher Education Act and No Child Left Behind" *Emily Feistritzer*	**193**
Chapter Sources		**203**
Index		**205**

PREFACE

One of the major goals of the No Child Left Behind Act of 2001 is to raise the achievement of students who currently fail to meet grade-level proficiency standards. Since student achievement is believed by many to depend in large part on effective teaching, the law also contains provisions designed to improve teacher quality. These provisions establish minimum teacher quality requirements and charge states and school districts with developing plans to meet them. This book examines implementation of the NCLB requirements and estimates the extent to which schools achieved the law's goal of placing a highly qualified teacher in every classroom.

Chapter 1 - In recent years, federal education legislation has placed an increased emphasis on assessment in schools. Perhaps most notably, Title I-A of the Elementary and Secondary Education Act (ESEA), as reauthorized by the No Child Left Behind Act (NCLB), requires states to test all students annually in grades 3 through 8 and once in high school in the areas of reading, mathematics, and science. These assessments are used as key indicators in an accountability system that determines whether schools are making progress with respect to student achievement. To receive Title I funding, states must also participate in the National Assessment of Educational Progress (NAEP), a standards-based national test given at grades 4 and 8. The Individuals with Disabilities Education Act (IDEA) requires states to use assessments to identify students with disabilities and track their progress according to individualized learning goals. In addition to assessments required by federal law, elementary and secondary school students generally participate in many other assessments, which range from small-scale classroom assessments to high-stakes exit exams.

This chapter provides a framework for understanding various types of assessments that are administered in elementary and secondary schools. It broadly discusses various purposes of educational assessment and describes comprehensive assessment systems. Common assessment measures currently used in education are described, including state assessments, NAEP, and state exit exams. The chapter also provides a description and analysis of technical considerations in assessments, including validity, reliability, and fairness, and discusses how to use these technical considerations to draw appropriate conclusions based on assessment results. Additionally, innovation in assessment is discussed, including the development and use of alternate assessments and performance assessments. Finally, this chapter provides a brief analysis of the use of assessments in accountability systems, including implications for curriculum, students, and testing.

Chapter 2 - One of the major goals of the No Child Left Behind Act of 2001 (NCLB) is to raise the achievement of students who currently fail to meet grade-level proficiency standards. Since student achievement is believed by many to depend in large part on effective teaching, the law also contains provisions designed to improve teacher quality. These provisions establish minimum teacher quality requirements and charge states and school districts with developing plans to meet them. These plans were to ensure that all schools had a *highly qualified teacher* in every classroom by the end of the 2005-2006 school year.

To be deemed *highly qualified*, NCLB requires that teachers possess a baccalaureate degree and a state teaching certificate, and that teachers also demonstrate subject-matter knowledge for their teaching level. Elementary school teachers must show knowledge of basic elementary school curricular areas. Middle and secondary school teachers must demonstrate a high level of competency in all subject areas taught. Demonstration of subject-matter knowledge and competency may be shown by passing a state certification exam or licensing test in the relevant subject(s).

This chapter examines implementation of the NCLB requirement and estimates the extent to which schools achieved the law's goal of placing a highly qualified teacher in every classroom. After describing the highly qualified teacher requirement in detail, the report analyzes data from a national survey of schools that provide information on teacher qualifications during the 1999- 2000 school year. These data suggest that more than four out of five teachers would have met the NCLB definition of a highly qualified teacher prior to the date of enactment. Monitoring data released by the Education Department indicate that the proportion of highly qualified teachers may have gone up slightly by the end of the 200 5-2006 school year, but that no state reached the 100% goal.

In addition to the findings of this analysis, knowledge gained through NCLB's implementation has important implications for future policy-making in the area of teacher quality. This chapter concludes with a discussion of issues that may be considered as the Elementary and Secondary Education Act reauthorization process unfolds. The teacher quality provisions, along with the rest of the Elementary and Secondary Education Act, will likely be considered for reauthorization by the 111th Congress.

Chapter 3 - Two of the major goals of the Elementary and Secondary Education Act (ESEA), as amended by the No Child Left Behind Act of 2001 (P.L. 107-110; NCLB), are to improve the quality of K- 12 teaching and raise the academic achievement of students who fail to meet grade-level proficiency standards. In setting these goals, Congress recognized that reaching the second goal depends greatly on meeting the first; that is, quality teaching is critical to student success. Thus, NCLB established new standards for teacher qualifications and required that all courses in "core academic subjects" be taught by a *highly qualified teacher* by the end of the 2005-2006 school year.

During implementation, the NCLB highly qualified teacher requirement came to be seen as setting minimum qualifications for entry into the profession and was criticized by some for establishing standards so low that nearly every teacher met the requirement. Meanwhile, policy makers have grown increasingly interested in the output of teachers' work; that is, their performance in the classroom and the effectiveness of their instruction. Attempts to improve teacher performance led to federal and state efforts to incentivize improved performance through alternative compensation systems. For example, through P.L. 109-149, Congress authorized the Federal Teacher Incentive Fund (TIF) program, which provides grants to support teacher performance pay efforts. In addition, there are various programs at all levels (national, state, and local) aimed at reforming teacher compensation systems. The most recent congressional action in this area came with the passage of the American Recovery and Reinvestment Act of 2009 (ARRA, P.L. 111-5) and, in particular, enactment of the Race to the Top (RTTT) program.

The U.S. Department of Education (ED) recently released a final rule of priorities, requirements, definitions, and selection criteria for the RTTT. The final rule established a definition of an *effective teacher* as one "whose students achieve acceptable rates (e.g., at least one grade level in an academic year) of student growth (as defined in this notice)." That is, to be considered effective, teachers must raise their students' learning to a level at or above what is expected within a typical school year. States, LEAs, and schools must include additional measures to evaluate teachers; however, these evaluations must be based, "in significant part, [on] student growth."

This chapter addresses issues associated with the evaluation of teacher effectiveness based on student growth in achievement. It focuses specifically on a method of evaluation referred to as *value-added modeling* (VAM). Although there are other methods for assessing teacher effectiveness, in the last decade, VAM has garnered increasing attention in education research and policy due to its promise as a more objective method of evaluation. The first section of this report describes what constitutes a VAM approach and how it estimates the so-called "teacher effect." The second section identifies the components necessary to conduct VAM in education settings. Third, the report discusses current applications of VAM at the state and school district levels and what the research on these applications says about this method of evaluation. The fourth section of the report explains some of the implications these applications have for large-scale implementation of VAM. Finally, the report describes some of the federal policy options that might arise as Congress considers legislative action around these or related issues.

Chapter 4 - Policymakers and researchers have focused on improving the quality of our nation's 3 million teachers to raise the achievement of students in key academic areas, such as reading and mathematics. Given the importance of teacher quality to student achievement and the key role federal and state governments play in supporting teacher quality, GAO's objectives included examining (1) the extent that the U.S. Department of Education (Education) funds and coordinates teacher quality programs, (2) studies that Education conducts on teacher quality and how it provides and coordinates research-related assistance to states and school districts, and (3) challenges to collaboration within states and how Education helps address those challenges. GAO interviewed experts and Education officials, administered surveys to officials at state educational agencies and state agencies for higher education in the fall of 2008, and conducted site visits to three states.

Chapter 5 - The federal government has invested billions of dollars to improve student academic performance, and many schools, teachers, and researchers are trying to determine the most effective instructional practices with which to accomplish this. The Conference Report for the Consolidated Appropriations Act for Fiscal Year 2008 directed GAO to study strategies used to prepare students to meet state academic achievement standards. To do this, GAO answered: (1) What types of instructional practices are schools and teachers most frequently using to help students achieve state academic standards, and do those instructional practices differ by school characteristics? (2) What is known about how standards-based accountability systems have affected instructional practices? (3) What is known about instructional practices that are effective in improving student achievement? GAO analyzed data from a 2006-2007 national survey of principals and 2005-2006 survey of teachers in three states, conducted a literature review of the impact of standards based accountability systems on instructional practices and of practices that are effective in improving student achievement, and interviewed experts.

Chapter 6 features testimony before the U. S. House of Representatives.

Chapter 7 - Teachers are the single largest resource in our nation's elementary and secondary education system. However, according to recent research, many teachers lack competency in the subjects they teach. In addition, research shows that most teacher training programs leave new teachers feeling unprepared for the classroom.

While the hiring and training of teachers is primarily the responsibility of state and local governments and institutions of higher education, the federal investment in enhancing teacher quality is substantial and growing. In 1998, the Congress amended the Higher Education Act (HEA) to enhance the quality of teaching in the classroom and in 2001 the Congress passed the No Child Left Behind Act (NCLBA), which established federal requirements that all teachers of core academic subjects be highly qualified.

This testimony focuses on (1) approaches used in teacher quality programs under HEA and NCLBA, (2) the allowable activities under these acts and how recipients are using the funds, and (3) how Education supports and evaluates these activities.

Chapters 8, 9, 10 and 11 feature testimony before the U. S. House of Representatives.

In: Teacher Quality and Student Achievement
Editor: Katherine E. Westley

ISBN: 978-1-61728-274-4
© 2010 Nova Science Publishers, Inc.

Chapter 1

ASSESSMENT IN ELEMENTARY AND SECONDARY EDUCATION: A PRIMER*

Erin D. Caffrey

SUMMARY

In recent years, federal education legislation has placed an increased emphasis on assessment in schools. Perhaps most notably, Title I-A of the Elementary and Secondary Education Act (ESEA), as reauthorized by the No Child Left Behind Act (NCLB), requires states to test all students annually in grades 3 through 8 and once in high school in the areas of reading, mathematics, and science. These assessments are used as key indicators in an accountability system that determines whether schools are making progress with respect to student achievement. To receive Title I funding, states must also participate in the National Assessment of Educational Progress (NAEP), a standards-based national test given at grades 4 and 8. The Individuals with Disabilities Education Act (IDEA) requires states to use assessments to identify students with disabilities and track their progress according to individualized learning goals. In addition to assessments required by federal law, elementary and secondary school students generally participate in many other assessments, which range from small-scale classroom assessments to high-stakes exit exams.

This report provides a framework for understanding various types of assessments that are administered in elementary and secondary schools. It broadly discusses various purposes of educational assessment and describes comprehensive assessment systems. Common assessment measures currently used in education are described, including state assessments, NAEP, and state exit exams. The report also provides a description and analysis of technical considerations in assessments, including validity, reliability, and fairness, and discusses how to use these technical considerations to draw appropriate conclusions based on assessment results. Additionally, innovation in assessment is discussed, including the development and

---

* This is an edited, reformatted and augmented version of a CRS Report for Congress publication dated January 2010.

use of alternate assessments and performance assessments. Finally, this report provides a brief analysis of the use of assessments in accountability systems, including implications for curriculum, students, and testing.

OVERVIEW

In recent years, federal education legislation has placed an increased emphasis on assessment in schools. Perhaps most notably, Title I-A of the Elementary and Secondary Education Act (ESEA), as reauthorized by the No Child Left Behind Act (NCLB), requires states to test all students annually in grades 3 through 8 and once in high school in the areas of reading, mathematics, and science. These assessments are used as key indicators in an accountability system that determines whether schools are making progress with respect to student achievement. To receive Title I funding, states must also participate in the National Assessment of Educational Progress (NAEP), a standards-based national test given at grades 4 and 8. The Individuals with Disabilities Education Act (IDEA) requires states to use assessments to identify students with disabilities and track their progress according to individualized learning goals. In addition to assessments required by federal law, elementary and secondary school students generally participate in many other assessments, which range from small-scale classroom assessments to high-stakes exit exams.

This report provides a framework for understanding various types of assessments that are administered in elementary and secondary schools. It broadly discusses various purposes of educational assessment and describes comprehensive assessment systems. Common assessment measures currently used in education are described, including state assessments, NAEP, and state exit exams. The report also provides a description and analysis of technical considerations in assessments, including validity, reliability, and fairness, and discusses of how to use these technical considerations to draw appropriate conclusions based on assessment results. Additionally, innovation in assessment is discussed, including the development and use of alternate assessments and performance assessments. Finally, this report provides a brief analysis of the use of assessments in accountability systems, including implications for curriculum, students, and testing.

While this report does not comprehensively examine all of the assessment provisions in federal education laws, it summarizes several of the major provisions and draws on examples from federal laws, such as IDEA and NCLB, to help situate assessment concepts in the context of federal policies.

ASSESSMENT FRAMEWORK

Educational assessment is a complex endeavor involving gathering and analyzing data to support decision-making about students and the evaluation of academic programs and policies. The most common type of assessment used in current education policy is achievement testing. Although educational assessment involves more than achievement testing, this report will use the words "assessment" and "test" interchangeably.

There are many ways to classify assessments in frameworks. The framework offered below is meant to provide a context for the remainder of the report and present an easily accessible vocabulary for discussing assessments. This framework addresses the various purposes of assessment, the concept of comprehensive assessment systems, and the scoring of assessments. After outlining a general assessment framework, this report will discuss current assessments in elementary and secondary schools, technical considerations in assessment, innovation in assessment, and the use of assessments in test-based accountability systems.

A Glossary is provided at the end of this report to provide definitions of common assessment and measurement terms. The Glossary provides additional technical information that may not be addressed within the text of the report. Additionally, an Acronym Reference is provided at the end of this report to provide an easily accessible list of common education and testing acronyms.

Purposes of Educational Assessment

Educational assessment does not take place in a vacuum. Generally, assessments are designed with a specific purpose in mind, and the results should be used for the intended purpose. It is possible that a test was designed for multiple purposes, and results can be interpreted and used in multiple ways. Often, however, test results are used for multiple purposes when the test itself was designed for only one. This "over-purposing" of tests is a major issue in education and can undermine test validity. In the sections below, four general purposes of assessment are discussed: instructional, predictive, diagnostic (identification), and evaluative.

Instructional

Instructional assessments are used to modify and adapt instruction to meet students' needs. These assessments can be informal or formal and usually take place within the context of a classroom. Informal instructional assessments can include teacher questioning strategies or reviewing classroom work. A more formal instructional assessment could be a written pretest in which a teacher uses the results to analyze what the students already know before determining what to teach. Another common type of instructional assessment is progress monitoring.[1] Progress monitoring consists of short assessments throughout an academic unit that can assess whether students are learning the content that is being taught. The results of progress monitoring can help teachers determine if they need to repeat a certain concept, change the pace of their instruction, or comprehensively change their lesson plans.

Predictive

Predictive assessments are used to determine the likelihood that a student or a school will meet a particular predetermined goal. One common type of predictive assessment used by schools and districts is a benchmark assessment, which is designed primarily to determine which students are on-track for meeting end-of-year achievement goals. Students who are not on-track to meet these goals can be offered more intensive instruction or special services to increase the likelihood that they will meet their goal. Similarly, entire schools or districts that are not on-track can undertake larger, programmatic changes to improve the likelihood of achieving the end goal.

Diagnostic (Identification)

Diagnostic assessments are used to determine a student's academic, cognitive, or behavioral strengths and weaknesses. These assessments provide a comprehensive picture of a student's overall functioning and go beyond exclusively focusing on academic achievement. Some diagnostic assessments are used to identify students as being eligible for additional school services like special education services or English language services. Diagnostic assessments to identify students for additional school services can include tests of cognitive functioning, behavior, social competence, language ability, and academic achievement.

Evaluative

Evaluative assessments are used to determine the outcome of a particular curriculum, program, or policy. Results from evaluative assessments are often compared to some sort of predetermined goal or objective. These assessments, unlike instructional, predictive, or diagnostic assessments, are not necessarily designed to provide actionable information on students, schools, or districts. For example, if a teacher gives an evaluative assessment at the end of a particular science unit, the purpose is to determine what the student learned rather than to plan instruction, predict future achievement, or diagnose strengths and weaknesses.

Assessments in accountability systems are conducted for an evaluative purpose. These assessments are administered to determine the outcome of a particular policy objective (e.g., determining a percentage of students who are proficient in reading). For example, currently under NCLB, state assessments are used for evaluative purposes to determine whether schools have made Adequate Yearly Progress (AYP).[2] State assessments will be discussed in more detail throughout this report.

Comprehensive Assessment System: Formative and Summative Assessments

One assessment cannot serve all the purposes discussed above. A comprehensive assessment system is necessary to cover all the purposes of educational assessment. One type of comprehensive assessment system is a combination of formative assessments and summative assessments. Generally speaking, formative assessments are those that are used during the learning process in order to improve curriculum and instruction, and summative assessments are those that are used at the end of the learning process to "sum up" what students have learned. In reality, the line between a formative assessment and a summative assessment is less clear. Depending on how the results of an assessment are used, it is possible that one assessment could be designed to serve both formative and summative functions. The distinction, therefore, between formative and summative assessments often is the manner in which the results are used. If an assessment has been designed so that results can inform future decision making processes in curriculum, instruction, or policy, the assessment is being used in a formative manner (i.e., for instructional, predictive, and diagnostic purposes). If an assessment has been designed to evaluate the effects or the outcome of curriculum, instruction, or policy, the assessment is being used in a summative manner (i.e., for diagnostic or evaluative purposes).

Formative Assessment

Formative assessment has received a lot of attention in recent years. That said, it is reasonably clear that there is not universal agreement over what constitutes a "formative assessment" in the field of education. It seems that teachers, administrators, policymakers, and test publishers use the term "formative assessment" to cover a broad range of assessments, from small-scale classroom assessments that track the learning of individual students to large-scale benchmark assessments that track the progress of a whole school or district to determine if they will meet certain policy goals. The confusion over exactly "What is formative assessment?" has led some in the testing industry to avoid the term altogether[3] and others to offer alternative names for certain types of formative assessment.[4] In this section, various types of assessments that have been described as formative assessments will be discussed, including classroom, interim, and benchmark assessments.

Formative assessments are often used in the classroom. They can be as informal as teacher questioning strategies or as formal as written examinations. Teachers use formative assessments for both instructional and predictive purposes. The results of formative assessment can be used to determine deficits in a student's knowledge and to adjust instruction accordingly. Teachers may adjust their instruction by changing the pace of instruction, changing the method of delivery, or repeating previously taught content. After these adjustments, teachers may administer another assessment to determine if students are learning as expected. The process of administering assessments, providing feedback to the student, adjusting instruction, and re-administering assessments is what makes the assessment "formative."

Black and William[5] conducted an international review of formative assessment practices in the classroom. A subset of this review was a quantitative synthesis of the effects of formative assessment on achievement. The authors report that "typical" effect sizes[6] in these studies range from 0.4 to 0.7, and that these effects are larger than most educational interventions. Moreover, Black and William note that formative assessment may help lower achieving students more than higher achieving students, which, if true, would increase the likelihood of narrowing the achievement gap. The review, however, uses a very broad definition of "formative assessment" and a very wide age range, making it difficult to isolate which methods of formative assessment are effective and for whom.

Perhaps in response to the apparent success of formative assessment at the classroom level, test publishers began promoting commercial formative assessment products in the form of interim assessments and benchmark assessments. Some testing experts believe that referring to interim and benchmark assessments as "formative" is inaccurate, but others believe that these assessments can be used in a formative way to determine how school or district practices need to change in order to meet policy goals. The latter position considers the use of interim or benchmark assessments as formative assessments at the school or district level as opposed to the classroom level. Instead of adjusting teaching practices to increase student learning, this type of formative assessment would require adjusting school or district practices to increase student achievement across the board. Interim and benchmark assessments can track the progress of students, schools, and districts toward meeting predetermined policy goals. For example, schools and districts report using benchmark assessments to determine if they are on-track to meet AYP goals as defined by NCLB.

The term "interim assessment" has been suggested to characterize assessments that fall between those which are purely formative and summative assessments.[7] Under this characterization, interim assessments are assessments used to track student achievement and to inform decisions at the classroom, school, or district level. Interim assessments can report on student achievement at the individual level or in the aggregate. The content and timing of the assessment is usually determined by the school or district, not the teacher, making it a less flexible classroom tool than a teacher-controlled, classroom-level formative assessment. Interim assessments can be used to inform classroom practice, but because teachers have less control over timing and content, the true value of interim assessment may lie at the school or district level. These assessments are usually used for predictive purposes—to determine whether a student, school, or district is likely to succeed on a later summative assessment and to identify those students who may need more intensive instruction. Another use of interim assessment may be to evaluate a short-term instructional program or a small aspect of the overall curriculum.

A benchmark assessment is a type of interim assessment that is widely used in schools and districts. Like other types of interim assessment, benchmark assessments are primarily used to predict the likelihood of success on a later summative assessment and to identify those students who may need more intensive instruction. They are also used to determine whether a student, school, or district is on-track to meet certain policy objectives, such as AYP.

The type of evidence provided by Black and William on the positive effects of teacher-controlled, classroom-level formative assessment is not necessarily relevant to the potential effects of benchmark assessments. Although little research has been conducted to determine the effect of benchmark assessments, the Regional Education Laboratory (REL) Northeast[8] conducted a study to determine whether the use of these assessments increased student achievement after two years of implementation in Massachusetts.[9] The study found no significant differences in mathematics achievement between schools that used benchmark assessments and those that did not. The study, however, had a number of limitations, and it is possible that two years of implementation may not have been long enough to observe an impact.

Summative Assessment

Summative assessments are tests given at the end of a lesson, semester, or school year to determine what has been learned. Summative assessments are used for diagnostic or evaluative purposes. Most test results that are reported by the school or media are based on summative assessments—state assessments, NAEP, international assessments, and state exit exams. Some forms of summative assessment are considered "high-stakes" assessments because they have rewards and consequences attached to performance. For example, some states require students to pass high-stakes high school exit exams or end of course exams in order to graduate. Furthermore, all states have high-stakes assessments used to determine AYP under NCLB. Although in this instance, the assessments have high stakes for schools and school districts, not necessarily for individual students.

Not all summative assessments have high-stakes school or district consequences attached to the results. An end-of-unit mathematics test, for example, is a summative assessment used

Assessment in Elementary and Secondary Education: A Primer

to determine a student's grade, but there are no school- or district-level consequences attached. On a larger scale, NAEP and international assessments are used to get an overall picture of national and international achievement, but, again, there are no major consequences associated with the results.

Relationships between Formative and Summative Assessment

Ideally, formative and summative assessments are administered in a comprehensive assessment system. In order for teachers and school administrators to use formative assessment to increase student achievement and predict outcomes on summative assessments, the two types of assessment must be closely aligned in terms of the test content and goals. One way to measure whether the assessments are in alignment is to determine the ability of a formative assessment to predict achievement on a summative assessment (i.e., determine predictive validity).

The REL Mid-Atlantic conducted an analysis of the predictive validity of benchmark assessments.[10] This analysis looked at the extent to which common, commercially developed benchmark assessments predicted performance on state assessments in Delaware, Maryland, New Jersey, Pennsylvania, and Washington, D.C. A review of four common assessments found that only one of these benchmark assessments showed strong evidence of predictive validity with state assessments. Moreover, none of the benchmark assessments demonstrated evidence of predictive validity for state assessments in Maryland and New Jersey. The ability of benchmark assessments to predict later performance on state assessments, therefore, seems to depend heavily on the benchmark assessment used and the state in which the assessment takes place. If this pattern is indicative of national use of benchmark assessments, there is evidence to suggest that these benchmarks are not serving a formative function within a comprehensive assessment system. Without having a strong predictive relationship between benchmark assessments and state assessments, school and district personnel may be unable to use the information from the benchmark assessment to predict future achievement on summative assessments, such as state assessments used for AYP.

Scores: How are Assessment Results Reported?

Test scores are reported in a variety of ways. Sometimes scores may compare an individual to a group of peers in the form of standard scores or percentiles. Other times, scores may indicate a student is "proficient" or "advanced" in a certain subject. Misinterpreting test scores or misunderstanding the way in which scores are reported can lead to unintended negative consequences, such as making an inappropriate conclusion regarding the effectiveness of a program or policy. The following sections describe common methods of score reporting in educational assessment, including scores from norm-referenced tests (NRTs), scores from criterion-referenced tests (CRTs), performance standards, and professional judgment. A brief discussion of the advantages and disadvantages of each method is provided.

Norm-Referenced Tests

An NRT is a standardized test in which results compare the performance of an individual with the performance of a large group of students. NRTs are sometimes referred to as scores of "relative standing." NRTs compare individual scores to a normative sample, which is a group of students with known demographic characteristics (age, gender, ethnicity, or grade in school). Comparisons are made using two statistical properties of the normative sample: the mean and the standard deviation.[11]

NRTs produce raw scores that are transformed into standard scores using calculations involving the mean and standard deviation. The standard score is used to report how a student performed relative to peers. Standard scores are often reported as percentiles because they are relatively easy for parents and educators to interpret, but there are many other types of standard scores that may be reported (e.g., z-scores, scale scores, or T-scores).

Commercially available cognitive and achievement tests are often norm-referenced. For example, the Stanford Achievement Test Series (SAT 10) is an NRT and was recently used in a national evaluation of the Reading First program.[12] Language proficiency tests used to identify students with Limited English Proficiency (LEP), such as the IPT Family of Tests, are NRTs. Tests to measure cognitive ability of students with disabilities, such as the Wechsler Intelligence Scale for Children (WISC), are also NRTs.

NRTs are particularly useful due to their ease of administration and scoring. Commercially available NRTs usually require no further development or validation procedures, so they are relatively cost-effective and time-efficient. NRTs can be easily administered to large groups of students at the same time and are useful for making comparisons across schools, districts, or states.

On the other hand, NRTs have been criticized for several reasons. Some criticize NRTs for measuring only superficial learning through multiple choice and short-answer formats instead of measuring higher-level skills such as problem solving, reasoning, critical thinking, and comprehension. Others have criticized NRTs for lacking instructional utility because they sample a wide range of general skills within a content area, but NRTs are rarely linked to the curriculum. In addition, results from NRTs can be difficult for educators to interpret because there is no designation of what score denotes mastery or proficiency.

Criterion-Referenced Tests

A CRT compares the performance of an individual to a predetermined standard or criterion. Like NRTs, CRTs are often standardized. They do not, however, report scores of "relative standing" against a normative sample. CRTs report scores of "absolute standing" against a predetermined criterion. CRTs are designed to determine the extent to which a student has mastered specific curriculum and content skills. "Mastery" of curriculum and content skills is usually determined through a collaborative process of professional judgment. Mastery can be defined in many ways. It may be defined as answering 80% of the items on an assessment correctly. Alternatively, it may be defined as meeting some level of proficiency within a content area based on an observation of the student performing the skills.

Unlike NRTs, CRTs are not designed to differentiate between students or compare an individual student to a normative group. Because comparisons are not being made, CRTs report either scale scores or raw scores, depending on how the assessment was designed. CRT results may be reported as grades, pass/fail, number correct, percentage correct, or performance standards. They may be measured through the use of multiple choice formats, short answer, rating scales, checklists, rubrics, or performance-based assessments. CRTs are flexible and can be designed to meet various educational needs.

The major advantage of CRTs is that they are versatile tests that can be used for instructional purposes. They can be directly linked to the curriculum, and the results from CRTs can be used for planning, modifying, and adapting instruction. Additionally, like commercially available NRTs, commercially available CRTs are relatively cost-effective and time-efficient. The disadvantage of CRTs is that they do not typically facilitate good comparisons across schools, districts, and states. When using CRTs, there is no normative sample, therefore, there is no common metric for comparisons. It is possible to design CRTs so that comparisons can be made, however, that would require (a) consistent standards across schools, districts, and states, and (b) consistent definitions of "mastery" across schools, districts, and states.

Performance Standards

Interest in CRTs increased throughout the 1 990s due to the emphasis on standards-based reform in education. Performance standards are a type of score reporting that evolved from CRTs and standards-based reform. A CRT can often report results as either a scale score or a performance standard. A performance standard is an objective definition of a certain level of performance in a content area that is expressed in terms of a cut score. The predetermined cut score denotes a level of mastery or level of proficiency within a content area. An assessment system that uses performance standards typically establishes several cut scores that denote varying levels of proficiency. For example, NAEP uses a system of performance standards with three achievement levels: basic, proficient, and advanced. Additionally, state assessments use performance standards to determine AYP under the NCLB accountability system. Definitions are provided for each performance standard, describing the competencies and abilities associated with the label.

Performance standards have the same advantages of CRTs. Performance standards can be directly linked to the curriculum and results can be used for planning, modifying, and adapting instruction. The main difference between reporting a score as a CRT or a performance standard is the "proficiency label," which can attach meaning to a score and provide an appropriate context. A CRT may report that a student scored 242 on a scale of 500, but the score of 242 may be meaningless to most educators and parents unless there is some context surrounding the score. Performance standards provide the context. If the proficiency cut score was predetermined to be 240, a score of 242 would be above the cut score, and therefore the student would be considered proficient in the content area.

Although they provide a meaningful context for assessment results, performance standards are criticized for their somewhat arbitrary cut scores. Cut scores are usually determined through a process of consensus and professional judgment, but there is rarely any meaningful difference between the abilities of a student who scores just below the cut score and a student who scores just above the cut score. Consider the example above in which a score of 240 denotes "proficiency". One student may score 238 and not be considered proficient, while another student may score 242 and be considered proficient. In reality, the cut score of the performance standard may be making an inappropriate distinction between two students who have similar abilities. Another criticism of performance standards is that they are insensitive to student growth. Suppose the cut score for the "advanced" level is 300.

A student in the previous example could move from a score of 242 to 299 within one year, making considerable progress; however, a score of 242 and a score of 299 are both considered to be within the same performance standard of "proficient."

Professional Judgment

Occasionally, assessment calls for professional judgment. On a daily basis within classrooms, teachers ask questions and make judgments about students' knowledge based on students' responses. In some cases, teachers may use their professional judgment to refer a child for a special education evaluation or a language assessment. Another application of professional judgment may be the use of a rubric to evaluate a student's performance against a predetermined standard. Although scoring rubrics can be quite prescriptive, there are occasionally value-laden decisions that require teachers to make judgments about the degree to which a student met the standard. Professional judgment has the advantage of being directly tied to the curriculum and sensitive to individual student performance, however, it is subjective and susceptible to personal biases.

Another type of professional judgment that is used in educational assessment is a process of professional consensus used to set performance standards. For example, the National Assessment Governing Board (NAGB) is responsible for setting the policy for NAEP. One of the activities of NAGB is to set appropriate student achievement levels (i.e., performance standards) that denote varying levels of proficiency. This process of defining and reviewing performance standards includes the professional judgment of a representative panel of teachers, education specialists, and members of the general public.

CURRENT ASSESSMENTS IN ELEMENTARY AND SECONDARY SCHOOLS

Students in elementary and secondary schools are assessed using a wide range of tests. The following sections describe some of the common types of assessments used in elementary and secondary schools; these assessments are situated within the framework described above. First, assessments that are required by federal law are discussed, followed by a discussion of assessments that are required by state policies, assessments that are administered at the discretion of local districts, and voluntary assessments.

The first three sections provide a discussion of assessments that are required by law: state assessments for AYP, NAEP, and assessments to identify students for special services. In the next section, state exit exams are discussed. These assessments are not required by federal law, but state policies often require that students participate in these assessments as a high school graduation requirement. The next section discusses benchmark assessments, in which local districts often have some control over the administration, scoring, and use of the assessment. The final section provides a discussion of international assessments. These assessments are voluntary assessments in which schools and students are periodically selected at random to participate.

State Assessments for AYP

Since the reauthorization of ESEA by the NCLB, a good deal of focus has been placed on state assessments used to calculate AYP.[13] States that participate in the Title I-A program[14] are required to administer standards-based assessments in reading and mathematics to students in each of grades 3-8, plus at least once in grades 10-12. Beginning with the 2007-2008 school year, states were also required to administer standards-based science assessments at least once in each of three grade level ranges (3-5, 6-9, and 10-12). At least 95% of all students (and at least 95% of students in all demographic subgroups used for AYP reporting) must participate in the state assessment in order for a school or LEA to make AYP.

NCLB allows states to develop individualized state standards and individualized assessments that appropriately measure these standards. Results from the state assessments are used in the determination of AYP within the NCLB accountability system. Although state assessments may be individualized, they are subject to several legislative requirements. NCLB requires that state assessments be used for the purposes for which they are valid and reliable, and they must meet professionally recognized technical standards. Assessments must be aligned with challenging academic content and academic achievement standards. They must produce coherent results that report whether students attained the achievement standards. Achievement standards must include, at a minimum, three levels. In a three-level system, these achievement levels are often referred to as basic, proficient, and advanced. The proficient and advanced levels denote "high achievement" while the basic level denotes a lack of proficiency.

The state educational agency (SEA) must provide evidence to the Secretary that the chosen assessments are consistent with the above requirements, including providing evidence of the technical quality of the instrument. As of January 2009, the U.S. Department of Education (ED) reported that 39 states had received Full Approval or Full Approval with Recommendations on their assessment systems in the areas of reading and mathematics.[15] Only 10 states, however, had received Full Approval or Full Approval with Recommendations for science assessments.[16]

States use both NRTs and CRTs in their state assessment systems. If a state chooses to use an NRT, it must use an "augmented" NRT, which is aligned with state content and performance standards. At the elementary and middle school level, 2 states use NRTs only, 35 states use CRTs only, and 14 states use a combination of NRTs and CRTs. At the high school level, 3 states use NRTs only, 37 states use CRTs only, and 11 states use a combination of NRTs and CRTs. Examples of NRTs used for state assessments include the Iowa Test of Basic Skills (ITBS) and the SAT 10. Examples of CRTs used for state assessments include the Texas Assessment of Knowledge and Skills (TAKS) and the New England Common Assessment Program (NECAP).[17]

The state assessments use a variety of test formats. Of 42 states with reported data, 7 states use multiple choice only, 1 state uses extended response only, and 34 states use a combination of formats. Of the 34 states that use a combination of testing formats, 34 states use multiple choice, 31 states use extended response, 24 states use short answer, and 4 states use fill-in-the blank.

State assessments are summative assessments used for evaluative purposes. Results from the augmented NRTs and CRTs are reported as the percentage of students reaching a performance standard (e.g., basic, proficient, advanced). Schools are held accountable for the percentage of students scoring "proficient" or above. The goal of NCLB is to achieve 100% proficiency by the end of school year 2013-2014.

The percentage of proficient students cannot be compared across states. Because each state had the discretion to develop its own assessment and choose its own cut scores denoting proficiency, there is no common measure of proficiency. If a State A chose a low cut score to denote proficiency and State B chose a high cut score to denote proficiency, State A may have a higher percentage of students reaching proficiency than State B. It would not be appropriate to conclude, however, that State A had higher student achievement levels overall.

National Assessment of Educational Progress

The NAEP is a series of assessments that have been administered since 1969. NAEP tests are administered to students in grades 4, 8, and 12, and they cover a variety of content areas, including reading, mathematics, science, writing, and, less frequently, geography, history, civics, social studies, and the arts. NAEP policies are established by NAGB, which is responsible for selecting the areas to be assessed, designing the assessment methodology, and developing guidelines for reporting and disseminating results. NAGB is an independent, bipartisan group of governors, state legislators, local and state school officials, educators, business representatives, and members of the general public. NAEP is administered uniformly to students within states (and some large urban districts) and serves as a common metric for understanding student achievement across the nation. NAEP is administered and scored by ED with assistance from contractors.[18]

There are several types of NAEP assessments. The NAEP *national assessment* began in 1969 and tests students in grades 4, 8, and 12 in all nine content areas (reading, mathematics, science, writing, geography, history, civics, social studies, and the arts); however, each subject is not assessed during every administration.[19] The NAEP *state assessment* began in 1990. The state assessment is administered every other year to students in grades 4 and 8 in the areas of reading and mathematics. States that receive Title I-A funding under NCLB are required to participate in these assessments. The NAEP *long-term trend* (LTT) assessments are given every four years and track the trends in reading and mathematics achievement since the 1970s. It is administered to a nationally representative sample of students ages 9, 13, and 17. The LTT differs from other NAEP assessments in that it has used identical questions since its original administration. The consistency of the questions allow for tracking overall national progress over time.

NAEP is a summative assessment used for evaluative purposes. NAEP is a CRT and, like state assessments, the results are reported as the percentage of students reaching a performance standard (e.g., basic, proficient, advanced). Unlike state assessments, however, the performance standards of basic, proficient, and advanced are consistent, which allows comparisons to be made across states. NAEP does not report results for individual students because no student is administered the entire NAEP assessment. Students who are selected to participate take only a sample of the possible items. The scores from all students are aggregated to produce results for groups and subgroups. NAEP reports achievement results for groups of students by grade and content area (e.g., grade 4 reading and grade 8 reading) and by subgroup (e.g., gender, ethnic minorities, students with disabilities).

It is important to note that the meaning of "proficiency" is not consistent across state assessments and NAEP. For any given state, the percentage of students who are proficient in reading on the state assessment and the percentage of students who are proficient in reading on NAEP can vary greatly. As discussed earlier, states had the discretion to design their own assessments and choose their own cut scores to denote proficiency. State assessments were not based on NAEP assessment frameworks and states did not choose cut scores consistent with NAEP. It is possible, however, to compare NAEP scores across states. For example, it is valid to compare the percentage of proficient students on a NAEP 4th grade reading assessment in State A to the percentage of proficient students on a NAEP 4th grade reading assessment in State B.

Assessments to Identify Students for Special Services

Schools are required by law to provide special services to eligible students with disabilities and LEP students. To receive special services through the schools, a student must be found "eligible" for services based on a battery of assessments. For eligible students with disabilities, IDEA requires that students receive special education and related services. For eligible LEP students, ESEA requires that students receive supplemental English language instruction. IDEA and ESEA provide general guidelines to determine a student's eligibility for services, but states and districts have some flexibility in the use and interpretation of assessments for eligibility determinations.

Students with Disabilities
IDEA defines a student with a disability as a student, "with mental retardation, hearing impairments (including deafness), speech or language impairments, visual impairments (including blindness), serious emotional disturbance (referred to in this title as 'emotional disturbance'), orthopedic impairments, autism, traumatic brain injury, other health impairments, or specific learning disabilities."[20] The law does not, however, provide educational definitions of these disability categories. Each state is required to develop its own educational definition of these disability categories outlined by IDEA. Because the definitions of these disability categories vary across states, the assessments used to identify a student with a disability is specific to the state and the suspected disability.

Although the actual assessments can vary across states, IDEA specifies several requirements for special education evaluations.[21] In conducting an evaluation, a local educational agency (LEA) must use a variety of assessment tools and strategies to gather relevant functional, developmental, and academic information, including information provided by the parent. The decision of which assessments to use depends on the disability in question and the domain to be assessed (i.e., functional, developmental, or academic). Most students with disabilities are assessed on a variety of skills and competencies outside of traditional academic assessments. For example, it is common in the assessment of students with disabilities to measure skills such as basic language, behavior and social competency, cognitive functioning, and motor skills. LEAs are responsible for interpreting the scores of these assessments and determining a student's eligibility for services based on state definitions of disability.

LEP Students

ESEA defines an LEP student as a student whose native language is a language other than English and whose difficulties in speaking, reading, writing, or understanding the English language may inhibit the individual from meeting proficient levels of achievement, succeeding in the classroom, or participating fully in society.[22] The law does not provide national eligibility criteria for LEP students. Based on the federal definition, each state determines their own eligibility criteria for LEP students to receive supplemental English language instruction.

Because the eligibility criteria vary across states, the assessments used to identify a student as an LEP student also varies across states. In general, there are two major components: a home language survey and an English language assessment. LEAs are responsible for interpreting the responses on the home language survey and interpreting scores on the English language assessment to determine LEP eligibility based on state criteria. In addition to this initial assessment, Title I-A of NCLB requires that LEP students be assessed annually in English language skills (i.e., reading, writing, speaking, and listening).

Summary

Assessments used to identify students for special services can be used as either formative or summative assessments, depending on their purpose and administration. Regardless of whether the assessment is formative or summative, these assessments are used for diagnostic purposes in order to determine a comprehensive profile of strengths and weaknesses for individual students. These assessments are a mixture of NRTs and CRTs, depending on the needs of the student and the eligibility criteria of the state.

State Exit Exams

Though not required by federal law, an increasing number of states require students to pass exit exams to graduate from high school. A state "exit exam" typically refers to one or more tests in different subject areas, such as language arts, mathematics, science, and social studies. These tests can usually be taken more than once throughout high school. Currently, 23 states require students to pass exit exams to receive a high school diploma, and 3 additional states plan to implement state exit exams by 2012. The exit exam requirement affects 68% of high school students today and will, according to projections, affect 74% of high school students by 2012.[23]

Exit exams can take several forms, including minimum competency exams, comprehensive exams, end-of-course exams, or some combination of the three. A minimum competency exam focuses on basic skills below the high school level. Comprehensive exams are aligned with state standards and typically assess 9th or 10th grade knowledge in several subject areas. End-of-course exams assess knowledge related to specific high school courses, such as Algebra I or U.S. History. In general, there has been a movement away from minimum competency exams toward comprehensive exams and end-of-course exams. Among the 23 states that currently use state exit exams, only 1 state uses minimum competency exams, 12 states use comprehensive exams, 5 states use end-of-course exams, and 5 states use a combination of comprehensive and end-of course exams. Although comprehensive exams are still the most commonly used type of state exit exam, states are moving toward using more end-of-course exams.

Very few studies of the impact of state exit exams on student achievement have been conducted. A recent national study examined the relationship between high school exit exams and achievement in reading and mathematics as measured by NAEP.[24] The results of this study indicate that high school exit exams do not lead to increases in reading and mathematics achievement and may reduce graduation rates. Furthermore, authors of this study reported that students who receive a diploma in states with required exit exams are not more successful in the labor market than students who receive diplomas in states that do not require exit exams. Other state-level studies have reported similar findings. Several reports on California's exit exam found that the exit exam may increase dropout rates and decrease enrollment in postsecondary education.[25]

State exit exams are summative assessments used for evaluative purposes. These assessments have high stakes for individual students, but there are no school- or district-level consequences associated with the results. Most exit exams are CRTs, aligned with state standards and specific curricula. Because exit exams can be taken more than one time, it is possible that they serve as a formative assessment for instructional purposes, as well. Performance on the first exit exam could serve to modify or adapt instruction in a formative way. States' use of exit exams as a formative assessment, however, has not been studied.

Benchmark Assessments

Benchmark assessments are mid-year assessments in core content areas that are usually administered to determine whether a school is on-track to meet its end-of-year goals. They are used at the discretion of school administrators and the particular type of benchmark assessment is chosen at the local level. Since NCLB increased the consequences associated with performance on state assessments, there has been more demand for commercially developed benchmark assessments that are aligned with state content standards and assessments. Typically, SEAs or LEAs hire the original test publisher or an independent contractor to conduct alignment studies between benchmark assessments and state content standards. Examples of commercially developed benchmark assessments include 4Sight Math and Reading, STAR Math and Reading, Study Island Math and Reading, and TerraNova Math and Reading.

Benchmark assessments are usually considered formative assessments and occasionally referred to as "interim assessments."[26] Most benchmark assessments report scores as performance standards. They can be used for instructional purposes if teachers use the results to identify deficits in students' knowledge and modify their instruction accordingly. Benchmark assessments are also used for predictive purposes, and well-designed benchmark assessments are closely aligned with a state assessment so that schools can predict the likelihood of making AYP.[27]

International Assessments

International assessments allow educators, administrators, and policymakers to get a sense of how students in the United States perform relative to other countries. Since the mid-1990s, students in the United States have participated in several international assessments, including the Program for International Student Assessment (PISA), the Progress in International Reading Literacy Study (PIRLS), and the Trends in International Mathematics and Science Study (TIMSS). Participation in international assessments is voluntary and the countries that choose to participate can vary from one administration to the next. Generally, a representative sample of schools and a representative sample of students within schools are selected to participate in international assessments.

The primary purpose of PISA is to report on broad subject-area "literacy" that is not directly tied to a particular curriculum or content framework. PISA assesses 15-year-olds' performance in reading literacy, mathematics literacy, and science literacy. The first administration of PISA was in 2000; it is administered every three years. During the 2006 administration, 57 countries participated in the assessment, including 30 countries within the Organization for Economic Cooperation and Development (OECD) and 27 countries outside of the OECD. PISA reports results in terms of "national averages" of students' scores; it does not report results for individual students.[28]

PIRLS is an assessment of reading achievement, behavior, and attitudes of 4th grade students in the United States and students who are in the equivalent of 4th grade in other countries. It was first administered in 2001 to students in 35 countries and most recently administered in 2006 to students in 40 countries. PIRLS reports results in two ways. First, it reports national averages, which allow countries to be compared to each other. Second, PIRLS reports the percentage of students in each country that reach international benchmarks.[29] Like PISA, PIRLS does not report results for individual students.[30]

TIMSS is an assessment of science and mathematics achievement of students in grades 4 and 8 in the United States and equivalent grades in other countries. It has been administered every four years since 1995. In 2007, 36 countries participated at grade 4 and 48 countries participated at grade 8. Like the other international assessments, TIMSS reports national averages which allow countries to be compared to each other, but it does not report results for individual students.[31] Several states have started using TIMSS results in international benchmarking studies. Within the context of these studies, some states can compare student performance within their state to other countries that participated in TIMSS.[32]

The aforementioned international assessments are summative assessments used for evaluative purposes. Usually, international assessment results are reported as a simple rank ordering of countries taking the assessment. Results describe which countries scored above the "international mean" and which scored below the mean. Because the "international mean" is highly variable depending on the countries that participate from administration to administration, it is quite possible that any particular country can score above the mean on one administration and below the mean on the next administration. Furthermore, this shift can happen even when students in that country make large gains in achievement.

TECHNICAL CONSIDERATIONS IN ASSESSMENT

This section will discuss technical considerations in assessment, such as validity, reliability, and fairness. It is generally the responsibility of the test developer to investigate technical characteristics of an assessment and to report any relevant statistical information to test users. Usually, this information is reported in testing manuals that accompany the assessment. It is the responsibility of the test user to administer the test as intended and to use the reported information concerning validity, reliability, and fairness to interpret test results appropriately.

Learning how to evaluate the validity, reliability, and fairness of an assessment allows test users to make appropriate inferences. An inference is a conclusion that is drawn from the result of a test. Inferences may be either appropriate or inappropriate based on a number of technical and contextual factors. This section will conclude with a discussion on how to avoid making inappropriate inferences from educational assessments. It will also highlight some of the issues to consider when making inferences from high-stakes assessments vs. low-stakes assessments.

Validity

Validity is arguably the most important concept to understand when evaluating educational assessments. When making instructional or policy decisions on the basis of an assessment, the question is often asked, "Is the test valid?" Validity, however, is not a property of the test itself. Validity is the degree to which a certain inference from a test is appropriate and meaningful.[33] The question to be asked, therefore, is "Is the inference being drawn from the test result valid?" The distinction between these questions may seem unimportant, but consider the following example. Often times, teachers, administrators, or policymakers would like to support multiple conclusions from the same assessment. Some of these conclusions, or inferences, may be valid and others may not. Consider the SAT Reasoning Test, which is taken by many high school students. The SAT is a college entrance examination, and its purpose is to measure critical thinking skills that are needed for success in college. Suppose a group of high school seniors in School A scored well on the SAT and a group of high school seniors in School B scored poorly. One possible valid inference from this result is that seniors from School A are more likely to succeed in college. There are, however, many possible inferences that may be less valid. For example, one could infer that School A had a better academic curriculum than School B. Or, one could infer that School A had better teachers than School B. Neither of these inferences may be valid because the SAT was designed for the purpose of predicting the likelihood of success in college and not for the purposes of evaluating teachers or curriculum. The validity of an inference, therefore, is tied inextricably to the purpose for which the test was created.

When an assessment is created or when a new use is proposed for an existing assessment, a process of validation should occur. Validation involves collecting evidence to support the use and interpretation of test scores based on the test construct. In testing, a construct is the concept or characteristic that a test is designed to measure. The process of validation includes, at a minimum, investigating the construct underrepresentation and construct irrelevance of the assessment instrument. Construct underrepresentation refers to the degree to which an assessment fails to capture important aspects of the construct. For example, if the assessment is designed to measure addition and subtraction skills, the entire construct would include addition, addition with carrying, subtraction, subtraction with borrowing, two-digit addition, two-digit addition with carrying, and so forth. If the assessment does not measure all the skills within a defined construct, it may be susceptible to construct underrepresentation, and the inference based on an assessment score may not reflect the student's actual knowledge of the construct. Similarly, construct irrelevance can threaten the validity of an inference. Construct irrelevance refers to the degree to which test scores are affected by the content of an assessment that is not part of the intended construct. Again, if an assessment was designed to measure addition and subtraction skills, any test items that contain multiplication or division would create construct irrelevance, and the inference based on the assessment score may not reflect the student's actual knowledge of the construct.

Construct underrepresentation is investigated by answering the question, "Does the assessment adequately cover the full range of skills in the construct?" Construct irrelevance is investigated by answering the question, "Are any skills within the assessment outside of the realm of the construct?" These two questions are investigated using statistical procedures that examine properties of the assessment itself and how the properties of the assessment interact with characteristics of individuals taking the test. One important consideration is to determine if the degree of construct underrepresentation or construct irrelevance differentially affects the performance of various subgroups of the population. If, for example, there was a moderate degree of construct irrelevance (e.g., multiplication questions on an assessment designed to measure addition and subtraction skills), students from advantaged subgroups may be more likely to score well on a test than students from disadvantaged subgroups, even if both subgroups have equal knowledge of the construct itself. The construct irrelevance, therefore, may lead to an invalid inference that advantaged students outperform disadvantaged students in a given construct (in this example, addition and subtraction skills).

There are many other types of evidence that may be collected during validation. For example, test developers might compare student scores on the assessment in question with existing measures of the same construct. Or, test developers might investigate how well the assessment in question predicts a later outcome of interest, such as pass rates on a high-stakes exam, high school graduation rates, or job attainment. Validation is not a set of scripted procedures but rather a thoughtful investigation of the construct and proposed uses of assessments.

Reliability

Reliability refers to the consistency of measurement when the testing procedure is repeated on a population of individuals or groups. It describes the precision with which assessment results are reported and is a measure of certainty that the results are accurate. The concept of reliability presumes that each student has a true score for any given assessment. The true score is the hypothetical average score resulting from multiple administrations of an assessment; it is the true representation of what the student knows and can do. For any given assessment, however, the score that is reported is not a student's true score, it is a student's observed score. The hypothetical difference between the true score and the observed score is measurement error. Reliability and measurement error are inversely related. The lower the measurement error, the higher the reliability. Furthermore, as reliability increases, it increases the likelihood that a student's observed score and a student's true score are reasonably equivalent.

Reliability can be reported in multiple ways. The most common expressions of reliability in educational assessment are the reliability coefficient, range of uncertainty, and consistency of classification.

Reliability Coefficient

The reliability coefficient is a number that ranges from 0 to 1. It is useful because it is independent of the scale of the assessment and can be compared across multiple assessments. A reliability coefficient of 0 implies that a score is due completely to measurement error; a reliability coefficient of 1 implies that a score is completely consistent and free of measurement error. There is no rule of thumb for deciding how high a reliability coefficient should be; however, most commercially available assessments report reliability coefficients above 0.8, and many have reliability coefficients above 0.9.

The most common types of reliability coefficients used in educational assessment are alternate- form coefficients, test-retest coefficients, inter-scorer agreement coefficients, and internal consistency coefficients. Alternate-form coefficients measure the degree to which the scores derived from alternate forms of the same assessment are consistent. For example, the SAT, which is used as a college entrance examination, has multiple forms that are administered each year. A high alternate-form reliability coefficient provides some certainty that a student's score on one form of the SAT would be reasonably equivalent to the student's score on another form of the SAT. Test-retest coefficients measure the stability of an individual student's score over time. If the NAEP reading subtest was administered to a student today and re-administered in two weeks, one would expect that the student would have comparable scores across the two administrations. A high test-retest reliability coefficient provides a measure of certainty that a student's score today is similar to the student's score in the near future. Inter-scorer agreement coefficients measure the degree to which two independent scorers agree when assessing a student's performance. A high inter-scorer agreement coefficient provides a measure of certainty that a student's score would not be greatly affected by the individual scoring the assessment.

Internal consistency coefficients are slightly more complicated. Internal consistency coefficients are a measure of the correlation of items within the same assessment. If items within an assessment are related, a student should perform consistently well or consistently poorly on the related items. For example, a mathematics assessment may test multiplication and division skills. Suppose a student is proficient with multiplication but has not yet mastered division. Within the mathematics assessment, the student should score consistently well on the multiplication items and consistently poorly on the division items. A high internal consistency coefficient provides a measure of certainty that related items within the assessment are in fact measuring the same construct.

The decisions regarding the type of reliability coefficients to investigate and report depend on the purpose and format of the assessment. For example, many assessments do not use alternate forms, and there would be no need to report an alternate-form coefficient. As another example, consider a test that was designed to measure student growth over a short period of time. In this case, it may not make sense to report a test-retest reliability coefficient because one does not expect any stability or consistency in the student's score over time. Test developers also consider the format of the test. In tests with multiple-choice or fill-in-the-blank formats, inter-scorer agreement may not be of great concern because the scoring is relatively objective; however, in tests with constructed responses, such as essay tests or performance assessments, it may be important to investigate inter-scorer agreement because the scoring has an element of subjectivity.

Range of Uncertainty—Confidence Intervals

As stated above, reliability describes the precision with which assessment results are reported and is a measure of certainty that the results are accurate. Often times, results can be reported with greater confidence if the observed score is reported along with a range of uncertainty. In educational assessment, the range of uncertainty is usually referred to as a confidence interval. Under the NCLB accountability system, some states use confidence intervals to report the results of state assessments. A confidence interval estimates the likelihood that a student's true score falls within a range of scores. The size of the confidence interval, or the size of the range, depends on how certain one needs to be that the true score falls within the range of uncertainty.

A confidence interval is calculated by using an estimated true score, the standard error of measurement (SEM)[34], and the desired level of confidence. The confidence interval is reported as a range of scores with a lower limit and an upper limit. In education, it is common to see 90%, 95%, or 99% confidence intervals. The following hypothetical example illustrates how the size of the confidence interval (i.e., the range of scores) can change as the degree of confidence changes.

If the estimated true score of a student is assumed to be 100 and the SEM is assumed to be 10:

- A 90% confidence interval would be 84 to 116 (a range of 32). In this case, about 90% of the time, a student's true score will be contained within the interval from 84 to 116. There is about a 5% chance that the student's true score is lower than 84 and about a 5% chance that the student's true score is higher than 116.
- A 95% confidence interval would be 80 to 120 (a range of 40). In this case, about 95% of the time, the student's true score will be contained within the interval from 80 to 120. There is about a 2.5% chance that the student's true score is lower than 80 and about a 2.5% chance that the student's true score is higher than 120.
- A 99% confidence interval would be 74 to 126 (a range of 52). In this case, about 99% of the time, the student's true score will be contained within the interval from 74 to 126. There is about a 0.5% chance that the student's true score is lower than 74 and about a 0.5% chance that a student's true score is higher than 126.

The illustration above demonstrates that the range of scores in a confidence interval increases as the desired level of confidence increases. A 90% confidence interval ranges from 84 to 116 (a range of 32) and a 99% confidence interval ranges from 74 to 126 (a range of 52).

Consistency of Classification

Consistency of classification is a type of reliability that is rarely reported but can be very important to investigate, especially when high-stakes decisions are made with the results of educational assessments. When assessments are used to place students and schools into discrete categories based on performance (e.g., proficient vs. not proficient or pass vs. fail), the consistency of classification is of interest.

Within school settings, consistency of classification is particularly important when using performance standards to place students in achievement levels based on state assessments (i.e., basic, proficient, advanced). If the classification of students into achievement levels for AYP purposes is not consistent over short periods of time, the accountability system may become highly variable and unreliable. Another example of the importance of consistency of classification is the use of state exit exams to award high school diplomas (i.e., pass/fail). Without consistency in classification, the system that awards diplomas to high school seniors may be unreliable. Consistency of classification has not been well studied in these instances, but statistical modeling demonstrates that it is possible to have considerable fluctuations in classification depending on the reliability of the assessment and the predetermined cut score used to categorize students.[35]

Consistency of classification is also relevant for decisions that determine eligibility for services, such as the classification of students with disabilities. Students who are suspected to have a disability are assessed using a wide-range of diagnostic assessments. Results of these assessments are interpreted based on state definitions of "disability" and, if students are determined to be eligible, they receive special education services. Some research has begun to investigate the consistency of states' "disability" classifications over time. In the Office of Special Education Program's most recent annual report to Congress, it was reported that approximately 17% of elementary students who received special education services in the year 2000 no longer received such services in 2002.[36] Similar results have been reported for students with disabilities in preschool.[37] While it is possible that students become "declassified" and ineligible for special education services due to their improvement in academic skills, it is likely that the rate of "declassification" is also affected by the reliability of assessments used to determine their initial eligibility and the cut scores that are used in state definitions of disability.[38]

Fairness

Fairness is a term that has no technical meaning in testing procedures, but it is an issue that often arises in educational assessment and education policy, generally. Educational assessments are administered to diverse populations, and all members of the population should be treated equally. The notion of fairness as "equal treatment", however, has taken several forms: (1) fairness as a lack of bias, (2) fairness as equitable treatment in the testing process, (3) fairness as equality in outcomes of testing, and (4) fairness as opportunity to learn.[39]

Fairness as a Lack of Bias

Bias is a common criticism in educational assessment, however, it is not well documented or well understood. Test bias exists if there are systematic differences in observed scores based on subgroup membership when there is no difference in the true scores between subgroups. For example, bias can arise when cultural or linguistic factors influence test scores of individuals within a subgroup, despite the individual's inherent ability. Or, bias can arise when a disability precludes a student from demonstrating his or her ability. Bias is a controversial topic and difficult to address in educational assessment. There is no professional consensus on how to mitigate bias in testing. There are statistical procedures, such as differential item functioning, that may be able to detect bias in specific test items, however, such techniques cannot directly address the bias in the interpretation of assessment results. Test bias, if present, undermines the validity of the inferences based on assessment results.

It is important to note that a simple difference in scores between two subgroups does not necessarily imply bias. If a group of advantaged students performs higher on a reading assessment than a group of disadvantaged students, the test may or may not be biased. If the advantaged students and the disadvantaged students have the same reading ability (true score), and the advantaged students still score higher on the reading assessment (observed score), bias may be present. If, however, the advantaged students have higher reading ability and higher scores on the reading assessment, the test may not be biased.

Fairness as Equitable Treatment in the Testing Process

Fairness as equitable treatment in the testing process is less controversial and more straightforward than the issue of bias. There is professional consensus that all students should be afforded equity in the testing process. Equity includes assuring that all students are given a comparable opportunity to demonstrate their knowledge of the construct being tested. It also requires that all students are given appropriate testing conditions, such as a comfortable testing environment, equal time to respond, and, where appropriate, accommodations for students with disabilities and LEP students.

Finally, equitable treatment affords each student equal opportunity to prepare for a test. This aspect of equitable treatment may be the most difficult to monitor and enforce. In some schools or districts, it is common practice to familiarize students with sample test questions or provide examples of actual test questions from previous assessments. In other districts, this type of test preparation may not be routine. Furthermore, some students receive test preparation services outside of the classroom from private companies, such as Kaplan, Inc. or Sylvan Learning. The amount of test preparation and the appropriateness of this preparation is not consistent across classrooms, schools, and districts and can undermine the validity of inferences drawn from assessments.

Fairness as Equality in Outcomes of Testing

There is no professional consensus that fairness should ensure equality in the outcomes of testing. On the other hand, when results are used for high-stakes decisions, such as the use of state exit exams for high school graduation, the issue of "equality in outcomes" can arise. The question of fairness arises when these tests are used to exclude a subgroup of students from certain privileges, like earning a high school diploma. For example, if a subgroup of advantaged students is more likely to pass a state exit exam than a subgroup of disadvantaged students, the advantaged students are more likely to graduate from high school, receive a diploma, pursue higher education, and obtain a job. The disadvantaged students are less likely to graduate from high school, which further disadvantages them in their pursuit of higher education or job attainment. "Equality in outcomes" is more likely to be a concern with high-stakes assessments, such as state assessments and state exit exams, than with low-stakes assessments, such as NAEP and international assessments.

Fairness as Opportunity to Learn

Fairness as opportunity to learn is particularly relevant to educational assessment. Many educational assessments, particularly state assessments used to determine AYP, are aligned with school curriculum and designed to measure what students know as a result of formal instruction. All students within a state are assessed against the same content and performance standards for AYP. If all students have not had an equal opportunity to learn, is it "fair" to assess all students against the same standard? If low scores are the result of a lack of opportunity to learn the tested material, it might be seen as a systemic failure rather than a characteristic of a particular individual, school, or district.

The difficulty with affording all students equal opportunity to learn is defining "opportunity to learn." Is exposure to the same curriculum enough to give students the opportunity to learn? Even if all students are exposed to the same curriculum, does the overall school environment influence a student's opportunity to learn? If students are exposed to the same curriculum within the same school environment, does the quality of the classroom teacher influence a student's opportunity to learn?

Using Assessment Results: Avoiding Inappropriate Inferences

Test users have a responsibility to examine the validity, reliability, and fairness of an assessment to make appropriate inferences about student achievement. Unfortunately, there is no simple checklist that will help determine if an inference is appropriate. Instead, test users must conduct a thoughtful analysis of the construct of the assessment, purpose of the assessment, the type of scores reported by the assessment, the evidence concerning the validity, reliability, and fairness of the assessment, and the context in which the assessment results will be used. If these issues are not carefully considered, inappropriate inferences can lead to a variety of unintended consequences.

The sections that follow provide some guidance in the form of sample questions that test users may wish to ask themselves before making an inference about a test score. These guidelines are not intended to be an exhaustive list of considerations but rather a starting point for learning to draw appropriate conclusions from assessments.

Construct

Questions about the construct: What is the content area being assessed (e.g., reading, mathematics)? What is the specific construct that is being measured within the content area (e.g., mathematics computation, mathematical problem solving, measurement, geometry)? Does the construct measure general knowledge within a content area, or is it specifically aligned with the curriculum?

Understanding the construct of an assessment can have important implications when comparing the results of two tests. Consider, for example, the international assessments described above, PISA and TIMSS. Both assessments measure mathematics achievement, but they measure different mathematical constructs. PISA was designed to measure basic "mathematical literacy" whereas TIMSS is curriculum-based and was designed to measure what students have learned in school. Results from the 2006 PISA administration reported that the average U.S. score in mathematics was lower than international average. Results from the 2007 administration of the TIMSS reported that the average U.S. score in mathematics was higher than the international average. Based on these results, a novice test user may be tempted to conclude that within one year, students in the U.S. improved in mathematics achievement compared to other countries. There are several reasons why this conclusion is inappropriate, one of which is that PISA and TIMSS measure very different constructs.[40]

Purpose

Questions about the purpose: What was the intended purpose of the assessment when it was designed (e.g., instructional, predictive, diagnostic, evaluative)? How will teachers, administrators, and policymakers use the results (e.g., formative assessment vs. summative assessment)?

Understanding the original purpose of the assessment will help test users determine how the results may be interpreted and how the scores may be used. For example, a state assessment that was designed for evaluative purposes may not lend itself to using scores to modify and adapt instruction for individual students. Most state assessments are strictly summative assessments, and it is difficult to use them in a formative manner because the results may not be reported in a timely fashion to the teachers and the items may not be sensitive to classroom instruction. Alternatively, a benchmark assessment that was designed for predictive purposes may report results in a more timely manner and allow teachers to target their instruction to students who scored poorly. Benchmark assessments are often aligned with state assessments, however, scores on benchmark assessments should not be considered definitive indicators of what state assessment scores will be.

Scores

Questions about scores: Does the score reported compare a student's performance to the performance of others (e.g., NRT)? Does the score reported compare a student's performance to a criterion or standard (e.g., CRT, performance standard)? Does the score determine whether a student is proficient within a certain content area (e.g., performance standards)? Does the score show growth or progress that a student made within a content area?

Misinterpreting scores is perhaps the most common way to make an inappropriate inference. To avoid an inappropriate inference, a test user should fully investigate the scale of the assessment and the way in which scores are reported. If scores are reported from NRTs, a student's score can be interpreted relative to the normative sample, which is a group of the student's peers. NRTs cannot, however, determine whether a student met a predetermined criterion or whether a student is proficient within a particular content area. If scores are reported from CRTs, either in the form of criterion-referenced scores or performance standards, a student's score can be interpreted relative to a predetermined standard or criterion. CRTs and performance standards, however, were not designed to make particularly meaningful comparisons between students who participated in the same assessment.

Because of the use of performance standards in state assessments, it is particularly important for test users to understand what they do and do not report. Performance standards are used primarily because they can be easily aligned with the state content standards and provide both a score and some meaningful description of what students know. Performance standards, however, can be particularly difficult to interpret. Students are classified into categories, such as basic, proficient, or advanced, based on their performance on an assessment. All students within the "proficient" category, however, did not score equally well. Furthermore, scores from performance standards do not lend themselves to interpret a student's growth. A student can score at the lower end of the proficient category, make considerable progress over the next year, and still be in the proficient category at the end of the year. Alternatively, a student could score at the high end of the basic category, make minimal progress over the next year, and move up into the proficient category. Because of these qualities of performance standards, test users should be very cautious equating the performance of students within the same category and making assumptions about growth based on movement through the categories.

Technical Quality

Questions about technical quality: Did the test developers provide statistical information on the validity and reliability of the instrument? Was the issue of fairness and bias addressed, either through thoughtful reasoning or statistical procedures? What kind of validity and reliability evidence was collected? Does that evidence seem to match the purpose of the assessment? Have the test developers reported reliability evidence separately for all the subgroups of interest?

Commercially available assessments are accompanied by a user's manual that reports validity and reliability evidence. Smaller, locally developed assessments do not always have an accompanying manual, but test developers should have validity and reliability evidence available upon request. It is a fairly simple process to determine whether evidence has been provided but a much more difficult task to evaluate the quality of the evidence. A thorough discussion of how to evaluate the technical quality of an assessment is beyond the scope of this report.[41] In light of the current uses of assessments in schools, however, some issues are noteworthy.

First, because schools are required to report state assessment results for various subgroups (i.e., students with disabilities and LEP students), it is important that validity and reliability be investigated for each subgroup for which data will be disaggregated. Doing so will reduce the likelihood of bias in the assessment against a particular subgroup.

Second, the type of reliability evidence provided should be specific to the assessment. For example, an assessment with constructed responses, such as essay tests or performance assessments, will have a degree of subjectivity in scoring. In this case, it is important to have strong evidence of inter-scorer reliability. In other cases when the assessment format consists of multiple choice or fill-in-the-blank items, inter-scorer reliability may be of lesser importance.

A test like the SAT Reasoning Test which relies on several alternate forms should report alternate- form reliability. Without a high degree of alternate-form reliability, some students will take an easier version of an assessment and others will take a more difficult version.

Unequal forms of the same assessment will introduce bias in the testing process. Students taking the easier version may have scores that are positively biased and students taking the harder version may have scores that are negatively biased.

Third, no assessment is technically perfect. All inferences based on an observed score will be susceptible to measurement error, and some may be susceptible to bias.

Context of the Assessment

Questions about the context: Is this a high-stakes or a low-stakes assessment? Who will be held accountable (e.g., students, teachers, schools, states)? Is the validity and reliability evidence strong enough to make high-stakes decisions? Are there confounding factors that may have influenced performance on the assessment? What other information could be collected to make a better inference?

The context in which an assessment takes place may have implications for how critical a test user must be about making an inference from a test score. In a low-stakes assessment, such as a classroom-level formative assessment that will be used for instructional purposes, conducting an exhaustive review of the reliability and validity evidence may not be a worthwhile endeavor. These assessments are usually short, conducted to help teachers adapt their instruction, and have no consequences if the inference is not completely accurate. On the other hand, for a high-stakes assessment, like a state exit exam for graduation, it is important to examine the validity and reliability evidence of the assessment to ensure that the inference is defensible. Consider the consequences of a state exit exam with poor evidence of validity due to a high degree of construct irrelevance. Students would be tested on content outside of the construct and may perform poorly, which may prevent them from earning a high school diploma. Or, consider a state exit exam with poor evidence of reliability due to a high degree of measurement error. Students who are likely to score near the cut score of the assessment may pass or fail largely due to measurement error.

Sometimes when making an inference for a high-stakes decision, certain protections are placed on the testing process or the test result. For example, in terms of a state exit exam for high school graduation, some states allow students to take the assessment multiple times to lessen the probability that measurement error is preventing them from passing. Or, in some cases, a state will consider collecting additional data (such as a portfolio of student work) to determine whether a student has met the requirements for receiving a high school diploma. In other high-stakes assessments, such as state assessments for AYP, some states use confidence intervals in addition to observed scores to report student achievement. Several states have chosen to use 95% or even 99% confidence intervals to increase the certainty of inferences based on test scores.

INNOVATION IN ASSESSMENT

Educators, measurements specialists, and policymakers are constantly calling for more research and development for innovative assessments. ED currently administers a grant program to encourage innovation in assessment. The Grants for Enhanced Assessment Instruments is a discretionary grant program awarded to SEAs. The objectives of this program are to: (1) improve the quality, validity, and reliability of state academic assessments; (2)

measure student academic achievement using multiple measures of student academic achievement from multiple sources; (3) chart student progress over time; and (4) evaluate student academic achievement through the development of comprehensive academic assessment instruments, such as performance and technology-based academic assessments.[42]

Funds have been appropriated for this program since FY2002 as follows: $17,000,000 for FY2002, $4,484,000 for FY2003, $11,680,000 for FY2005, $7,563,200 for FY2006, $7,563,200 for FY2007, and $8,732,480 for FY2008 (estimated).[43] A total of 33 grants have been awarded to at least 22 states, and several states have received multiple awards. It is common for states to work together in a collaborative effort with one state taking the lead. If collaboration is taken into account, nearly all states have received funds under this program.

Although these grant projects are complex and often focus on more than one issue of assessment, these projects can be grouped by the main focus of their work. Of the 33 awards, 9 projects are developing assessments for LEP students, 8 projects are developing alternate assessments for students with disabilities, 4 projects study the use of accommodations for students with disabilities and LEP students, 4 projects address issues of accessibility and universal design in assessments, 4 projects study issues of technical adequacy and alignment, 2 projects are developing performance-based assessments, 1 project is developing a science assessment, and 1 project is developing a comprehensive assessment system.[44]

The following sections broadly describe current innovation in assessment. Some innovation efforts are driven by policy, such as the development of alternate assessments and performance- based assessments. Other innovations are driven by issues of equity (universal design of assessments) and statistical measurement (linking assessments).

Alternate Assessments[45]

In December 2003, ED finalized NCLB regulations that authorized states to use results from an alternate assessment based on *alternate* achievement standards (AA-AAS) in AYP determinations for students with the most significant cognitive disabilities.[46] AA-AAS are assessments that differ from general state assessments in form and complexity. They are designed to be a more appropriate measure of what students with the most significant cognitive disabilities know and can do. ED regulations allow up to 1% of all proficient and advanced scores based on AA-AAS to count in AYP determinations for an LEA.

Later, in April 2007, ED finalized NCLB regulations that authorized states to use results from an alternate assessment based on *modified* achievement standards (AA-MAS) in AYP determinations for other students with disabilities.[47] AA-MAS are assessments that also differ from general state assessments in both form and complexity, however, they must be aligned with grade-level content. ED regulations allow up to 2% of all proficient and advanced scores based on AA-MAS to count in AYP determinations for an LEA.

The following sections briefly describe ED regulations and guidance regarding AA-AAS and AAMAS.

Alternate Assessments based on Alternate Achievement Standards

Students with significant cognitive disabilities[48] are eligible to take AA-AAS. A student's Individualized Education Plan (IEP) team may make the decision regarding the type of assessment that is appropriate (i.e., general state assessment or alternate assessment). LEAs and states are held to a 1% cap in the number of proficient and advanced scores that may be counted in AYP determinations.

An alternate assessment differs from a general state assessment in format and complexity. Often times, alternate assessments take the form of a performance assessment or a portfolio assessment. Performance on alternate assessments is compared to alternate achievement standards, which can be based on a limited sample of content that is linked to grade-level content but does not fully represent grade-level content. For example, the content standards may include some of the prerequisite skills that are linked to grade-level content but not necessarily representative of grade-level content. Students who take AA-AAS may participate in "out-of-level" testing, provided that the assessment has a documented and validated standards-setting processes. A student in fifth grade, therefore, may be eligible to take a third grade assessment provided that the standards-setting process is consistent with ED regulations.

The alternate achievement standards may be defined for "grade clusters" (e.g., one achievement standard for all students in grades 3-5). Like general state assessments, alternate achievement standards must have at least three defined achievement levels with performance descriptors, and cut scores must be provided.

Alternate Assessments based on Modified Achievement Standards

Other students with disabilities,[49] who do not have significant cognitive disabilities, may also be eligible to take an alternate assessment. This second type of alternate assessment is based on modified achievement standards. The student's IEP team must provide evidence that the student would not reach proficiency within one year (the year covered by the IEP) even with significant growth. LEAs and states are held to a 2% cap in the number of proficient and advanced scores that may be counted in AYP determinations; however, they may exceed the 2% cap if they are below the 1% cap described above. States shall not exceed a 3% cap of proficient and advanced scores that may be counted in AYP determinations from both types of alternate assessments (AAAAS and AA-MAS).

Performance is measured against modified achievement standards, which must be aligned with grade-level content. Modified achievement standards are designed to be challenging to the students taking this assessment, however, they may be less difficult than the grade-level achievement standards of general state assessments. These assessments may contain easier test items or easier formats. For example, a general state assessment may use multiple choice formats with four possible answers whereas an AA-MAS may have only two possible answers. Another example is using shorter reading passages with simplified language for a reading comprehension assessment.

Because modified assessment standards must be based on grade-level content, they may not be established for "grade clusters" (e.g., 3-5) and "out-of-level" testing is not permitted. Like general state assessments, modified achievement standards must have at least three defined achievement levels with performance descriptors, and cut scores must be provided.

Performance Assessments

NCLB requires that assessments use, "multiple up-to-date measures of student academic achievement, including measures that assess higher-order thinking skills and understanding."[50] Critics of current assessment measures argue that state assessments do not assess higher-order thinking skills in large part due to their multiple-choice and short-answer formats. Furthermore, they argue that higher-order thinking skills can be better measured through performance assessments.[51] Advocates for the use of performance assessments believe that they are better suited for measuring "21st Century Skills," such as critical thinking and problem solving skills, collaboration, and creativity and innovation.[52]

Performance assessments are authentic tasks that assess what a student knows and can do. They are tools that allow teachers to collect information on how the student can use what they have learned. Performance assessments can take many forms, including science experiments that students design and carry out, computer programs that students create, persuasive essays, research projects, or applying mathematical problem solving to a real-world scenario. Performance assessments are usually instructionally relevant and useful tools for teachers. Because most performance assessments are scored by teachers using predetermined standards, results are available in a timely manner and teachers can use the results to modify and adapt instruction. On the other hand, unless they are well-designed measures with clear scoring guidelines, performance assessments can be subject to bias in scoring.

Several states use performance assessments as part of their state testing program. For example, a consortium of schools in New York and the state of Wyoming use performance assessments to determine whether students have mastered the standards required for graduation. Connecticut uses "rich science exams" to assess students' science reasoning skills. Some schools in California use the Mathematics Assessment Resource System (MARS) performance tasks to measure complex mathematical reasoning. Although states have developed and used performance assessments for state-level decision making, performance assessments are generally not used in federal accountability systems (except in limited cases in which alternate assessments are used).

In debates over reauthorization of the ESEA, some have proposed refocusing traditional accountability systems under NCLB into locally controlled accountability systems that use performance assessments.[53] Advocates of this approach believe that the use of performance assessments can be consistent with NCLB notions of accountability and standards-based reform. Furthermore, this approach may promote teacher "buy-in" to accountability practices and encourage more collaborative work. On the other hand, use of locally controlled performance assessments may exacerbate the current problem of having different standards, assessments, and scoring procedures across states, districts, and schools. In addition, it would require substantial investment and professional development to scale-up performance assessment practices to create a large-scale accountability system. There is evidence to suggest, however, that it may be possible to build accountability systems based on performance assessments if there is ongoing capacity building and professional development within schools.[54]

Universal Design of Assessments

Universal design is a concept central to disability policy and is currently a focus of assessment design within IDEA. The universal design of assessments is based on a set of principles that promote fairness and equity in educational assessment. These principles require that assessments (1) be inclusive of the entire population, (2) have precisely defined constructs, (3) contain accessible, non-biased items, (4) be amenable to accommodations, (5) have simple, clear, and intuitive instructions and procedures, and (6) maintain maximum readability, comprehensibility, and legibility.[55] By using these principles in assessment design, proponents believe that items will be relatively free of bias against students with disabilities and other students who may be affected by test bias.

IDEA requires that the SEA apply universal design principles in the development and administration of educational assessments.[56] In addition, although not required by NCLB, there has been some interest in using universal design in the development of state assessments because of the requirement that all students, including students with disabilities, participate in the assessment. By the 2004-2005 school year, more than half of the states requested test developers to use principles of universal design in test construction for state assessments.[57] In general, research has demonstrated that students with disabilities perform better on assessments that incorporate universal design. [58] This research, however, has been conducted on relatively small- scale assessments with a small number of students, and it is unclear if results would generalize to large-scale, high-stakes state assessments.

Linking Assessments

The process of linking assessments incorporates the use of statistical analyses to connect the scores from one test with those of another, regardless of the equivalence of the scales. The most common example of linking is the Fahrenheit and Celsius temperature scales. These two systems express temperature using two different scales, but they are easily linked with a simple equation. This process is fairly simple because there is a common understanding of what constitutes "temperature." The process of linking educational assessments, however, is much more complex because there is less agreement on what constitutes "reading achievement" or "mathematics achievement."

If statistical linkages could be achieved, it would allow policymakers to interpret performance across state assessments using a common metric. Comparing all states to a common metric would, in essence, allow states to be compared to each other, even if they use different assessments and different performance standards. Furthermore, linking techniques based on a common metric may allow individual states to be compared to international assessments. If linking assessments became a common practice, it could greatly reduce the number of assessments administered to students because student performance could be compared across assessments without the necessity of all students participating in the same assessment. Administering fewer assessments may reduce the testing burden and increase the amount of time schools could use for instruction.

Congress asked a committee from the National Research Council (NRC) to study the feasibility of developing a common metric to link scores from existing commercial and state assessments to each other and to NAEP.[59] To determine the feasibility of linking these assessments, the committee considered the validity and practicality of making statistical linkages. After a review of studies attempting to link NAEP with state assessments and an independent evaluation, the NRC concluded that (1) comparing state assessments to each other using a common metric was not feasible, and (2) linking state assessments to NAEP is problematic and any inferences drawn from these links may be misleading. The inferences drawn from linking two tests can be adversely affected by differences in content, format, and the use of the tests being linked, as well as the consequences attached to the two tests. If two tests vary greatly along these dimensions (as many state assessments and NAEP tend to vary) the inferences drawn from the linkage may not be valid.[60]

There has been some progress, however, linking assessments in limited contexts. For example, studies have demonstrated that it may be feasible to link NAEP results for grade 8 mathematics to results on the TIMSS.[61] Statistical linking is more feasible in this case because NAEP and TIMSS use similar constructs, testing frameworks, and scoring, and they test students in the same grade. The statistical linkage between NAEP and TIMSS allows individual states to be compared to other countries in mathematics performance. This type of linkage could be particularly useful, given the recent increased interest in international benchmarks.[62]

USE OF ASSESSMENTS IN ACCOUNTABILITY SYSTEMS: IMPLICATIONS FOR CURRICULUM, STUDENTS, AND TESTING

NCLB greatly increased the emphasis on student assessment. Under NCLB, student scores on state assessments are used as key indicators in an accountability system that determines whether schools are making progress with respect to student achievement. Some have viewed this shift towards test-based accountability as a positive move because it places more emphasis on developing rigorous content standards in reading, mathematics, and science and teaching to the standards. Test-based accountability as implemented by NCLB also leads to increased attention on traditionally underperforming subgroups of students, including disadvantaged students, students with disabilities, and LEP students. On the other hand, test-based accountability has been criticized for narrowing the curriculum and focusing all instruction on the tested subjects of reading and mathematics at the expense of other subjects. The current practice of test-based accountability may also create incentives to set low expectations for proficiency and to focus on a subset of children who are near the proficiency level instead of focusing on children at all achievement levels. Another criticism is that the increased emphasis on test-based accountability can lead to score inflation, which may inhibit policymakers from measuring the actual impact of accountability.

In the sections below, the potential positive and negative implications of test-based accountability are discussed, including implications for curriculum, students, and testing. It is important to note that the issues discussed below are specific to current test-based accountability systems under NCLB; however, all test-based accountability systems may not have the same positive and negative implications.

Implications for Curriculum

One potentially positive outcome of test-based accountability has been an increased focus on state-level content standards and teaching to those standards. Under NCLB, states are required to develop rigorous content standards for reading and mathematics, which many see as core subjects that will lead to improved learning in other content areas. There is some evidence that using content standards and assessments can help teachers focus their instruction and obtain feedback on the effectiveness of their instruction.[63] There are also some data to suggest that high- performing schools have a stronger alignment between state content standards and school curriculum. Furthermore, schools that include teachers in the development of these standards tended to have a higher degree of teacher "buy-in" to the standards.[64]

On the other hand, test-based accountability may be affecting the curriculum in less desirable ways. One criticism of test-based accountability systems is that they lead to a narrowing of the curriculum. There are several ways in which these systems might narrow the curriculum. First, the time spent administering the actual assessments, sometimes called the "testing burden," could detract from classroom instruction. Second, test-based accountability systems may lead to increases in test preparation, leaving less time for instruction. There is some evidence to suggest that teachers feel pressure to "teach to the test" and engage in test preparation activities at the expense of instruction. Test-preparation activities take several forms, including altering typical classroom assignments to conform to the format of an expected response on the state assessment (e.g., if the state assessment requires a five paragraph constructed response, teachers may assign a disproportionate number of five-paragraph essays).[65] Third, in test-based accountability systems, teachers report reallocating instructional time towards tested subjects and away from non-tested subjects. Surveys of teachers have consistently reported that their instruction emphasizes reading and mathematics over other subjects like history, foreign language, and arts.[66] Although there is consistency in the survey results, it is difficult to understand the extent to which instructional time is reallocated towards tested subjects. Most of these reports do not collect data through experimental observation, but rather they rely on self-reported data from teachers and administrators, which is often less reliable.

Implications for Students

NCLB requires states to disaggregate student assessment data for major subgroups, including racial/ethnic groups, economically disadvantaged students, students with disabilities, and LEP students. Schools are held accountable for the performance of each of these subgroups, and each subgroup shares a common goal of reaching 100% proficiency in reading and mathematics by 2014. Designing an accountability system in this way has increased the attention given to the achievement of certain subgroups that may have been previously masked by overall student performance. In general, disaggregating data by subgroups has been seen as a positive step in terms of equity in education because the performance of all subgroups "counts" towards AYP. Supporters of disaggregation believe that it leads to increased access to rigorous academic curriculum for students who otherwise may not have had access to such curriculum due to low expectations of performance.

Along with the increased attention to subgroups of students, there has been increased attention to the achievement gaps between white students and minority students and between economically advantaged students and disadvantaged students. Over the last several decades, a general goal of public education has been to "close the achievement gap," and thus, improve equity in education. By disaggregating assessment results, NCLB has led to consistent measurement of the achievement gap and allows researchers to examine the size of the achievement gap over time.

One of the unintended consequences of NCLB accountability is the way instruction may be focused on students just below the "proficient" level, possibly at the expense of other students.[67] In the current test-based accountability system, the goal is for 100% of students to reach proficiency by 2014. In an effort to raise the percentage of proficient students, schools and teachers may target instructional time and resources towards those students who are near proficiency. Since time and resources are a zero-sum game, fewer instructional resources may be available for students who are far below proficiency or even those who achieve at advanced levels. This disincentive to focus instructional resources on all children has led to possible alternative methods of measuring achievement, including growth models.[68] Within certain accountability systems, the use of growth models may give teachers and schools credit for student growth, even if the growth occurs far below the proficiency level.

Implications for Testing

Test-based accountability systems use high-stakes assessments to make decisions about students, teachers, and schools. Under NCLB, individual schools are held accountable for student achievement, and if schools fail to meet their AYP goals, there are consequences. In an effort to avoid these consequences, schools often make conscious efforts to prepare students for high- stakes assessments. Although these efforts are often undertaken with good intentions, they can lead to score inflation. Score inflation is a phenomenon in which scores on high-stakes assessments tend to increase at a faster rate than scores on low-stakes assessments. The validity of an inference is greatly reduced when score inflation is present.

Test preparation can take many forms, and it is difficult to distinguish appropriate test preparation from inappropriate test preparation. Many schools provide test preparation to young students who have little experience with standardized testing, and this form of test preparation can actually increase the validity of a test score because it is less likely that students will do poorly due to unfamiliarity with the testing process. Other test preparation strategies, such as working more effectively or working harder, are also usually desirable. Test preparation begins to affect validity in a negative way, however, when there are excessive amounts of alignment between test items and curriculum, excessive coaching of a particular type of item that will appear on the test, or even outright cheating.

Studying the prevalence of score inflation is difficult because school districts may be reluctant to give researchers access to test scores for the purpose of investigating possible inflation. Nevertheless, several studies have documented the problem of score inflation by comparing gains on state assessments (high-stakes) to those made on NAEP (low-stakes).[69]

Studies have consistently reported discrepancies in the overall level of student achievement, the size of student achievement gains, and the size of the achievement gap. The discrepancies indicate that student scores on state assessments may be inflated and that these inflated scores may not represent true achievement gains as measured by another test of a similar construct. In this case, the validity of the inference made from state assessments may be questioned.

One possible way to reduce the problem of score inflation is to consistently use a low-stakes "audit" assessment, such as NAEP, to corroborate gains on state assessments.[70] If gains on state assessments generalize to another "audit" assessment, it increases the likelihood that gains are due to true achievement gains. This type of corroboration may help policymakers separate the policies that lead to true student achievement from those that lead to score inflation.

APPENDIX A. GLOSSARY

alternate-form reliability	A reliability statistic that measures the degree to which scores from alternate forms of the same assessment are consistent.
assessment	Any systematic method of obtaining information from tests and other sources, used to draw inferences about characteristics of people, objects, or programs.
benchmark assessment	A type of interim assessment that is either commercially developed or created by school districts for the purpose of predicting the likelihood that students will meet a predetermined future goal, such as passing the annual state assessment. It can be used as either a formative or summative assessment, depending on the timing of the test and how the results are used by teachers.
bias	In a statistical context, a systematic error in a test score. In discussing fairness in testing, bias may refer to construct underrepresentation or construct irrelevance of test scores that differentially affect the performance of various subgroups of test takers.
confidence interval	In educational assessment, a range of values that is likely to contain a student's score. The size of the confidence interval depends on the level of confidence desired (e.g., 95% confidence) in the interpretation of test scores. Higher levels of confidence create larger confidence intervals.
construct	The concept or characteristic that a test is designed to measure.
construct irrelevance	The extent to which test scores are influenced by factors that are irrelevant to the construct that the test is intended to measure. Such extraneous factors

Assessment in Elementary and Secondary Education: A Primer   35

construct underrepresentation distort the meaning of test scores from what is implied in the proposed interpretation.

The extent to which a test fails to capture important aspects of the construct that the test is intended to measure. In this situation, the meaning of test scores is narrower than the proposed interpretation implies.

criterion-referenced score A score from a test that allows its users to make interpretations in relation to a functional performance level, as distinguished from those interpretations that are made in relation to the performance of others. Examples of criterion-referenced interpretations include comparisons to cut scores (performance standards), interpretations based on expectancy tables, and domain-referenced score interpretations.

fairness In testing, the principle that every test taker should be assessed in an equitable way.

formative assessment A type of assessment that is used during the learning process in order to improve curriculum and instruction. It is a process of assessment that teachers use within the classroom to determine gaps in a student's knowledge and to adjust instruction accordingly. Formative assessment takes place within a relatively short time frame and is mainly used to inform the teaching process.

generalizability The extent to which one can draw conclusions for a larger population based on information from a sample population. Or, the extent to which one can draw conclusions about a student's ability on an entire content area based on a sample of test items from that content area.

inference A meaningful conclusion based on the results of an assessment.

inter-scorer agreement A reliability statistic that measures the degree to which two independent scorers agree when assessing a student's performance.

interim assessment A type of assessment that falls between formative assessment and summative assessment. The term is not widely used but sometimes describes assessments that are used to evaluate a student's knowledge and skills within a limited time frame and to inform decisions at the classroom, school, and district level. Interim assessments may serve a variety of purposes, including instructional, predictive, or evaluative, depending on how they are designed.

internal consistency A reliability statistic that measures the correlation between related items within the same assessment.

mean	The arithmetic average of a group of scores.
measurement error	Inaccuracy in an assessment instrument that can misrepresent a student's true score through fluctuations in the observed score. Measurement error reduces the reliability of the inference based on the observed score. Measurement error is not the same as bias, which is systematic error in the assessment instrument that tends to misrepresent scores consistently in one direction.
normative group	A group of sampled individuals designed to represent some larger population, such as test takers throughout the country. The group may be defined in terms of age, grade, or other demographic characteristics, such as socioeconomic status, disability status, or racial/ethnic minority status.
norm-referenced score	A score from a test that allows its users to make interpretations in relation to other test takers' performance within the normative group.
observed score	A score that is a result of an assessment; a reported score. In measurement, the observed score is often contrasted with the true score.
performance standard	An objective definition of a certain level of performance in some content area in terms of a cut score or a range of scores on a test. The performance standard often measures the level of proficiency within a content area.
reliability	The degree to which test scores for a group of test takers are consistent over repeated applications of a measurement procedure and hence are inferred to be dependable and repeatable for an individual test taker; the degree to which scores are free of errors of measurement for a given group.
score inflation	A phenomenon in which scores on high-stakes assessments tend to increase at a faster rate than scores on low-stakes assessments. Score inflation can be influenced by both positive factors (such as working harder or teaching more efficiently) or negative factors (such as excessive test preparation or cheating).
standard deviation	A statistic that shows the spread or dispersion of scores in a distribution of scores. The more widely the scores are spread out, the larger the standard deviation.
standard error of measurement	The standard deviation of an individual's observed scores from repeated administrations of a test under identical conditions. Because such data cannot

generally be collected, the standard error of measurement is usually estimated from group data. The standard error of measurement is used in the calculation of confidence intervals.

summative assessment
In education, summative assessments are generally given at the end of a lesson, semester, or school year to "sum up" what the student knows and has learned. They are used for evaluative purposes.

test-retest reliability
A reliability statistic that measures the stability of a student's score over time.

true score
In classical test theory, the average of the scores that would be earned by an individual on an unlimited number of perfectly parallel forms of the same test. In educational assessment, a true score is a hypothetical, error-free estimation of true ability within a content area.

validation
The process through which the validity of the proposed interpretation of test scores is investigated.

validity
The degree to which accumulated evidence and theory support specific interpretations of test scores entailed by proposed uses of a test.

variability
The spread or dispersion of scores in a group of scores; the tendency of each score to be unlike the others. The standard deviation and the variance are the two most commonly used measures of variability.

variance
A measure of the spread or dispersion of scores. The larger the variance, the further the scores are from the mean. The smaller the variance, the closer the scores are to the mean.

APPENDIX B. ACRONYM REFERENCE

AA-AAS Alternate Assessment based on Alternate Achievement Standards
AA-MAS Alternate Assessment based on Modified Achievement Standards
AYP Adequate Yearly Progress
CRT Criterion-referenced Test
ED U.S. Department of Education
ESEA Elementary and Secondary Education Act
IDEA Individuals with Disabilities Education Act
IEP Individualized Education Program
LEA Local Educational Agency
LEP Limited English Proficiency
NAEP National Assessment of Educational Progress
NAGB National Assessment Governing Board

NCLB	No Child Left Behind
NRT	Norm-referenced Test
PIRLS	Progress in International Reading Literacy Study
PISA	Program for International Student Assessment
SEA	State Educational Agency
TIMSS	Trends in International Mathematics and Science Study

End Notes

[1] See for example, Stanley L. Deno, "Curriculum-based Measures: Development and Perspectives," Research Institute on Progress Monitoring, at http://www.progressmonitoring.net/CBM_Article_Deno.pdf.

[2] For more information on AYP, see CRS Report RL3373 1, *Education for the Disadvantaged: Reauthorization Issues for ESEA Title I-A Under the No Child Left Behind Act*, by Rebecca R. Skinner and CRS Report RL32495, *Adequate Yearly Progress (AYP): Implementation of the No Child Left Behind Act*, by Rebecca R. Skinner.

[3] Scott J. Cech, "Test Industry Split Over 'Formative' Assessment," *Education Week*, September 17, 2008, at http://www.edweek.org/ew/articles/2008/09/17/04formative_ep.h28.html.

[4] Marianne Perie, Scott Marion, Brian Gong, and Judy Wurtzel, "The Role of Interim Assessments in a Comprehensive Assessment System: A Policy Brief," Achieve, Inc., The Aspen Institute, and The National Center for the Improvement of Educational Assessment, Inc., November 2007.

[5] Paul Black and Dylan William, "Assessment and Classroom Learning," Assessment in Education, vol. 5, no. 1 (March 1998), pp.7-75.

[6] An effect size is a statistic that quantifies the strength of a relationship between two variables. It defines the magnitude and the direction of the relationship. In this case, the effect size is a measure of the strength of the relationship between the use of formative assessment and student achievement. A positive effect size indicates that the use of formative assessment can lead to increases in student achievement.

[7] Marianne Perie, Scott Marion, Brian Gong, and Judy Wurtzel, "The Role of Interim Assessments in a Comprehensive Assessment System: A Policy Brief," Achieve, Inc., The Aspen Institute, and The National Center for the Improvement of Educational Assessment, Inc., November 2007.

[8] The Regional Education Laboratories (RELs) are part of the National Center for Educational Evaluation and Regional Assistance, U.S. Department of Education. The REL program consists of a network of 10 laboratories that conduct applied research, implement development projects and studies, and provide technical assistance.

[9] Susan Henderson, Anthony Petrosino, Sarah Guckenburg, and Stephen Hamilton, *A Second Follow-up Year for "Measuring How Benchmark Assessments Affect Student Achievement,"* (REL Technical Brief, REL Northeast and Islands 2007-No. 002). Washington, D.C.: U.S. Department of Education, Institute of Education Sciences, National Center for Education Evaluation and Regional Assistance, Regional Education Laboratory Northeast and Islands, April 2008.

[10] Richard S. Brown and Ed Coughlin, The Predictive Validity of Selected Benchmark Assessments Used in the Mid- Atlantic Region (Issues & Answers Report, REL 2007-No.017), Washington, D.C.: U.S. Department of Education, Institute of Education Sciences, National Center for Education Evaluation and Regional Assistance, Regional Educational Laboratory, Mid-Atlantic, November 2007.

[11] The mean is the arithmetic average of scores in the normative sample. The standard deviation is a measure of the degree of dispersion or variability within the normative sample. In simple terms, the mean is the average score and the standard deviation is a measure of how spread out students' scores are from the average score.

[12] Beth C. Gamse, Robin Tepper Jacob, Megan Horst, Beth Boulay, and Fatih Unlu, *Reading First Impact Study Final Report* (NCEE 2009-4038), Washington, D.C.: U.S. Department of Education, Institute of Education Sciences, National Center for Education Evaluation and Regional Assistance, November 2008; For more information on Reading First, see CRS Report RL3 1241, *Reading First and Early Reading First: Background and Funding*, by Gail McCallion and CRS Report RL3 3246, *Reading First: Implementation Issues and Controversies*, by Gail McCallion.

[13] For more information, see CRS Report RL3 1407, *Educational Testing: Implementation of ESEA Title I-A Requirements Under the No Child Left Behind Act*, by Rebecca R. Skinner and Erin D. Caffrey.

[14] Currently, all states participate in ESEA, Title I-A.

[15] U.S. Department of Education, "State Standards and Assessment Update," January 2009 at http://www.ed.gov/admins/lead/account/statesystems.html.

[16] U.S. Department of Education, State Status Chart, http://www.ed.gov/policy/elsec/guid/stateletters/ssc.xls.

[17] This information is available through the Council of Chief State School Officers' state assessment profiles for school year 2007-2008.

[18] The Commissioner from the National Center for Education Statistics (NCES), U.S. Department of Education is responsible by law for carrying out NAEP activities.

[19] For a schedule of NAEP national assessments, see http://nces.ed.gov/nationsreportcard/about/assessmentsched.asp.

[20] For a more comprehensive definition, see IDEA, §602(3).

[21] IDEA, §614

[22] For a more comprehensive definition, see ESEA, §9101(25).

[23] For more information on end-of-course exams, see Center on Education Policy, *State High School Exit Exams: A Move Toward End-of-Course Exams,* August 2008.

[24] Eric Grodsky, John R. Warren, and Demetra Kalogrides, "State High School Exit Examinations and NAEP Long-term Trends in Reading and Mathematics, 197 1-2004.," *Educational Policy*, (in press).

[25] D.E. (Sunny) Becker and Christina Watters, "Independent Evaluation of the California High School Exit Examination (CAHSEE): 2007 Evaluation Report, October 2007 at http://www.cde.ca.gov/ta/tg/hs/documents/evalrpt07.pdf; Andrew C. Zau and Julian R. Betts, "Predicting Success, Preventing Failure: An Investigation of the California High School Exit Exam," 2008 at http://www.ppic.org/content/pubs/report/R_608AZR.pdf.

[26] See the earlier discussion of "Formative Assessment" in this report.

[27] The general level of alignment of benchmark assessments and state assessments has not been thoroughly studied. There is some evidence to suggest that performance on benchmark assessments does not strongly predict performance on state assessments, which may suggest a lack of alignment. See, for example, Richard S. Brown and Ed Coughlin, The Predictive Validity of Selected Benchmark Assessments Used in the Mid-Atlantic Region (Issues & Answers Report, REL 2007-No.017), Washington, D.C.: U.S. Department of Education, Institute of Education Sciences, National Center for Education Evaluation and Regional Assistance, Regional Educational Laboratory, Mid-Atlantic, November 2007.

[28] For information on the results of the 2006 PISA administration, see http://nces.ed.gov/surveys/pisa/pisa2006highlights.asp.

[29] International benchmarks are independently determined for the PIRLS assessment by percentile groups (i.e., top 10%, upper quartile, median, lower quartile).

[30] For more information on the results of the 2006 PIRLS administration, see http://nces.ed.gov/pubs2004/pirlspub/index.asp.

[31] For more information on the results of the 2007 TIMSS administration, see http://nces.ed.gov/timss/results07.asp.

[32] For more information on the TIMSS benchmarking studies, see http://nces.ed.gov/timss/benchmark.asp.

[33] For a thorough discussion of validity, see AERA, APA, NCME, "Standards for Educational and Psychological Testing," (Washington, DC: American Psychological Assiciation, 1999).

[34] The standard deviation of an individual's observed scores from repeated administrations of a test under identical conditions. Because such data cannot generally be collected, the standard error of measurement is usually estimated from group data. The standard error of measurement is used in the calculation of confidence intervals.

[35] Daniel Koretz, "Error and Reliability: How Much We Don't Know What We're Talking About," in *Measuring Up: What Educational Testing Really Tells Us* (Cambridge, MA: Harvard University Press, 2008), pp. 143-178.

[36] U.S. Department of Education , *28th Annual Report to Congress on the Implementation of the Individuals with Disabilities Education Act, 2006*, Vol. 1, Washington, DC, 2006, http://www.ed.gov/about/reports/annual/osep/2006/ parts-b-c/28th-vol-1 .pdf.

[37] Elaine Carlson, Tamara Daley, and Amy Shimshak, et al., *Changes in the Characteristics, Services, and Performance of Preschoolers with Disabilities from 2003-04 to 2004-05*, U.S. Department of Education, PEELS Wave 2 Overview Report, Washington, DC, June 10, 2008, http://ies.ed.gov/ncser/pdf/20083011.pdf.

[38] Students who receive special education services are reevaluated periodically for eligibility. If the reevaluation determines that the student is no longer eligible to receive special education services, he or she becomes "declassified." "Declassification" refers to a process by which a student who once received special education services is no longer eligible to receive such services.

[39] For a comprehensive discussion of fairness in testing, see AERA, APA, NCME, "Standards for Educational and Psychological Testing," (Washington, DC: American Psychological Assiciation, 1999).

[40] Other reasons that this conclusion would be inappropriate include differences in countries participating in the assessments, differences in sampling procedures of students participating in the assessments, and differences in the level of development of participating countries.

[41] For a comprehensive discussion on evaluating the technical quality of assessments, see AERA, APA, NCME, "Standards for Educational and Psychological Testing," (Washington, DC: American Psychological Assiciation, 1999).

[42] For a full program description, see http://www.ed.gov/programs/eag/index.html.

[43] No grants were awarded in FY2004 because funds were not appropriated for this program.

[44] For more information on the individual grant projects, see http://www.ed.gov/programs/eag/awards.html.

[45] For a comprehensive discussion on alternate assessments, see CRS Report R4070 1, *Alternate Assessments for Students with Disabilities*, by Erin D. Caffrey.

[46] 34 C.F.R. §200

[47] 34 C.F.R. §200

[48] "Significant cognitive disability" is not specifically defined in IDEA. To be eligible to take an AA-AAS, the student must have a disability as defined by IDEA, §620(3) and meet specific state criteria that define a "significant cognitive disability."

[49] As defined by IDEA, §620(3).

[50] P.L. 107-110 § 111 1(b)(2)(I)(vi)

[51] George H. Wood, Linda Darling-Hammond, Monty Neil, et al., *Refocusing Accountability: Using Local Performance Assessments to Enhance Teaching and Learning for Higher Order Skills,* The Forum for Education and Democracy, May 2007, http://www.forumforeducation.org/node/368.

[52] To view the complete framework of 21st century skills, see http://www.21stcenturyskills.org/index.php?option=com_content&task=view&id=254&Itemid=120.

[53] Forum on Educational Accountability, *Assessment and Accountability for Improving Schools and Learning: Principles and Recommendations for Federal Law and State and Local Systems*, August 2007, pp. 1-55, http://www.edaccountability.org/AssessmentFullReportJUNE07.pdf.

[54] David Niemi, Eva L. Baker, and Roxanne M. Sylvester, "Scaling Up, Scaling Down: Seven Years of Performance Assessment Development in the Nation's Second Largest School District", *Educational Assessment*, vol. 12, no. 3&4, (2007), 195-214.

[55] Sandra J. Thompson, Christopher J. Johnstone, and Martha L. Thurlow, *Universal Design Applied to Large Scale Assessments*, National Center on Educational Outcomes, NCEO Synthesis Report 44, Minneapolis, MN, June 2002, http://education.umn.edu/NCEO/OnlinePubs/Synthesis44.html.

[56] P.L. 108-446 §612(a)(16)(E)

[57] Christopher J. Johnstone, Martha L. Thurlow, and Michael Moore, et al., *Using Systematic Item Selection Methods to Improve Universal Design of Assessments* , National Center for Educational Outcomes, Policy Directions 18, Minneapolis, MN, September 2006, http://education.umn.edu/NCEO/OnlinePubs/Policy18/.

[58] Robert P. Dolan, Tracey E. Hall, and Manju Banerjee, et al., "Applying Principles of Universal Design to Test Delivery: The Effect of Computer-based Read-aloud on Test Performance of High School Students with Learning Disabilities," *The Journal of Technology, Learning, and Assessment*, vol. 3, no. 7 (February 2005); Robert P. Dolan and Tracey E. Hall, "Developing accessible tests with universal design and digital technologies: Ensuring we standardize the right things," in *Large-scale Assessment and Accommodations: What works* , ed. C.C. Liatusis and L.L. Cook (Arlington, VA: Council for Exceptional Children, 2007), pp. 95-111; Christopher J. Johnstone, *Improving Validity of Large-scale Tests: Universal Design and Student Performance* , National Center for Educational Outcomes, Technical Report 37, Minneapolis, MN, December 2003, http://education.umn.edu/NCEO/OnlinePubs/ Technical37.htm.

[59] P.L. 105-78, §306

[60] Michael J. Feuer, Paul W. Holland, and Bert F. Green, et al., *Uncommon Measures: Equivalence and Linkage Among Educational Tests* (Washington, D.C.: National Academy Press, 1999).

[61] Gary W. Phillips, *Expressing International Educational Achievement in Terms of U.S. Performance Standards: Linking NAEP Achievement Levels to TIMSS*, American Institutes for Research, Washington, DC, April 2007, http://www.air.org/news/documents/naep-timss.pdf; Gary W. Phillips, *Chance Favors the Prepared Mind: Mathematics and Science Indicators for Comparing States and Nations*, American Institutes for Research, Washington, DC, November 14, 2007,
http://www.air.org/publications/documents/phillips.chance.favors.the.prepared.mind.pdf.

[62] Michele McNeil, "Panel to Spur International Benchmarks," *Education Week*, September 17, 2008.

[63] L. Mabry, J. Poole, and L. Redmond, et al., "Local Impact of State Testing in Southwest Washington," *Education Policy Analysis Archives*, vol. 11, no. 22 (July 18, 2003), http://epaa.asu.edu/epaa/v11n22/.

[64] Deepa Srikantaiah, Ying Zhang, and Lisa Swayhoover, *Lessons from the Classroom Level: Federal and State Accountability in Rhode Island*, Center on Education Policy, November 25, 2008, http://www.cep-dc.org/document/docWindow.cfm?fuseaction=document.viewDocument&documentid=249&documentFormatId=3846.

[65] Deepa Srikantaiah, Ying Zhang, and Lisa Swayhoover, *Lessons from the Classroom Level: Federal and State Accountability in Rhode Island*, Center on Education Policy, November 25, 2008, http://www.cep-dc.org/document/docWindow.cfm?fuseaction=document.viewDocument&documentid=249&documentFormatId=3846.

[66] Laura Hamilton, "Assessment as a Policy Tool," *Review of Research in Education*, vol. 27 (2003), pp. 25-68; Laura S. Hamilton and Mark Berends, *Instructional Practices Related to Standards and Assessment*, RAND, WR-374-EDU, Washington, DC, April 2006,
http://www.rand.org/pubs/working_papers/2006/RAND_WR374.pdf; Patricia Velde Pederson, "What is Measured Is Treasured: The Impact of the No Child Left Behind Act on Nonassessed Subjects," *Clearing*

House: A Journal of Educational Strategies, Issues and Ideas, vol. 80, no. 6 (July/August 2007), pp. 287-291; Jennifer McMurrer, *Choices, Changes, and Challenges: Curriculum and Instruction in the NCLB Era*, Center on Education Policy, December 2007, http://www.cep-dc.org/_data/n_0001/resources/ 1%2007.pdf.

[67] Jennifer Booher-Jennings, "Below the Bubble: "Educational Triage" and teh Texas Accountability System," *American Educational Research Journal*, vol. 42, no. 2 (Summer 2005), pp. 231-268; Laura S. Hamilton and Mark Berends, *Instructional Practices Related to Standards and Assessment*, RAND, WR-374-EDU, Washington, DC, April 2006, http://www.rand.org/pubs/working_papers/2006/RAND_WR374.pdf.

[68] CRS Report RL33032, *Adequate Yearly Progress (AYP): Growth Models Under the No Child Left Behind Act*, by Wayne C. Riddle.

[69] B. Fuller, K. Gesicki, and E. Kang, et al., *Is the No Child Left Behind Act Working? The Reliability of How States Track Achievement*, University of California, Berkeley PACE, Working Paper 06-1, Berkeley, CA, 2006; S.P. Klein, Linda S. Hamilton, and Daniel F. McCaffrey, et al., *What Do Test Scores in Texas Tell Us?*, RAND, Santa Monica, CA, 2000; Daniel Koretz and S. I. Barron, *The Validity of Gains on the Kentucky Instructional Results Information System (KIRIS)*, RAND, MR-792-PCT/FF, Santa Monica, CA, 1998; Robert L. Linn and C. Haug, "Stability of School- building Accountability Scores and Gains," *Educational Evaluation and Policy Analysis*, vol. 24, no. 1 (2002), pp. 29- 36.

[70] Daniel Koretz, *Measuring Up: What Educational Testing Really Tells Us* (Cambridge, MA: Harvard University Press, 2008), pp. 247-248.

In: Teacher Quality and Student Achievement
Editor: Katherine E. Westley

ISBN: 978-1-61728-274-4
© 2010 Nova Science Publishers, Inc.

Chapter 2

A HIGHLY QUALIFIED TEACHER IN EVERY CLASSROOM: IMPLEMENTATION OF THE NO CHILD LEFT BEHIND ACT AND REAUTHORIZATION ISSUES FOR THE 111TH CONGRESS[*]

Jeffrey J. Juenzi

SUMMARY

One of the major goals of the No Child Left Behind Act of 2001 (NCLB) is to raise the achievement of students who currently fail to meet grade-level proficiency standards. Since student achievement is believed by many to depend in large part on effective teaching, the law also contains provisions designed to improve teacher quality. These provisions establish minimum teacher quality requirements and charge states and school districts with developing plans to meet them. These plans were to ensure that all schools had a *highly qualified teacher* in every classroom by the end of the 2005-2006 school year.

To be deemed *highly qualified*, NCLB requires that teachers possess a baccalaureate degree and a state teaching certificate, and that teachers also demonstrate subject-matter knowledge for their teaching level. Elementary school teachers must show knowledge of basic elementary school curricular areas. Middle and secondary school teachers must demonstrate a high level of competency in all subject areas taught. Demonstration of subject-matter knowledge and competency may be shown by passing a state certification exam or licensing test in the relevant subject(s).

This report examines implementation of the NCLB requirement and estimates the extent to which schools achieved the law's goal of placing a highly qualified teacher in every classroom. After describing the highly qualified teacher requirement in detail, the report analyzes data from a national survey of schools that provide information on teacher qualifications during the 1999- 2000 school year. These data suggest that more than four out

---

[*] This is an edited, reformatted and augmented version of a CRS Report for Congress publication dated April 2009.

of five teachers would have met the NCLB definition of a highly qualified teacher prior to the date of enactment. Monitoring data released by the Education Department indicate that the proportion of highly qualified teachers may have gone up slightly by the end of the 200 5-2006 school year, but that no state reached the 100% goal.

In addition to the findings of this analysis, knowledge gained through NCLB 's implementation has important implications for future policy-making in the area of teacher quality. This report concludes with a discussion of issues that may be considered as the Elementary and Secondary Education Act reauthorization process unfolds. The teacher quality provisions, along with the rest of the Elementary and Secondary Education Act, will likely be considered for reauthorization by the 111th Congress.

INTRODUCTION

It is widely believed that good teachers are critical to student learning. A large body of academic research has produced strong evidence that teacher quality is positively related to student performance. However, the strength of this research finding depends on the measure used to indicate "quality." Studies that use credentials such as degree attainment or teacher certification show weaker impacts on student performance than studies that use direct measures of teachers' pedagogical and subject-matter knowledge.[1] Nevertheless, credentials are more readily available to local school administrators that hire teachers and more easily incorporated into state and federal policy. In recent years, education policy governing the attainment of teaching credentials has evolved to incorporate pedagogy and subject expertise. General state certification exams have been replaced or enhanced with testing for knowledge of subject matter. Some states have developed multi-tiered, knowledge-based certification systems. Teacher preparation programs in some states have begun requiring that candidates obtain a major or minor in a subject as a prerequisite for or in conjunction with an education degree.[2]

Teaching credential reforms that incorporate subject-matter knowledge have also been enacted in federal education policy. Most recently, the Elementary and Secondary Education Act of 1965 (ESEA), as amended by the No Child Left Behind Act of 2001 (NCLB) (P.L. 107-110), requires that all public school teachers, in states participating in the ESEA Title I-A program for Education of the Disadvantaged, be *highly qualified* by demonstrating subject knowledge for their teaching level. Elementary school teachers must show knowledge of basic elementary school curricular areas. Middle and secondary school teachers must demonstrate a high level of competency in all subject areas taught. Subject-matter knowledge and competency may be demonstrated by passing a state certification exam or licensing test in the relevant subject(s).[3]

One of the major goals of NCLB is to raise the achievement of students who currently fail to meet grade-level proficiency standards. Since student achievement has been shown to be dependent in large part on teacher quality, the law seeks to improve achievement by setting higher minimum teacher quality requirements. In complying with the law, schools are prevented from hiring substandard teachers, such as those with emergency or provisional certification, those without a baccalaureate degree, or those with limited subject knowledge.

For some time, it was thought that schools hired substandard teachers because a shortage existed in the overall supply of qualified teachers. That idea has been challenged in recent years by research that revealed the shortage is in fact a distribution problem. Some so-called "hard-to staff" schools find it difficult to maintain a staff of qualified teachers, while other schools have an adequate supply (and in some cases an oversupply) of quality teachers.[4]

The reasons for the uneven distribution in the teacher supply are still a matter of debate. Some argue that rules providing priority in reassignment options to teachers with seniority and the late decision deadline given to resigning teachers relegates the least-qualified teachers to less desirable schools. Others point to working conditions and other factors that make these schools less desirable to quality teachers in the first place. Whatever the reasons for the uneven distribution of quality teachers, the persistence of hard-to-staff schools may undermine the impact of NCLB teacher quality standards in reducing the student achievement gap.

This report examines implementation of the NCLB requirement of a highly qualified teacher in every public school classroom. The first section of the report describes the *highly qualified teacher* (HQT) requirement and how it has been specified through regulation, guidance, and policy statements issued by the Education Department (ED). In the second section, the report analyzes data from a national survey of schools to assess the extent to which they are meeting the NCLB challenge. Finally, the report discusses issues regarding these requirements that may be considered as the ESEA reauthorization process unfolds during the 111th Congress.

THE HIGHLY QUALIFIED TEACHER REQUIREMENT

NCLB requires that each state educational agency (SEA) receiving ESEA Title I, Part A funding (compensatory education of disadvantaged students) must have a plan to ensure that, by no later than the end of the 2005-2006 school year, all public school teachers teaching in core academic subjects within the state will meet the definition of a HQT.

Definition of a Highly Qualified Teacher

According to ESEA, Section 9101(23), the definition of an HQT has two basic components. First, to be deemed highly qualified, a teacher must possess full state teaching certification (i.e., must not have had any certification requirements waived on an emergency, temporary, or provisional basis) as well as a baccalaureate degree. The second component of the definition is that an HQT must demonstrate subject-matter knowledge in the areas that she or he teaches. The manner in which teachers satisfy the second component depends on the extent of their teaching experience and the level at which they teach. These subject knowledge requirements are as follows:

- **New elementary school teachers** must pass a rigorous state test demonstrating subject knowledge and teaching skills in reading, writing, math, and other basic elementary school curricular areas.

- **New middle or secondary school teachers** must demonstrate a high level of competency in all subjects taught by (1) passing rigorous state academic tests in those subjects, **or** (2) completing an academic major (or equivalent course work), graduate degree, or advanced certification in each subject taught.

- **Experienced school teachers** must meet (1) the requirements described above for new teachers (depending upon his or her level of instruction), or (2) demonstrate competency in all subjects taught using a "high objective uniform state standard of evaluation" (HOUSSE).

These provisions indicate that the tests used to demonstrate subject-matter knowledge may include state certification or licensing exams. Section 9101(23) states that a demonstration of subject-matter knowledge by an elementary school teacher "may consist of passing a State- required certification or licensing test or tests in reading, writing, mathematics, and other areas of the basic elementary school curriculum." For a middle or secondary school teacher, Section 9101(23) states that a demonstration of subject-matter knowledge "may consist of a passing level of performance on a State-required certification or licensing test or tests in each of the academic subjects in which the teacher teaches."

Implementing the Definition

Following passage of NCLB, ED further specified the HQT definition through regulation, non-regulatory guidance, and other means. In general, these policy statements addressed concerns about the scope and application of the HQT requirements. Among a wide variety of implementation issues, ED sought to clarify what constitutes "core" subject matter, how states should develop and apply a HOUSSE, how the HQT requirements may be differentially applied to different types of teachers and in different types of educational settings, and when various aspects of the requirement must be completed.

Subject Matter

Early in the implementation of these provisions, some asked whether they apply to *all* teachers, including vocational education teachers, special education teachers, or others not teaching core academic subjects. According to ESEA Section 9101(11), "The term 'core academic subjects' means English, reading or language arts, mathematics, science, foreign languages, civics and government, economics, arts, history, and geography." Final regulations for the Title I program published on December 2, 2002, in the *Federal Register* apply these requirements only to core academic subject teachers. ED noted that these requirements would apply to a *vocational education* teacher or a *special education* teacher providing instruction in a core academic subject.[5]

ED addressed other subject matter issues in subsequent guidance and policy letters. A March 2004 policy announcement modified earlier non-regulatory guidance (issued in January 2004), which stated that *science* teachers teaching more than one field of science (e.g., biology and chemistry) would have to be highly qualified in each of the fields taught. Under the new flexibility, states determine whether science teachers need to be highly qualified in each science field they teach or highly qualified in science in general, based on how the state currently certifies teachers in these subject areas.

This new flexibility, along with other changes, was incorporated into the revised non-regulatory guidance issued on August 3, 2005.[6] The guidance clarifies that *social studies* is not considered a core subject and that certification in social studies or possession of a "composite social studies degree" does not necessarily indicate that a teacher is highly qualified to teach related subjects (e.g., economics and history). States are to determine whether a social science teacher is qualified to teach the specific subject he or she is assigned to teach.

High Objective Uniform State Standard of Evaluation (HOUSSE)

According to NCLB, a teacher who is not new to the teaching profession may demonstrate subject matter knowledge through the states' HOUSSE method. In defining its HOUSSE, the SEA must set standards for both grade appropriate academic subject knowledge and teaching skills that are aligned with challenging state academic and student achievement standards. The HOUSSE must provide objective information about teachers' content knowledge in all subjects taught and be applied uniformly statewide to all teachers in the same subjects and grade levels. Finally, the statute states that the HOUSSE may use multiple measures of teacher competency and may consider, but not be based primarily on, time teaching the relevant subjects.

Non-regulatory guidance, published on September 12, 2003, included suggestions on the development of HOUSSE procedures. According to the guidance, states should consider several factors when developing their HOUSSE procedures, including whether the proposed HOUSSE measures provide an "objective" way of determining whether a teacher has adequate subject- matter knowledge. The latest (August 2005) guidance defines *new* teachers as those with less than one year of teaching experience and teachers who are *not new* as those with more than one year of experience. However, the guidance indicates that states have the authority to determine who is new to the profession and who is not. States may also design their HOUSSE procedures to allow a teacher to go through the process a single time to demonstrate competency in multiple subjects.

Different Teachers

NCLB states that full certification includes "certification obtained through alternative routes to certification." The December 2002 final regulations indicated that teachers who were participating in an alternative certification program will be considered highly qualified on a provisional basis. Such teachers have a maximum of three years in which to become fully certified without being in violation of the highly qualified requirements regarding certification. This allowance is made only for a teacher in an alternative certification program who is receiving high-quality professional development, intensive supervision, and is making satisfactory progress toward full certification.

Concerns had been raised that the HQT requirements would limit participation in *international* teacher exchange programs. In a policy letter issued on March 24, 2003, the Secretary addressed these concerns by indicating how teachers from other countries could be considered highly qualified in the state in which they teach. The Secretary pointed out that each state has the full authority to define and enforce its own requirements for certification and licensure and make accommodations for foreign teachers. Accommodations could also be made in developing tests and other ways of demonstrating subject-matter expertise. In making this point, the Secretary clarified that one such demonstration provided in the law is coursework equivalent to an academic major.

These changes were included in the September 2003 updated guidance, along with clarification on the issue of *middle school* teachers. When determining whether teachers of core academic subjects in grades 6 through 8 should meet competency requirements for elementary or middle school teachers, the guidance advises states to "examine the degree of rigor and technicality of the subject matter that a teacher will need to know in relation to the state's content standards and academic achievement standards for the subjects in those grade levels." In addition, states may choose to consider teachers with middle school certification to be "highly qualified," and states may approve tests that are specifically developed for middle school teachers if the tests are "rigorous content-area assessments that are developed specifically for middle school teachers and aligned with middle school content and academic standards."

Different Settings

In a March 31, 2004 policy letter, the Secretary announced that additional flexibility could be applied in the implementation of the HQT requirements with regard to teachers in small rural school districts.[7] In small rural districts, ED provided that teachers teaching core academic subjects who meet the highly qualified requirements in at least one of the subject areas they teach may have an additional three years to meet these requirements in the other subjects they might teach. For current teachers, this three-year grace period began with the 2004-2005 school year, meaning that rather than facing a deadline of the end of the 2005-2006 school year to be highly qualified in all core subjects taught, current rural teachers may have until the end of the 2006- 2007 school year. For newly hired teachers, a full three-year grace period can be provided from the date of hiring. But those newly hired teachers will have to be highly qualified in one of their core subject areas when hired. States decide whether to offer this flexibility to eligible rural districts.

Section 9101(23) states that charter school teachers must meet "the requirements set forth in the State's public charter school law." ED's guidance clarifies that this only refers to the requirements for certification and indicates that such teachers must meet all other HQT requirements. The guidance also states that teachers in juvenile and correctional institutions or "other alternative settings" must meet HQT standards only if such settings are considered LEAs under state law.

Deadlines for Implementation

Each SEA was to submit its plan to meet the HQT deadline along with its Consolidated State Application for State Grants on July 12, 2002. The plan was to establish annual measurable objectives for each local educational agency (LEA) and school that, at a minimum, included annual increases in the percentage of HQTs at each LEA and school to ensure that the 2005-2006 deadline was met. In turn, each LEA was also to have a plan to meet this deadline. In addition, beginning with the first day of the 2002-2003 school year, any

LEA receiving ESEA Title I funding must ensure that all teachers hired after that date who are teaching in Title I-supported programs are highly qualified. States and LEAs must also submit annual reports to ED describing progress on the state-set annual objectives.

The Consolidated State Performance Reports (CSPR), for the 2003-2004 school year due in January of 2005, were to contain the first data on the status of meeting the HQT requirement. However, ED reported widespread problems in state data systems and offered a series of regional data workshops to support states in collecting data.[8] This includes the additional data on teachers who are not highly qualified that was required to be submitted in the January 2006 CSPR. ED announced these workshops in a policy letter to chief state school officers dated October 21, 2005.

The letter also announced additional flexibility in meeting the HQT deadline. The Secretary stated that the letter's purpose was "to assure you that States that do not quite reach the 100% goal by the end of the 2005-2006 school year will not lose federal funds if they are implementing the law and making a good-faith effort to reach the HQT goal in NCLB as soon as possible."[9] Instead, states that "meet the law's requirements and the Department's expectations in these areas but fall short of having highly qualified teachers in every classroom" would be given an *additional year* to reach the 100% goal.

In a letter dated March 21, 2006, the Secretary requested that each state submit a revised plan to meet the 2006-2007 goal. The letter also established a schedule for reviewing these plans, monitoring their implementation, and assessing the state's progress.[10] The Secretary's latest letter to chief state school officers on this policy (dated July 23, 2007) stated that all but one state had a plan approved.[11] The letter also stated that data submitted in the 2005-2006 CSPR indicated that no state had reached 100% HQT (further examination of these data will be undertaken in the next section of this report). The Secretary reiterated ED's earlier position that no penalties would be imposed on states making a good-faith effort to reach the HQT goal.

Figure 1 provides a graphic diagram of the major HQT requirements as defined in NCLB and further specified in ED regulation and guidance.

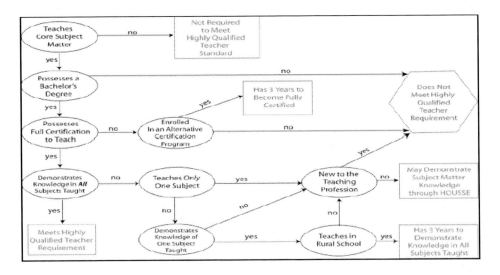

Figure 1. Diagram of Highly Qualified Teacher Requirement

MEETING THE HIGHLY QUALIFIED TEACHER CHALLENGE

Given that the NCLB goal of placing a highly qualified teacher in every classroom by the 2005- 2006 school year was not reached, the analysis in this section will focus on the extent to which progress was made in meeting this challenge. Specifially, data gathered prior to the law's passage will be compared to the most recent data available to see whether the nation's schools witnessed a measurable increase in the proportion of highly qualified teachers.

The only nationally representative source of pre-NCLB information on teacher quality is the Schools and Staffing Survey (SASS), which collects data on teachers' assignments, education, and certification.[12] Conducted every four years by ED's National Center for Education Statistics, the SASS survey fielded during the 1999-2000 school year provides a snapshot of the teaching force prior to passage of NCLB. Since the 2007-2008 SASS data have not yet been released, the only source of post-NCLB data on teacher quality comes from the law's reporting requirements. Each year, states must submit to ED, as part of their Consolidated State Performance Reports (CSPRs), "the percentage of classes being taught by highly qualified teachers in the State."[13]

It is important to note that the *units of analysis* for these two data sources are different. In the SASS data, the "objects" being measured in the survey are teachers; thus, these data are designed to address such questions as, "how many teachers are highly qualified?" Conversely, in the CSPR data the units of analysis are classes; thus, these data are designed to address such questions as, "how many classes are taught by highly qualified teachers?" Although the pre- and post-NCLB data come from different sources and use different units of analysis, these data do appear to show improvement in teacher quality over the years in which the law was implemented.

The Percentage of HQTs Prior to NCLB

According to the 1999-2000 SASS survey, just under 3 million teachers were employed in the public schools and, for about 6%, that year was their first year of teaching.[14] Virtually all teachers (99.3%) held a baccalaureate degree at the time of the survey; the large majority (95.9%) also held some form of state teaching certification. Nearly one-third of all teachers did not teach a "core" academic subject during the 1999-2000 school year; these non-core teachers are not subject to the HQT requirement and are omitted from this analysis.[15]

The SASS data suggest that *prior to the passage of NCLB, more than eight out of ten teachers met the HQT requirement.* Of the 2.1 million teachers who taught at least one core subject in 1999-2000, 1.73 million taught a single subject and 339,000 taught two subjects.[16] Nine in ten single-subject teachers reported that they held full state certification in the subject they taught. Half of all two-subject teachers reported that they held full state certification in both of their subjects. Taken together, 84.5% of all single and two-subject teachers held a baccalaureate degree and reported being certified in the subject(s) they taught. Since NCLB considers state certification in all fields taught adequate demonstration of subject-matter knowledge, 84.5% of teachers met the HQT requirement. **Table 1** presents the qualifications of core subject teachers for the 1999- 2000 school year.

Table 1. Qualifications of Core Subject Teachers, 1999-2000

	Number	Percent
Core Subject Teachers	2,068,306	100%
Certified in all Subjects Taught	1,747,343	84.5
Highly Qualified Teachers	**1,747,343**	**84.5**
In Alternative Certification Program	64,009	3.1
Certified in 1 of 2 Subjects & SRSA	9,246	0.4
Provisionally Highly Qualified Teachers	**1,820,598**	**88.0**

Source: CRS analysis of the U.S. Department of Education, National Center for Education Statistics' 1999-2000 Schools and Staffing Survey.

Table 2. Percentage of Core Subject Classes Taught by Highly Qualified Teachers

	2003-2004	2004-2005	2005-2006	2006-2007
Total	86.5%	90.6%	92.2%	94.2%
Elementary	na	93.0	94.0	95.9
High-Poverty	na	89.6	90.4	93.5
Low-Poverty	na	95.0	95.8	96.6
Secondary	na	89.0	90.9	93.0
High-Poverty	na	84.6	85.7	88.7
Low-Poverty	na	91.9	93.8	95.4

Source: U.S. Department of Education, Consolidated State Performance Reports, various years.

An additional 3.1% of all teachers were participating in an alternative certification program at the time of the survey. NCLB considers such teachers to be provisionally HQT and gave them three years to complete their program and become fully certified. Also given provisional HQT status (this time through regulation instead of statute) were another 0.4% of teachers who taught two subjects, held certification in only one, and were located in LEAs eligible for participation in the Small Rural School Achievement (SRSA) program (ESEA Title VI-B). According to the guidance (discussed above), these teachers have additional time to demonstrate subject-matter knowledge in the field in which they are not highly qualified— one year in the case of veteran teachers and three years for new teachers. Thus, a total of 3.5% of all 1999-2000 teachers would have been temporarily deemed highly qualified teachers (combining those in alternative certification programs and those in SRSA schools who were uncertified in one of their two subjects).

The Percentage of Classes Taught by HQTs after NCLB

NCLB reporting requirements (under the CSPR) ask states to tabulate the proportion of *classes* taught by highly qualified teachers, rather than the proportion of *teachers* who were highly qualified. Consequently, the CSPR data focus on a different unit of analysis and are not completely compatible with the estimates produced by the SASS survey. However, given that the SASS data show that a large majority of core subject teachers (83.6%) are also single-subject teachers, the proportion of core subject HQTs and the proportion of core subject classes taught by HQTs should not be greatly different.

According to the CSPR, *more than nine out of ten classes were taught by a highly qualified teacher*. By the 100% HQT deadline contained in NCLB (the 2005-2006 school year), 92.2% of all core subject classes were taught by a highly qualified teacher; and by the extended deadline of 2006-2007, that figure had risen to 94.2%. The CSPR data also provide this information disaggregated by level of school and poverty status. **Table 2** presents the percentage of core subject classes taught by highly qualified teachers.[17]

Although there was improvement each year and in all subgroups, the CSPR data show that classes taught by HQTs were not evenly distributed across school level or school poverty status. In each year, classes in elementary schools were more likely to be taught by HQTs than classes in secondary schools. The gap was four percentage points in 2004-2005 (93.0% versus 89.0%) and about three percentage points in 2005-2006 (94.0% versus 90.9%) and 2006-2007 (95.9% versus 93.0%). Also in each year, classes in low-poverty schools were more likely to be taught by an HQT than classes in high-poverty schools.

Summary of Findings

The 1999-2000 SASS data show that prior to passage of NCLB, there was a very high proportion (84.5%) of core subject teachers who were highly qualified by the law's definition. Although they are not comparable to the SASS data, the CSPR data appear to show improvement in teacher quality over the years in which NCLB was implemented. The 2003-2004 CSPR data show a higher proportion of HQT-led classes (86.5%) than was suggested by the SASS data, and the subsequent years show a steady increase over time—from 90.6% in 2004-2005 to 92.2% in 2005- 2006 and 94.2% in 2006-2007.

REAUTHORIZATION ISSUES

The current funding authority for the ESEA expired after FY2007.[18] Legislative action to reauthorize and amend the ESEA, along with the HQT requirements, will likely occur during the 111th Congress. Numerous proposals have already been forwarded that cover a number of important issues likely to be raised during the reauthorization process. Most of these proposals would amend the HQT definition or make exceptions for certain teachers or schools. Many of the proposals make changes similar to the waivers and increased flexibility already announced by ED during its implementation of the law and include such areas as multiple subject matter teachers, definition of subject matter, middle school teachers, and rural, urban, and poor schools.

Multiple Subject Teachers

Although the analysis in this report indicates that less than one in five teachers teaches more than one subject, those who did teach more than one subject were much less likely to be

HQT. Among multiple subject teachers in this analysis, half did not meet the HQT standard. This small group— fewer than six percent of all teachers—may present a large problem for schools and states attempting to meet the 100% HQT requirement. Solutions have been proposed for certain kinds of schools (such as rural and hard-to-staff schools, discussed below); however, some proposals seek to address the problem for teachers in all schools generally. These amendments would allow teachers teaching multiple subjects to demonstrate knowledge in one subject area using the existing methods and provide a second method for other subject(s) taught. For example, multiple subject teachers who are HQT in one of their subjects could be given a certain amount of time to accumulate coursework equivalent to an academic minor in the subject(s) for which they lack sufficient knowledge.

Definition of Subject Matter

The issue of multiple subject teachers is in part created by the definition of subject matter in NCLB. Specifically, section 9101(11) of the statute states that, "The term 'core academic subjects' means, English, reading and language arts, mathematics, science, foreign languages, civics and government, economics, arts, history, and geography." As mentioned earlier, ED addressed issues related to science and social studies teachers in its non-regulatory guidance. States were given the authority to determine whether teachers qualified to teach in one field of science or social studies were qualified in other fields in those areas. Some have proposed legislative solutions that would recognize "generalist" certificates in these and other areas as proof of subject-matter knowledge.

Middle School Teachers

Many of the teachers found not to meet the HQT standard are teaching middle school students. The problem posed by this group of teachers is that some have duties similar to elementary teachers, while others are more like secondary school teachers. That is, some middle school teachers work in so-called "self-contained" classroom settings where they are responsible for teaching multiple subjects to the same group of students. Meanwhile, other middle school teachers work in "departmental" settings, in which they teach the same subject to different groups of students over the course of a single day. According to NCLB, middle school teachers are to be treated like secondary school teachers with regard to demonstration of subject-matter expertise. Thus, those teaching multiple subjects in self-contained classrooms must be certified to teach in several subjects—or prove subject knowledge in each area by the other permitted means. The proposals to recognize "generalist" certification mentioned above would remedy this problem. Other proposals include expanding the allowable types of experience and forms of evaluation permitted in state HOUSSE methods for veteran middle school teachers.

Rural, Urban, and Poor Schools

The multi-subject issue just discussed is compounded in small, rural schools, which appear to have an especially difficult time meeting the 100% HQT requirement.[19] This analysis revealed that only a small fraction (0.4%) of schools benefit from the SRSA waiver. SRSA schools are largely defined as those located in areas classified as "rural" according to the U.S. Census Bureau locale codes. ED analysis has found the Census locale code classifications of rural areas to be at best crude and in some cases grossly inaccurate .[20] One proposal would give rural schools until the 2009-2010 school year to meet the HQT deadline; however, the proposal would provide this option only to SRSA schools. Another proposal would give the Secretary the authority to waive the HQT requirement for any rural school that could demonstrate that the requirement would impose an undue hardship on the school because of population and geographic constraints.

Research has shown that schools in poor neighborhoods and central city locations have higher rates of underqualified teachers.[21] Although no legislative amendments have been proposed to address issues regarding urban or poor schools, some of the proposals presented here that concern "hard-to-staff" schools could be adopted to relieve the burden imposed by the HQT requirement. However, given the high turnover rates at these schools, short-term waivers and deadline extensions may not provide sufficient relief. At the same time, such flexibility might weaken NCLB's emphasis on improving instructional quality—especially for disadvantaged pupils attending schools in high poverty areas.

End Notes

[1] Michael B. Allen, *Eight Questions on Teacher Preparation: What Does the Research Say?*, Education Commission of the States, July 2003; Linda Darling-Hammond and Gary Sykes, "Wanted: A National Teacher Supply Policy for Education," *Education Policy Analysis Archives*, vol. 11, no. 33 (September 2003); Dan Goldhaber and Emily Anthony, "Can Teacher Quality Be Effectively Assessed?," The Urban Institute, Research Paper no. 410958, April 27, 2004; Leslie G. Vandervoort and David C. Berliner, "National Board Certified Teachers and Their Students' Achievement," *Education Policy Analysis Archives*, vol. 12, no. 46, (September 2004); Eric A. Hanushek, et al., "The Market for Teacher Quality," National Bureau of Economic Research, Working Paper no. 11154, February 2005.

[2] The College of Education at the University of Kentucky provides a compilation of teacher certification requirements for all 50 states. The compilation is available online at http://www.uky.edu/Education/TEP/usacert.html. The National Association of State Directors of Teacher Education and Certification annually publishes a similar compilation, *The NASDTEC Manual on the Preparation & Certification of Educational Personnel*, that is available at http://www.nasdtec.org.

[3] Teachers may also demonstrate knowledge by having majored in the relevant subject(s), and experienced teachers may do so through the HOUSSE method explained later in this report.

[4] Richard M. Ingersol, *Teacher Turnover, Teacher Shortages, and the Organization of Schools*, Center for the Study of Teaching and Policy, Research Report, January 2001; Patrick J. Murphy and Michael M. DeArmond, From the *Headlines to the Frontlines: The Teacher Shortage and Its Implications for Recruitment Policy*, Center on Reinventing Public Education, Research Paper, July 2003; the American Association for Employment in Education, *Educator Supply and Demand in the United States 2001*, Research Report, 2002; Recruiting New Teachers, Inc., *The Urban Teacher Challenge*, Research Report, January 2000.

[5] The application of HQT requirements to special education teachers was subsequently modified under the Individuals with Disabilities Education Act. For more information, see CRS Report RL32913, *The Individuals with Disabilities Education Act (IDEA): Interactions with Selected Provisions of the No Child Left Behind Act (NCLB)*, by Richard N. Apling and Nancy Lee Jones.

[6] The most recently revised ESEA Title II non-regulatory guidance is available online at http://www.ed.gov/programs/ teacherqual/guidance.pdf.

[7] Rural school teachers are defined as those teaching in schools eligible for the Small Rural School Achievement (SRSA) Program (ESEA Title VI-B). The policy letter announcing this flexibility is available at http://www.ed.gov/policy/elsec/guid/secletter/040331.html.

[8] A GAO report dated July 2003 anticipated these data systems problems: U.S. Government Accountability Office, *No Child Left Behind Act: More Information Would Help States Determine Which Teachers Are Highly Qualified*, GAO- 03-631.

[9] The Secretary's letter is available at http://www.ed.gov/policy/elsec/guid/secletter/051021.html.

[10] The Secretary's letter is available at http://www.ed.gov/programs/teacherqual/cssoltr.doc.

[11] The Secretary's letter is available at http://www.ed.gov/policy/elsec/guid/secletter/070723.html.

[12] The SASS sample is drawn from ED's Common Core of Data, which contains virtually every school in the country.

[13] §1111(h)(4)(G).

[14] This figure does not include those employed as teacher aides (or paraprofessionals). Although NCLB does contain a separate series of requirements for paraprofessional quality, individuals employed to assist teachers were not included in the SASS sample. For information on the requirements for paraprofessionals, see CRS Report RS22545, *Paraprofessional Quality and the No Child Left Behind Act of 2001*, by Jeffrey J. Kuenzi.

[15] Although "social studies" is not part of the statutory definition of a "core academic subject," it is used in this analysis because it encompasses subjects that are in statute but not in the survey; namely, economics, history, and geography. SASS survey respondents could also categorize themselves as "Kindergarten" and/or "Elementary" teachers; those choosing these categories were also considered core subject teachers in this analysis. Special education teachers who teach core subjects are required to be HQT; however, they were omitted from this analysis because the SASS instrument design prevented clear distinction between those who taught core subjects and those who did not.

[16] Those who reported their teaching assignment field as, "Kindergarten" or "Elementary," were counted as single-subject teachers. Additional analysis of SASS data reveal that only a small fraction (less than 2%) of these teachers taught more than two subjects in 1999-2000. Therefore, the analysis in this report only considers teachers' first two teaching assignments.

[17] NCLB required that states submit these data starting in the 2002-2003 school year; however, according to ED, "several states reported that they did not have the mechanisms to accurately report these data the first year, ... [so] the 2003-04 data will serve as the baseline." U.S. Department of Education Issue Brief, *A Summary of Highly Qualified Teacher Data*, May 2008, available at http://www.ed.gov/programs/teacherqual/resources. The data for 2003 -2004 were not disaggregated in a manner comparable to later years.

[18] A one-year automatic extension, through FY2008, was provided under the General Education Provisions Act.

[19] Based on anecdotal evidence from ED monitoring visits provided during a February 27, 2006, phone conversation with an ED official.

[20] Douglas E. Geverdt, *Review of NCES School Locale Tabulation and Analysis, U.S. Census Bureau, Technical Memorandum*, December 22, 2005.

[21] Wuejin Lu, *Teacher Quality: A National Survey of Secondary Public School Teachers Using SASS 1999-2000*, unpublished manuscript, and CRS analysis available from the author.

Chapter 3

VALUE-ADDED MODELING FOR TEACHER EFFECTIVENESS[*]

Erin D. Caffrey and Jeffrey J. Kuenzi

SUMMARY

Two of the major goals of the Elementary and Secondary Education Act (ESEA), as amended by the No Child Left Behind Act of 2001 (P.L. 107-110; NCLB), are to improve the quality of K- 12 teaching and raise the academic achievement of students who fail to meet grade-level proficiency standards. In setting these goals, Congress recognized that reaching the second goal depends greatly on meeting the first; that is, quality teaching is critical to student success. Thus, NCLB established new standards for teacher qualifications and required that all courses in "core academic subjects" be taught by a *highly qualified teacher* by the end of the 2005-2006 school year.

During implementation, the NCLB highly qualified teacher requirement came to be seen as setting minimum qualifications for entry into the profession and was criticized by some for establishing standards so low that nearly every teacher met the requirement. Meanwhile, policy makers have grown increasingly interested in the output of teachers' work; that is, their performance in the classroom and the effectiveness of their instruction. Attempts to improve teacher performance led to federal and state efforts to incentivize improved performance through alternative compensation systems. For example, through P.L. 109-149, Congress authorized the Federal Teacher Incentive Fund (TIF) program, which provides grants to support teacher performance pay efforts. In addition, there are various programs at all levels (national, state, and local) aimed at reforming teacher compensation systems. The most recent congressional action in this area came with the passage of the American Recovery and Reinvestment Act of 2009 (ARRA, P.L. 111-5) and, in particular, enactment of the Race to the Top (RTTT) program.

---

[*] This is an edited, reformatted and augmented version of a CRS Report for Congress publication dated January 2010.

The U.S. Department of Education (ED) recently released a final rule of priorities, requirements, definitions, and selection criteria for the RTTT. The final rule established a definition of an *effective teacher* as one "whose students achieve acceptable rates (e.g., at least one grade level in an academic year) of student growth (as defined in this notice)." That is, to be considered effective, teachers must raise their students' learning to a level at or above what is expected within a typical school year. States, LEAs, and schools must include additional measures to evaluate teachers; however, these evaluations must be based, "in significant part, [on] student growth."

This report addresses issues associated with the evaluation of teacher effectiveness based on student growth in achievement. It focuses specifically on a method of evaluation referred to as *value-added modeling* (VAM). Although there are other methods for assessing teacher effectiveness, in the last decade, VAM has garnered increasing attention in education research and policy due to its promise as a more objective method of evaluation. The first section of this report describes what constitutes a VAM approach and how it estimates the so-called "teacher effect." The second section identifies the components necessary to conduct VAM in education settings. Third, the report discusses current applications of VAM at the state and school district levels and what the research on these applications says about this method of evaluation. The fourth section of the report explains some of the implications these applications have for large-scale implementation of VAM. Finally, the report describes some of the federal policy options that might arise as Congress considers legislative action around these or related issues.

INTRODUCTION

Two of the major goals of the Elementary and Secondary Education Act (ESEA), as amended by the No Child Left Behind Act of 2001 (P.L. 107-110; NCLB), are to improve the quality of K-12 teaching and raise the academic achievement of students who fail to meet grade-level proficiency standards. In setting these goals, Congress recognized that reaching the second goal depends greatly on meeting the first; that is, quality teaching is critical to student success. Thus, NCLB established new standards for teacher qualifications and required that all courses in "core academic subjects" be taught by a *highly qualified teacher* by the end of the 2005-2006 school year.[1]

During implementation, the NCLB highly qualified teacher requirement came to be seen as setting minimum qualifications for entry into the profession and was criticized by some for establishing standards so low that nearly every teacher met the requirement.[2] Meanwhile, policy makers have grown increasingly interested in the output of teachers' work; that is, their performance in the classroom and the effectiveness of their instruction. Attempts to improve teacher performance led to federal and state efforts to incentivize improved performance through alternative compensation systems. For example, through P.L. 109-149, Congress authorized the Federal Teacher Incentive Fund (TIF) program, which provides grants to support teacher performance pay efforts.[3] In addition, there are various programs at all levels (national, state, and local) aimed at reforming teacher compensation systems.[4] The most recent congressional action in this area came with the passage of the American Recovery and

Reinvestment Act of 2009 (ARRA, P.L. 111-5) and, in particular, enactment of the Race to the Top (RTTT) program.

Under the RTTT program, the U.S. Department of Education (ED) makes $4.35 billion in discretionary grant funding available to states for the purpose of school reform. Eligibility for funds is dependent on four broad areas of school reform outlined by ED:

- adopting standards and assessments that prepare students to succeed in college and the workplace and to compete in the global economy;
- building data systems that measure student growth and success, and inform teachers and principals about how they can improve instruction;
- recruiting, developing, rewarding, and retaining effective teachers and principals, especially where they are needed most; and
- turning around the lowest-achieving schools.

Two of the four school reform areas specifically address teacher improvement and teacher effectiveness. By articulating these reform areas, ED has provided an incentive to states to become more systematic about using student data to inform teacher instruction and to measure teacher effectiveness. The latter point is elaborated on in the discussion that follows pertaining to the definition of effectiveness (i.e., "effective teacher") included in ED's RTTT final rule.

In November 2009, ED released a final rule of priorities, requirements, definitions, and selection criteria for the RTTT, which provided details on how states are expected to address the four school reform areas.[5] In the area of teacher effectiveness, the final rule proposed a definition of an *effective teacher* as one "whose students achieve acceptable rates (e.g., at least one grade level in an academic year) of student growth (as defined in this notice)."[6] That is, to be considered effective, teachers must raise their students' learning to a level at or above what is expected within a typical school year. States, LEAs, and schools must also include additional measures to evaluate teachers; however, these evaluations must be based, "in significant part, [on] student growth."

This report addresses issues associated with the evaluation of teacher effectiveness based on student growth in achievement. It focuses specifically on a method of evaluation referred to as *value-added modeling* (VAM). Although there are other methods for assessing teacher effectiveness, in the last decade, VAM has garnered increasing attention in education research and policy due to its promise as a more objective method of evaluation. Considerable interest has arisen pertaining to the feasibility of using VAM on a larger scale—for instance, to meet RTTT program eligibility requirements concerning the evaluation of teacher performance. This report has been prepared in response to numerous requests for information on this topic. While no federal program has specified VAM as the approach that should be used to link teacher performance to student achievement, this examination of the feasibility of implementation and relevant policy implications may generate insights that are helpful in consideration of the use of VAM and alternative approaches to linking student achievement to teacher performance.

The first section of this report describes what constitutes a VAM approach and how it estimates the so-called "teacher effect." The second section identifies the components necessary to conduct VAM in education settings. Third, the report discusses current applications of VAM at the state and school district levels and what the research on these applications says about this method of evaluation. The fourth section of the report explains some of the implications these applications have for large-scale implementation of VAM. Finally, the report describes some of the federal policy options that might arise as Congress considers legislative action around these issues.

WHAT IS VALUE-ADDED MODELING?

VAM is a quasi-experimental[7] method that uses a statistical model to establish a causal link between a variable and an outcome. In education, VAM has been used to establish a link between teachers and the achievement of students within their classroom. This method of modeling is seen as promising because it has the potential to promote education reform and to create a more equitable accountability system that holds teachers and schools accountable for the aspects of student learning that are attributable to effective teaching while not holding teachers and schools accountable for factors outside of their control (e.g., the potential impact of socioeconomic status on student learning).

VAM is actually a flexible set of statistical approaches that can incorporate many different types of models. Some models use student achievement as an outcome and others use student growth. Some models attempt to link teachers to student achievement while other models attempt to link both teachers and schools to student achievement. Although many types of VAM approaches are possible, this report refers to all of these approaches as VAM. There are common elements across these VAM approaches that have policy implications, and these common elements will be explored in the following sections.

VAM is not necessarily equivalent to other "value-added assessment" systems. Some use the term "value-added assessment" to include any method of analyzing student assessments to ascertain growth in learning by comparing students' current level of learning to their own past level of learning.[8] There are some "value-added assessment" systems that do not use VAM,[9] and there are other "value-added assessment" systems that do use VAM.[10] While there are many "value-added assessment" systems, many of them do not use statistical modeling to compare a student's actual growth to a level of expected growth (e.g., one year of academic achievement, average student growth for a school, or some other measure of expected growth). Without comparing actual growth to some pre-defined level of expected growth, a "value-added assessment" system may not be estimating teacher effectiveness. Because the focus of this report is on the estimation of teacher effectiveness—a prominent provision in the RTTT grant competition—only VAM approaches, and not other "value-added assessment" systems, are considered.

The "Teacher Effect"

There are numerous factors that influence student achievement, including past educational experiences, home and neighborhood experiences, socioeconomic status, disability status, the classroom teacher, and so on. VAM recognizes that there are multiple factors that contribute to learning and is therefore designed with the intention of isolating the teacher's effect on student learning. The "teacher effect" is an estimate of the teacher's unique contribution to student achievement as measured by student performance on assessments. It is isolated from other factors that may influence achievement, such as socioeconomic status, disability status, English language learner (ELL) status, and prior achievement. One important feature of the teacher effect is that it is a statistical *estimate* of teacher effectiveness. The teacher effect is simply a statistical value or number, whereas teacher effectiveness is the actual phenomenon being estimated. Another important characteristic of the teacher effect is that it cannot determine *why* a teacher is effective or ineffective, nor does it provide any information on the specific characteristics of what makes a teacher effective. The teacher effect is no more or less than an estimate of the amount of influence a teacher has on the achievement of students in his or her classroom in the content areas being assessed.

Defining a teacher effect is critical to the utility of VAM. If VAM is used to estimate teacher effectiveness, it may be advisable to define the teacher effect consistently across schools, districts, or states, depending on the conclusions one would like to make about teachers (i.e., comparisons of teacher effectiveness across schools, comparisons of teacher effectiveness across districts, or comparisons of teacher effectiveness across states). A teacher effect can be defined in multiple ways depending on two major features: (1) the "plausible alternative," and (2) the other factors in the model (e.g., socioeconomic status, disability status, ELL status, prior achievement, and so on).

The first feature—the "plausible alternative"—defines a teacher effect relative to some other realistic alternative. For example, the teacher effect can be defined relative to the average teacher within a school, average teacher within a district, average teacher within a state, or some other alternative. In current applications of VAM, teacher effects are often estimated relative to the average teacher within a district. Defining the teacher effect in this way may make sense if the goal is to provide information about teacher effectiveness relative to others in the district; however, this definition makes it difficult to make comparisons of teachers across districts within a state. If policy makers pursue the use of VAM approaches, the policy may need to clearly describe the desired comparisons to be made.

The second feature—the other factors in the model—defines how precisely a teacher effect is isolated from other factors that are not attributable to the teacher but can nonetheless affect student achievement. VAM approaches usually include "covariates," which are factors that are thought to affect student achievement but are not attributable to the teacher. For example, one covariate that is often used in VAM is socioeconomic status. By adding covariates in VAM, the model attempts to essentially remove the influence of other factors on student learning. By doing this, the teacher effect is isolated and the modeled teacher effect does not, in theory, reflect student learning that is attributable to these other factors. To maintain consistency in the definition of a teacher effect, VAM approaches may need to use the same covariates across settings.

The use of covariates influences the amount of student achievement that can be directly attributed to a teacher. For example, if a large number of covariates are added to the model, much of a student's achievement may be attributed to these factors, leaving a small amount that can be influenced by the teacher. In this scenario, the teacher effect may be accurately isolated, but the magnitude of the effect may be small. If a small number of covariates are added to the model, much of a student's achievement is available to be explained. In this scenario, the teacher effect may not be well isolated, but the magnitude of the effect has the potential to be large. If policy makers pursue the use of VAM approaches, the policy may need to clearly describe the covariates of interest that should be included in a model that attempts to isolate the teacher effect.

The use of covariates in VAM is appealing because it allows the teacher effect to more accurately reflect his or her contribution to student performance; however, the use of covariates also introduces several conceptual difficulties for policy. For example, consider the use of socioeconomic status as a covariate. If a student comes from a family of low socioeconomic status, it is likely that this will explain a portion of his or her achievement within the model. Historically, students from families of low socioeconomic status tend to have lower scores on student assessments than students from families of higher socioeconomic status. Should policy assume that socioeconomic status may influence student scores and not make teachers responsible for attaining equitable achievement of students from low socioeconomic status? Or, should policy acknowledge that a factor like socioeconomic status is outside of the control of a classroom teacher and should be taken into consideration when evaluating that teacher? As another example, assume that one of the covariates in the model is disability status. If the model allows a student's disability status to explain a portion of achievement, is that acceptable? Or, should policy expect teachers to be equally effective in teaching students with disabilities and students without disabilities? These are important underlying questions that can inform the use of VAM. Answers to these questions are difficult and depend on the overall goal of education policy.

Components of Conducting a Value-Added Model

Using VAM to estimate teacher effectiveness has the potential to provide clear, useful information to teachers, principals, and policy makers about which teachers are influencing student learning in a positive way. If principals and policy makers can identify effective teachers, they may be able to begin the process of understanding what makes them effective and promote policies and practices that may increase the effectiveness of other teachers. Although the positive potential for using VAM to gauge teacher effectiveness is considerable, VAM is conceptually complex and computationally difficult. The sections below discuss some of these complexities, including the database requirements that must be in place prior to using VAM and the decisions that must be made when calculating a teacher effect. Although there are many statistical issues to consider, the sections below primarily discuss how the statistical complexities of VAM may influence policy decisions regarding the use of VAM to estimate teacher effectiveness.[11]

Database Requirements

To conduct an analysis using VAM, a sophisticated database must be in place, possibly for several years before an analysis can be carried out. The first requirement of a database for VAM is that it must have longitudinal data; that is, the database must include test scores from multiple grades for individual students. Ideally, the test scores would come from the same assessment, and that assessment would have known psychometric properties, such as reliability and validity.[12] Second, the database must have variables that link students to teachers. In some cases, this link could be fairly simple. For example, an elementary school teacher who is completely responsible for teaching a class of 20 students could be linked to the assessment scores of these students in a relatively straightforward way. In other cases, this link is not as clear. For example, many students are taught by multiple teachers, such as a regular education classroom teacher and a special education teacher or an English language teacher. In higher grades, students often have multiple teachers—one for each subject. Linking multiple teachers to a student's assessment score is a difficult process that requires some forethought: What fraction of the student's learning should be accounted for by each teacher? In higher grades, which teacher should be responsible for student performance on a reading assessment (e.g., history teacher, English teacher, etc.), given that most students do not explicitly learn "reading skills" in higher grades? Similarly, which teacher is responsible for student performance on a mathematics assessment (e.g., geometry teacher, algebra teacher, trigonometry teacher, etc.), given that a "mathematics" assessment may have items from multiple mathematics courses? Are all teachers responsible? If so, what fraction of student performance should be attributed to each teacher?

A third requirement for databases is general information about the students, teachers, and schools that can be used as covariates in the model. At the student level, information about student race/ethnicity, socioeconomic status, disability status, and ELL status may be included in the database. In addition, any information on the student's family and neighborhood characteristics may be included. At the teacher and school level, information about teacher preparation programs, years of experience, and characteristics of the school may be useful covariates in VAM. In reality, however, information on students, teachers, and schools in large-scale databases is often limited, inaccurate, or missing completely, which may make the use of covariates in VAM inconsistent. Policy regarding the use of VAM may wish to consider which covariates are of interest when estimating teacher effectiveness, and ensure that schools and districts have the capacity to collect this information and report it accurately.

Estimating Teacher Effects

Once an appropriate database is in place, an analyst can construct a specific model using a VAM approach designed to isolate the teacher effect, thus estimating teacher effectiveness. The estimation of a teacher effect requires the analyst to make decisions about the specific model to be used and the covariates to be included. These decisions can affect the results and influence the level of certainty of the teacher effect. The following sections discuss common factors that can influence the calculation of the teacher effect: general issues of statistical modeling; covariates, confounding factors, and missing data; and the use of student assessments.

General Issues of Statistical Modeling

There are many types of VAM approaches that can estimate teacher effectiveness.[13] Models differ along at least two dimensions: (1) how student achievement is conceptualized, and (2) how teacher effectiveness is conceptualized. In terms of how student achievement is conceptualized, some models use a single score on an assessment while others use "growth" or "gain scores" from one year to the next. While there are advantages and disadvantages to both methods, the important policy implication to consider is that teacher effects from VAM using a single score and teacher effects from VAM using gain scores may not be directly comparable. Furthermore, the way in which student achievement is conceptualized can affect the magnitude of the teacher effect. In some cases, teachers may be found to be "more effective" using a single score on an assessment than when using gain scores. In other cases, the opposite may be true. Again, an important consideration in the use of VAM is to predetermine the types of comparisons to be made with the results. Teacher effects may not be easily compared across different types of models with different conceptualizations of student achievement.

In terms of how teacher effectiveness is conceptualized, some models consider teachers "fixed effects" while others consider teachers "random effects."[14] Analysts may choose to use either "fixed effects" or "random effects" based on the goal of the VAM analysis. If the outcome of interest is to determine the effectiveness of teachers in a particular school or district relative to each other, it may make sense to consider teachers a "fixed effect." In this scenario, teachers within the same school or district could be compared to each other but not to teachers who were not included in the VAM analysis. If the outcome of interest is to determine the effectiveness of teachers relative to a "hypothetical teacher," it may make sense to consider teachers a "random effect."[15] In this scenario, teachers could be compared more broadly to the hypothetical situation defined by the model. Both methods have advantages and disadvantages in modeling teacher effectiveness. Some researchers have suggested that using a "fixed effect" model may be preferable when using teacher effects within an accountability system;[16] however, some current applications of VAM use a "random effects" model (e.g., the Tennessee Value-Added Assessment System; TVAAS). There are many statistical implications for specifying teachers as either "fixed effects" or "random effects," but, once again, an important policy consideration is the potential to make comparisons of teacher effectiveness. The teacher effect from a "fixed effects" VAM analysis and the teacher effect from a "random effects" VAM analysis may not be easily compared. It may be of interest, therefore, to specify the comparisons of interest before making these modeling decisions.

Covariates, Confounding Factors, and Missing Data

Analysts must also make decisions about the components that constitute the VAM: covariates, confounding factors, and missing data. Decisions about how to include these components can affect the calculation of a teacher effect.

Characteristics of a student or a student's environment that are believed to affect academic achievement but are not attributable to the teacher are called covariates. As discussed above, a covariate is included in a VAM analysis to "factor out" the amount of a student's academic performance for which the teacher is not responsible. By doing so, the teacher effect should be a true representation of the influence of the teacher on achievement and not the influence of so- called "uncontrollable" factors on achievement (i.e., the influence of covariates). Some of the most relevant covariates in education are factors such as socioeconomic status, disability status, ELL status, and expenditure per student. Although these are commonly discussed covariates, there may be many more covariates that affect student achievement—some of which are not apparent or cannot be easily measured. For example, some research has demonstrated that parental level of education or individual student motivation can influence student achievement, but this information is unlikely to be included as covariates in a VAM analysis because it is generally not available in statewide databases. Furthermore, there may be other covariates that influence student achievement that have not yet been uncovered.

Without knowing all the variables that affect student achievement (and how to measure them), the teacher effect is not completely isolated from any influence of characteristics of a student or a student's environment that is not attributable to the teacher. This introduces bias into the teacher effect due to the influence of unknown factors. That is, a student's learning, or lack thereof, is mistakenly attributed to the teacher when, in reality, the learning may be a function of unmeasured school or community characteristics. Nevertheless, in practical terms, the use of *known* factors (e.g., covariates such as socioeconomic status) to measure teacher effects may be the most accurate method currently available to gauge how much a teacher contributes to student learning. In practice, however, it is possible that even the most accurate method may not be sufficiently precise to provide useful information to teachers and principals due to the unknown factors that are left out of the estimate of teacher effectiveness. This gap between the current state of research and the current needs of practice continues to be negotiated as VAM is used and studied in schools and districts.

Another potential source of bias in the teacher effect may arise due to confounding factors. A confounding factor is something within the culture of the school, community, or neighborhood that can influence the teacher effect. This source of bias may negatively affect teachers who work in low-performing schools where the factors that cannot be measured likely influence student achievement in negative ways. For example, students in low-performing schools may live in communities with more widespread problems that affect student achievement, such as health problems (e.g., malnutrition and undiagnosed vision or hearing problems) or neighborhood factors (e.g., low expectations for academic success or lack of community resources for after- school activities). Although VAM can estimate a teacher effect that reduces the influence of confounding factors, it is difficult to completely isolate the "true" teacher effect from these factors. As such, policy regarding teacher effectiveness may again consider the appropriate comparisons of teacher effects. If teacher effects are to be compared within a school, the influence of confounding factors is less likely to be a problem because most students within a single school will be influenced by similar health and community factors. If teacher effects are to be compared across schools, districts, or states, the influence of confounding factors may introduce bias into the comparisons because of the diversity of health and community factors across schools, districts, and states.

Finally, the issue of missing data can affect the teacher effect. In district-wide or statewide longitudinal databases, there generally is missing data. Due to high levels of student mobility and absence rates, information collected on students may be incomplete. In addition, cultural factors or language barriers may not allow for certain parent and community data to be collected. There are several methods that researchers use to deal with the problem of missing data;[17] however, these methods have not been well tested in the context of VAM.

It is unknown at this time how missing data would affect the teacher effect; however, student data that is missing in a nonrandom way may create bias. If student data is missing on a large number of students who are highly mobile or have numerous absences, this missing data is nonrandom (i.e., students who are frequently absent have a greater chance of having missing data than students who are not frequently absent). Since students who are highly mobile or have numerous absences are likely to perform at a lower level than other students, the missing data may bias the teacher effect depending on how an analyst chooses to deal with missing data. For example, if students who have missing data are excluded from the analysis, the teacher effect may be positively biased and the teacher may appear more effective than his or her true level of effectiveness. Alternatively, if students who have missing data are assigned an "average" value for their missing data, the teacher effect may be negatively biased because the covariates explaining low achievement are not appropriately used in the model.

Use of Student Assessments

Student achievement is measured through the use of assessments.[18] Results of student assessments are used for many purposes, one of which is to evaluate programs and policies. If states choose to incorporate VAM within teacher evaluation systems, it is unclear at this time whether the VAM analyses would be conducted with existing state assessments or whether states would choose to develop new assessments. Currently, states are required by NCLB to conduct assessments in reading, mathematics, and science for grades 3 through 8 and once in high school.[19] If states choose to use existing assessments, VAM can only provide an estimate of teacher effectiveness for teachers who provide instruction in tested subjects (i.e., reading, mathematics, and science) and for teachers of students in the tested grades (i.e., grades 3 through 8 and once in high school). Using existing assessments may exclude a large number of teachers from an evaluation system using VAM (e.g., teachers of students younger than grade 3 or in non- tested secondary grades; teachers of geography, social studies, history, art, music, etc.). In this scenario, teachers within the same school could not all be evaluated using the same system, which may complicate decisions regarding teacher performance, promotion, and tenure. Furthermore, an evaluation system that does not treat all teachers equally has the potential to create internal conflict among a group of teachers within the same school. If states wish to include all teachers in a VAM system, they may need to develop new assessments for currently untested grades and subjects. To create a comprehensive and consistent teacher evaluation system with VAM, states may need to consider the feasibility and cost of developing new assessments in untested grades and subjects.

Regardless of whether states use new or existing assessments, there are several features of assessments in general that may affect their use in a VAM system that estimates teacher effectiveness. One feature of assessments that may complicate the measurement of the teacher effect is scaling. Ideally, scores from different grades in a longitudinal data system would be vertically linked to a single scale so that achievement at one grade could be compared to achievement at other grades. In most statewide assessment systems, scores across multiple grades are not vertically linked onto a single scale. If scores are not vertically linked, the calculation of teacher effects across grades may be inconsistent. For example, students may appear to make large gains from 3rd grade to 4th grade, and the teacher effect may be relatively large. The same group of students could appear to make small gains from 4th grade to 5th grade, and the teacher effect would be relatively small. It is possible that the group of students learned the same amount from 3rd to 4th grade as it did from 4th grade to 5th grade; however, the scaling of the test or the items on the test may have been more suited to measuring the gain from 3rd to 4th grade than to measuring the gain from 4th to 5th grade. Thus, without vertical scaling, it is difficult to equate the amount of gain made across grades, and therefore it is difficult to compare the teacher effect across grades.

Another issue related to using student assessment scores in VAM is the timing of the assessment. Currently, state assessments used in accountability systems are administered once per year, typically in the spring. Using this "posttest-only" model of student assessment, a student's gain score would be measured as the difference in achievement in spring of the previous grade to the spring of the current grade. One problem with this model may be the drop in student achievement that occurs over the summer recess. If this drop in achievement affected all students equally, it may not be a problem for VAM. Research has demonstrated, however, that the drop in student achievement during the summer recess may be related to socioeconomic status and ethnicity.[20] In practice, this may translate into negatively biased teacher effects for teachers of minority student groups of low socioeconomic status.

In theory, it may be beneficial to test students twice per year, once in the fall and once in the spring, so that a student's gain score would be measured as the difference in achievement across one grade in school, presumably with one teacher. This "pretest-posttest" model of student assessment may reduce the problem of decreased achievement over the summer recess; however, it introduces more testing into the school year, which may be burdensome. Furthermore, a past evaluation of federal programs found evidence that the "pretest-posttest" model may introduce *more* bias into the teacher effect than the "posttest-only" model.[21] Due to the uncertainty related to "posttest-only" models and "pretest-posttest" models in VAM, it is unclear when school administrators and policy makers should schedule assessments to accommodate VAM.

Another consideration in the use of student assessments to measure teacher effectiveness is the potential for score inflation.[22] Score inflation refers to increases in scores that do not reflect increases in actual student achievement. In the case of score inflation, increases in scores can be attributed to an inappropriate focus on the specific types of items on the test, "teaching to the test," or even cheating. Score inflation is a difficult phenomenon to study, so it is unclear how prevalent score inflation is in educational testing. Increasing the stakes of student achievement, however, may inappropriately incentivize teachers and schools to engage in activities that promote score inflation. If estimates of teacher effectiveness are to be used for high-stakes decisions for teachers (such as promotion, compensation, tenure, and dismissal), policy makers may consider implementing certain protections against score inflation (e.g., the use of multiple measures of student assessment, the use of a low-stakes "audit" assessment, etc.).

Practical Applications and Research Results of Value-Added Modeling

Despite the complexities associated with the use of VAM, it is currently used on a limited basis for both teacher and school evaluation. It is not known how many schools or districts have VAM in place; however, the popularity of "value-added" systems continues to grow. Often times, the schools and districts that choose to implement VAM to estimate teacher effectiveness provide limited information on the details of their procedures and their statistical models. There are, however, several large-scale examples of VAM. Two often-cited applications of VAM are the Tennessee Value-Added Assessment System (TVAAS) and the Dallas Value-Added Accountability System (DVAAS). Both TVAAS and DVAAS (pronounced "T-VAS" and "D- VAS") are used as a part of larger, comprehensive evaluation systems that offer monetary incentives for teachers and schools.

Although the available information on the use of VAM is fairly limited, the findings of several research studies may be able to supplement information on VAM and provide policy guidance. The following section discusses VAM in the field, including the current large-scale applications in Tennessee and Dallas. In addition, relevant research findings are reported and discussed in terms of how they may be able to inform future policy surrounding the use of VAM to estimate teacher effectiveness.

VAM in the Field

The TVAAS is perhaps the most widely cited application of VAM. The TVAAS was developed in the mid-1980s by the Tennessee Department of Education and two statisticians from the University of Tennessee.[23] TVAAS is a statewide system that uses student performance on the state assessment to analyze student gain scores.[24] The student gain scores are used to estimate both teacher effects and school effects. The TVAAS system uses prior student records to remove the influence of factors not attributable to teachers (e.g., socioeconomic status or prior achievement); however, the model does not use covariates in the traditional sense.[25] Teachers' records, including the estimate of teachers' effects, are reported only to the necessary school administrators and not to the public. Teachers are typically awarded a salary bonus for high performance on the TVAAS. In some cases, principals and teams of teachers are also eligible for monetary awards based on high performance on the TVAAS.

The Dallas Public Schools began developing a ranking system for effective schools in 1984. Over time, the DVAAS was developed by an Accountability Task Force as part of a comprehensive accountability system that incorporated school improvement planning, principal and teacher evaluation, and school and teacher effectiveness. In past years, the DVAAS was used to estimate "Teacher Effectiveness Indices" and "Classroom Effectiveness Indices." The indices represent a composite measurement of multiple outcomes, such as results from qualitative evaluations, student achievement, graduation rates, etc. In its current form, the DVAAS mainly measures "School Effectiveness Indices." The DVAAS uses a VAM that incorporates covariates to control for preexisting differences in student characteristics. The covariates in the DVAAS model include ethnicity, gender, English language proficiency, socioeconomic status, and students' prior achievement. The DVAAS model also controls for school-level variables, such as mobility, crowding, percent minority, and socioeconomic status. Unlike some of the other VAM approaches used in accountability systems, the DVAAS uses multiple indicators, such as student assessment scores, attendance rates, dropout rates, graduation rates, and other indicators selected by the Accountability Task Force. Scores from student assessments, however, are weighted more heavily and contribute more to the overall estimation of school effectiveness than the other indicators.[26] Because the DVAAS primarily measures School Effectiveness Indices, monetary awards are typically awarded for an entire school. The school then decides how to distribute the awards among teachers and staff at the school.[27]

The TVAAS and DVAAS have been in place (in some form) for over 20 years. Although these systems appear to have operated successfully, a perceived lack of transparency has created confusion among accountability analysts and policy makers who have tried to evaluate these systems.[28] It is difficult to determine the exact models that were used to produce the results reported through the TVAAS and DVAAS systems. If policy makers and administrators choose to use these current systems as examples in the use of VAM for teacher effectiveness, more transparency in model specification may be necessary to replicate the results from Tennessee and Dallas. If these systems cannot be replicated reliably, policy makers may not be able to ensure that the estimate of the teacher effect is meaningful, and teachers may not buy in to a system that is perceived to be unreliable. Furthermore, if these systems are not well understood, they may not be able to serve as appropriate models as other districts and states choose to implement VAM programs to estimate teacher or school effectiveness.

Research Findings

In addition to the use of VAM in states and districts, researchers also have explored the potential use of VAM to estimate teacher effectiveness using data from multiple educational settings. This work may be able to inform the development of policy regarding viable methods for estimating teacher effectiveness because results may have implications for how teacher effects are measured and how teacher effects can be interpreted. In a critical review of the literature on the use of VAM to estimate teacher effectiveness, a team of researchers determined that results generally support the existence of teacher effects; however, the magnitude of teacher effects may have been overstated in some cases. Furthermore, researchers generally expressed concerns about the stability of teacher effects over time.[29]

Researchers who have explored the stability of teacher effectiveness estimates report mixed results. The results suggest that the correlation between the estimate of a teacher's effectiveness from year to year is "modest."[30] Furthermore, the estimated effectiveness of pre-tenure teachers does not necessarily predict their effectiveness post-tenure. For example, one study categorized pre-tenure teachers of reading into quintiles based on their estimated effectiveness; then, the researchers calculated the same teachers' post-tenure effectiveness and categorized the teachers into quintiles. Although many ineffective pre-tenure teachers remained ineffective, 11% of pre- tenure ineffective teachers became effective teachers when measured post-tenure. In the area of mathematics, the estimate of teacher effectiveness seemed to be more stable, with only 2% of ineffective pre-tenure teachers becoming effective post-tenure teachers.[31]

Other researchers have studied the stability of teacher effectiveness estimates and reached similar conclusions. That is, when teachers are ranked by effectiveness and separated into quintiles, the rankings change over time. In general, about one-third to one-fourth of teachers remained within the same effectiveness quintile; however, approximately 10% to 15% of teachers move from the bottom quintile of effectiveness to the top, and an equal number move from the top quintile of effectiveness to the bottom.[32] These results may serve to caution policy makers and school administrators from making tenure and dismissal decisions based solely on teacher effectiveness rankings. It may be possible to use teacher effectiveness rankings as part of an overall evaluation; however, researchers have not studied such evaluation systems.

Although the results suggest that VAM may not accurately rank teachers according to effectiveness, there may be other potential conclusions that can be made using VAM. Some research suggests that VAM can be used to determine whether teacher effectiveness is significantly different from the average teacher effectiveness. In one study, approximately one- fourth to one-third of teachers could be identified as distinct from the average level of teacher effectiveness.[33] If other studies are able to corroborate these results, this information could have implications for the way policy makers and school administrators use the estimates of teacher effectiveness. If one-fourth to one-third of teachers can be accurately identified as significantly less effective or significantly more effective than the average teacher, policy makers may be able to support some high-stakes decisions for teachers based on VAM in limited contexts.

Researchers who conduct VAM studies generally caution policy makers about making high-stakes decisions based on the measurement of teacher effectiveness. Currently, VAM may not produce estimates that are stable enough to support decisions regarding promotion, compensation, tenure, and dismissal. VAM measures of teacher effects, however, may be useful in a more comprehensive system of evaluation for teachers and schools.

Implications of Large-Scale Implementation

To date, VAM has been used in limited contexts to estimate teacher effectiveness. With the introduction of the RTTT program, however, states may now be incentivized to find new, rigorous methods to evaluate teachers, one of which may be VAM. If states begin to consider the use of VAM to evaluate teachers, there are many questions regarding large-scale implementation that may require some forethought. These questions largely concern the statewide longitudinal data requirements, capacity for data collection and analysis, and transparency of VAM for teacher evaluation.

Data Requirements

There are specific database requirements for VAM analyses. States that pursue the use of VAM may need to have comprehensive statewide longitudinal data systems in place for at least a year (possibly longer) before they can measure teacher effects using student achievement or student growth as an outcome. In addition, if states consider collecting additional student-level information to use as covariates in VAM, there may be new confidentiality and security policies that must be developed and implemented to ensure that students' and teachers' personally identifiable information is protected.

Using VAM to estimate teacher effectiveness may require states to consider the resources, time, and expertise involved with establishing an appropriate database. Although a number of states have already developed statewide longitudinal data systems, either on their own or through an ED grant,[34] it is unclear how many of these data systems currently link teachers to student achievement data. If existing statewide longitudinal data systems do not have this link in place, states may not be able to use data from their current longitudinal data system to estimate teacher effectiveness with VAM. If states choose to create the link between teachers and student achievement from this point forward, it may take a year or more before VAM can be used to estimate teacher effectiveness.[35] Creating a comprehensive statewide longitudinal data system with teachers linked to student achievement is a large investment; however, the potential for future analyses may extend beyond analyses of teacher effectiveness. States would face a tradeoff between the time and resources necessary to create and maintain the database and the potential information that may be revealed by it.

Capacity

States may also consider whether they have the capacity to conduct VAM analyses in terms of human resources and computing requirements. Measuring a teacher effect with VAM is quite complex computationally and requires an experienced analyst who can make defensible decisions about covariates, confounding factors, and missing data. Although it is possible that accountability analysts may already be trained in this methodology, it is unlikely that most of them possess the necessary skills to conduct VAM in the absence of further training. In addition to human capital requirements, VAM requires sophisticated software to create and run these models.[36] If districts and states choose to use these standard software packages, there is an associated cost with purchasing the software and maintaining licenses for this software. Furthermore, although these software packages are currently available on the market, it is unclear whether they can compute some of the more complex models that are used in research.[37]

Transparency

Due to the complexity of VAM, transparency can be difficult. The estimate of teacher effectiveness using VAM may not be universally accepted if it is not well conceived and communicated to all the appropriate stakeholders. Furthermore, if teacher effectiveness is to be used, in part, for decisions regarding teacher compensation, promotion, tenure, and dismissal, teachers need to understand how their performance will be measured. One way to make the process of estimating teacher effectiveness more transparent is to involve teachers and other school personnel throughout the process. For example, the DVAAS used an Accountability Task Force comprised of parents, teachers, principals, and community and business representatives to design the accountability system for teachers and schools. It may be important for the sustainability of the system to get "buy-in" from teachers and other stakeholders at the beginning of the process. Another way to increase the transparency of VAM may be to allow a second team of analysts to have access to the data in order to corroborate findings. If teacher effectiveness data are to be used for high-stakes decisions, it may be beneficial to have two separate groups of analysts reaching the same conclusions. Replication may increase the scientific rigor of the process and provide additional protection for teachers who are being evaluated using VAM.

The emphasis on transparency of VAM procedures may need to be balanced with an emphasis on student and teacher privacy. As the VAM procedures become more transparent, more information about students and teachers becomes available to analysts or teams of analysts. Although names and other personally identifiable information are typically removed from databases before any analysis takes place, states may need to ensure that appropriate privacy policies are in place before they implement VAM. States may also need to consider implementing policies regarding who may have access to data for analysis purposes and who may have access to the results of the data analysis.

Federal Policy Options

Although VAM approaches have been used successfully in district- and state-level contexts to estimate teacher and school effectiveness, research findings related to VAM and implications of large-scale implementation raise issues that may be relevant to the development of federal policy. At this time, it is unclear whether the current applications of VAM can be generalized to a large- scale federal effort or if future research and development is necessary for large-scale implementation. Perhaps other policy alternatives to evaluate teacher effectiveness independent of VAM may be considered (e.g., increasing teachers' and principals' capacity to use student achievement data to inform practice, better use of teacher data to inform teacher evaluation, etc.). If the use of VAM for teacher effectiveness is seen as promising for federal policy, however, there are several short-, mid-, and long-term objectives that may be able to further this goal.

In the short term, federal policy could continue to incentivize states to create databases that can be used for VAM. For example, the RTTT program prohibits eligible states from having any legal, statutory, or regulatory barriers to creating databases that link teachers to student achievement data for the purposes of teacher and principal evaluation. Linking teachers to student achievement data is an essential short-term objective for the use of VAM (or other models of teacher evaluation). Another short-term objective may be to ensure that the student assessments currently in place in elementary and secondary schools are relatively stable and remain in place for a number of years.[38] A consistent measure of student achievement simplifies longitudinal databases and increases the likelihood that VAM can be conducted. In addition to using consistent measures of student achievement, developing consistent measures of potential covariates for VAM analysis may be useful. In some cases, measures of covariates already exist and are collected routinely by schools (e.g., measures of socioeconomic status, disability status, ELL status, etc.). In other cases, however, new measures of covariates of interest may need to be developed (e.g., family characteristic measures, school violence measures, school climate measures, neighborhood measures, etc.), and schools may need to increase the capacity for data collection.

Another short-term objective may be to improve analysts' access to school, district, and state longitudinal databases. In other contexts, analysts have reported difficulty in accessing databases containing high-stakes student achievement data.[39] Although these databases include sensitive information about test scores, analysts who are granted access to actual data may be able to conduct studies on the feasibility of VAM in a typical school context. The federal government may have a role in incentivizing schools, districts, and states to share their longitudinal databases with analysts who are interested in conducting experimental VAM analyses. The potential information gained from granting data access to analysts, however, may need to be weighed against the privacy concerns for students, teachers, principals, districts, and even states. Privacy policies, confidentiality agreements, and strict protection of identification numbers may be necessary before data access can be granted to analysts outside of the system.

In the mid-term, federal policy could provide startup funding for model demonstration projects of VAM systems in real school contexts. One way to do this may be to scale up current applications of VAM, such as the TVAAS and DVAAS, to other districts or states within the nation. Another way may be to incentivize the development of new teacher accountability systems in which VAM is part of a comprehensive evaluation system. If model demonstration projects of VAM are successful, these models may continue to be scaled up and generalized to new contexts. While the VAM approaches are being generalized, researchers and practitioners may be able to develop "practice guides" that may allow the use of VAM to become more widespread.

Another mid-term objective may be to increase the capacity to carry out VAM in an efficient way. Currently, there is no easily accessible software that can carry out some of the more complicated VAM analyses,[40] and there are few analysts who are qualified to conduct these complicated analyses. The development of more sophisticated, user-friendly modeling software may allow VAM to become more feasible in educational settings. In addition, building human capacity in the use of VAM may be necessary. The federal government has provided funding for capacity building in the past through grants administered by ED. In the current context, grants could be provided for training pre- or post-doctoral fellows in VAM techniques or retraining current accountability specialists in VAM techniques. In addition, the federal government could provide funding to train teachers and principals to make better use of student achievement data and teacher effectiveness data to inform their practice.

In the long term, federal policy may be able to build on successful model demonstration projects of VAM in school settings. In addition, the capacity to conduct this work on a larger scale may be in place. Once VAM is implemented on a larger scale, further evaluation may be warranted. Some researchers advocate using alternative measures of teacher effectiveness to validate the results of VAM.[41] Using alternative measures of teacher effectiveness to validate VAM may potentially lead to more "buy-in" from teachers who are evaluated using VAM. It may also allow teachers, principals, and policy makers to gain a better understanding of what characteristics of teachers make them effective. Currently, a teacher effect can estimate the magnitude of teacher effectiveness; however, the teacher effect cannot, by itself, point to the characteristics of teachers that make them effective. By combining VAM with alternative measures of teacher effectiveness, research and practice may eventually be better able to identify characteristics of effective teachers.

End Notes

[1] According to ESEA Section 9101(11), "The term 'core academic subjects' means English, reading or language arts, mathematics, science, foreign languages, civics and government, economics, arts, history, and geography." For more information on the teacher quality requirements, see CRS Report RL3 3333, *A Highly Qualified Teacher in Every Classroom: Implementation of the No Child Left Behind Act and Reauthorization Issues for the 111th Congress*, by Jeffrey J. Kuenzi.

[2] According to a study conducted for the Education Department by the RAND Corporation, "By 2006–07, the vast majority [over 90 percent] of teachers met their states' requirements to be considered highly qualified under NCLB." See http://www.ed.gov/rschstat/eval/teaching

[3] For more information on TIF, see CRS Report R40576, *Compensation Reform and Incentive Pay for Teachers*, by Jeffrey J. Kuenzi.

[4] For more information on compensation reform, see CRS Report R40576, *Compensation Reform and Incentive Pay for Teachers*, by Jeffrey J. Kuenzi.

[5] U.S. Department of Education, "Race to the Top Fund; Final Rule," 74 *Federal Register* 59688-59834, November 18, 2009.

[6] U.S. Department of Education, "Race to the Top Fund; Final Rule," 74 *Federal Register* 59804, November 18, 2009. The definition states, "Effective teacher means a teacher whose students achieve acceptable rates (e.g., at least one grade level in an academic year) of student growth (as defined in this notice). States, LEAs, or schools must include multiple measures, provided that teacher effectiveness is evaluated, in significant part, by student growth (as defined in this notice). Supplemental measures may include, for example, multiple observation-based assessments of teacher performance."

[7] Experimental methods rely on random assignment, such as random assignment of teachers to schools or random assignment of students to teachers. In school settings, random assignment does not occur. Teachers are not hired at random and students are not placed in classrooms at random. For this reason, schools are typically observational settings in which quasi-experimental methods are necessary. A quasi-experimental method uses statistical techniques to approximate experimental conditions; however, this approximation is not perfect, and results will contain a certain amount of uncertainty due to the nonrandom nature of the data.

[8] For example, see http://www.effwa.org/pdfs/Value-Added.pdf.

[9] The Pennsylvania Value-Added Assessment System (PVAAS) measures student growth but does not seem to link student growth to teachers (see http://www.pde.state.pa.us/a_and_t/cwp/view.asp?A=108&Q=108916).

[10] The Tennessee Value-Added Assessment System (TVAAS) links student achievement data and uses VAM to estimate teacher effects (see http://addingvalue.wceruw.org/Related%20Bibliography/Articles/Sanders%20&%20Horn.pdf).

[11] For a more comprehensive discussion of statistical issues that influence the estimate of teacher effectiveness using VAM, see Daniel F. McCaffrey, J.R. Lockwood, and Daniel M. Koretz, et al., *Evaluating Value-Added Models for Teacher Accountability* (Santa Monica, CA: RAND Corporation, 2003).

[12] For a discussion of reliability and validity, see CRS Report R405 14, *Assessment in Elementary and Secondary Education: A Primer*, by Erin D. Caffrey.

[13] For example, some common types of VAM approaches include the covariate adjustment model, the gain score model, and multivariate models.

[14] Specifying teachers as "fixed effects" assumes that the observed teachers (i.e., teachers in the current VAM analysis) are the only teachers of interest. Specifying teachers as "random effects" assumes that teachers are sampled from a larger population of interest.

[15] The "hypothetical teacher" would be defined by the analyst for the specific purposes of the model. It could be defined as an average teacher, an effective teacher, or an ideal teacher, depending on the goals of the analysis.

[16] For example, see Daniel F. McCaffrey, J.R. Lockwood, and Daniel M. Koretz, et al., *Evaluating Value-Added Models for Teacher Accountability* (Santa Monica, CA: RAND Corporation, 2003), pp. 64-68.

[17] In statistical models, imputation is often used to substitute some value for a missing data point (e.g., hot-deck imputation or regression imputation). Another way some statisticians correct for missing data is to delete all cases that have missing data and exclude them from the analysis.

[18] For more information on assessment in education, see CRS Report R40514, *Assessment in Elementary and Secondary Education: A Primer*, by Erin D. Caffrey.

[19] For more information on federal testing requirements, see CRS Report RL3 1407, *Educational Testing: Implementation of ESEA Title I-A Requirements Under the No Child Left Behind Act*, by Rebecca R. Skinner and Erin D. Caffrey.

[20] K.L. Alexander, D.R. Entwisle, and L.S. Olson, "Schools, achievement, and inequality: A seasonal perspective," *Educational Evaluation and Policy Analysis*, vol. 23, no. 2 (2001), pp. 171-191.

[21] Robert Linn, "Assessments and accountability," *Educational Researcher*, vol. 29, no. 2 (2000), pp. 4-14. Linn reported that a number of factors introduced bias into the "pretest-posttest" model. Some of these factors include student selection, scale conversion errors, administration conditions, administration dates compared to norming dates, practice effects, and teaching to the test.

[22] For more information about score inflation, see CRS Report R40514, *Assessment in Elementary and Secondary Education: A Primer*, by Erin D. Caffrey, pp. 34-3 5.

[23] Drs. William L. Sanders and Robert A. McLean.

[24] Tennessee uses the Tennessee Comprehensive Assessment Program (TCAP), which includes both criterion-referenced and norm-referenced items. In the TVAAS system, only norm-referenced items are used to determine gain scores. The gain scores in the TVAAS model are compared to national norms. For more information about criterion- referenced and norm-referenced assessments, see CRS Report R40514, *Assessment in Elementary and Secondary Education: A Primer*, by Erin D. Caffrey.

[25] The TVAAS uses prior information on each student as a "blocking factor" rather than using individual covariates, such as socioeconomic status, disability status, ELL status, etc. In this model, each student is used as his or her own control. Using a "blocking factor" is another statistical method to factor out the influence of non-teacher variables on student achievement.

[26] The DVAAS system uses both criterion-referenced and norm-referenced student assessments.

[27] William J. Webster and Robert L. Mendro, "The Dallas Value-Added Accountability System," in *Grading Teachers, Grading Schools: Is Student Achievement a Valid Evaluation Measure?*, ed. J. Millman (Thousand Oaks, CA: Corwin Press, Inc., 1997), pp. 8 1-99. For additional information about the DVAAS, see http://www.dallasisd.org/eval/research/ articles.htm.

[28] For example, see Yeow Meng Thum and Anthony Bryk, "Value-Added Productivity Indicators: The Dallas System," in *Grading Teachers, Grading Schools: Is Student Achievement a Valid Evaluation Measure?*, ed. Jason Millman (Thousand Oaks, CA: Corwin Press, Inc., 1997), pp. 100-109; Gary Sykes, "On Trial: The Dallas Value-Added Accountability System," in *Grading Teachers, Grading Schools: Is Student Achievement a Valid Evaluation Measure?*, ed. Jason Millman (Thousand Oaks, CA: Corwin Press, Inc., 1997), pp. 110-119; Daniel F. McCaffrey, J.R. Lockwood, and Daniel M. Koretz, et al., *Evaluating Value-Added Models for Teacher Accountability* (Santa Monica, CA: RAND Corporation, 2003), pp. 19-24.

[29] Daniel F. McCaffrey, J.R. Lockwood, and Daniel M. Koretz, et al., "Literature Review," in *Evaluating Value-Added Models for Teacher Accountability* (Santa Monica, CA: RAND Corporation, 2003), pp. 17-50.

[30] Daniel Aaronson, Lisa Barrow, and William Sander, "Teachers and Student Achievement in the Chicago Public High Schools," *Journal of Labor Economics*, vol. 25, no. 1 (2007), pp. 95-135; Daniel F. McCaffrey, Tim Sass, and J.R. Lockwood, *The Intertemporal Stability of Teacher Effect Estimates*, National Center on Performance Incentives, Working Paper 2008-22, 2008.

[31] Dan Goldhaber and Michael Hansen, *Assessing the Potential of Using Value-Added Estimates of Teacher Job Performance for Making Tenure Decisions*, National Center for Analysis of Longitudinal Research Data in Education Research, Brief 3, November 2008, pp. 1-12.

[32] Daniel F. McCaffrey, Tim Sass, and J.R. Lockwood, *The Intertemporal Stability of Teacher Effect Estimates*, National Center on Performance Incentives, Working Paper 2008-22, 2008; Cory Koedel and Julian R. Betts, *Re- Examining the Role of Teacher Quality in the Educational Production Function*, National Center on Performance Initiatives, Working Paper 2007-03, Nashville, TN, 2007.

[33] Daniel F. McCaffrey, J.R. Lockwood, and Daniel Koretz, et al., "Models for Value-Added Modeling of Teacher Effects," *Journal of Educational and Behavioral Statistics*, vol. 29, no. 1 (Spring 2004), pp. 67-101.

[34] The Institute of Education Sciences (IES), the research arm of ED, administers a grant competition for states to develop statewide longitudinal data systems. For more information, see http://www.nces.ed.gov/Programs/SLDS/.

[35] Sometimes VAM averages the "teacher effect" over several years to make the estimate of teacher effectiveness more reliable. In these cases, it may take three or four years before teacher effectiveness data are reported.

[36] There are several software packages that are available to conduct these analyses. Many researchers currently use hierarchical linear modeling software, which is available from Scientific Software International. In addition, SAS has developed "Schooling Effectiveness—SAS EVAAS K-12" software.

[37] Daniel F. McCaffrey, J.R. Lockwood, and Daniel M. Koretz, et al., *Evaluating Value-Added Models for Teacher Accountability* (Santa Monica, CA: RAND Corporation, 2003), p. 115.

[38] The current, state-led effort towards common core standards and common assessments may influence states' decisions regarding assessment measures in future years. For more information about the common core standards initiative, see http://www.corestandards.org/.

[39] For example, see Daniel Koretz, *Measuring Up* (Cambridge, MA: Harvard University Press, 2008), pp. 242-245.

[40] Daniel F. McCaffrey, J.R. Lockwood, and Daniel M. Koretz, et al., *Evaluating Value-Added Models for Teacher Accountability* (Santa Monica, CA: RAND Corporation, 2003), p. 115.

[41] See footnote 40.

In: Teacher Quality and Student Achievement
Editor: Katherine E. Westley

ISBN: 978-1-61728-274-4
© 2010 Nova Science Publishers, Inc.

Chapter 4

TEACHER QUALITY: SUSTAINED COORDINATION AMONG KEY FEDERAL EDUCATION PROGRAMS COULD ENHANCE STATE EFFORTS TO IMPROVE TEACHER QUALITY[*]

United States Government Accountability Office

WHY GAO DID THIS STUDY

Policymakers and researchers have focused on improving the quality of our nation's 3 million teachers to raise the achievement of students in key academic areas, such as reading and mathematics. Given the importance of teacher quality to student achievement and the key role federal and state governments play in supporting teacher quality, GAO's objectives included examining (1) the extent that the U.S. Department of Education (Education) funds and coordinates teacher quality programs, (2) studies that Education conducts on teacher quality and how it provides and coordinates research-related assistance to states and school districts, and (3) challenges to collaboration within states and how Education helps address those challenges. GAO interviewed experts and Education officials, administered surveys to officials at state educational agencies and state agencies for higher education in the fall of 2008, and conducted site visits to three states.

WHAT GAO RECOMMENDS

GAO recommends that the Secretary of Education implement a strategy for sustained coordination among program offices. A key purpose would be to aid information and resource sharing, and strengthen linkages among its efforts to help improve teacher quality. While

---

[*] This is an edited, reformatted and augmented version of a U. S. Government Accountability Office publication dated July 2009.

Education will consider forming a cross-program group, it favors short-term, issue-specific coordination. We continue to believe sustained coordination is needed.

WHAT GAO FOUND

Education allocates billions of federal dollars for teacher quality improvement efforts through many statutorily authorized programs that nine offices administer. Education officials said these offices share information with one another as needed, and from time to time Education has established and completed broader collaborative efforts. Yet, GAO found little sustained coordination and no strategy for working systematically across program lines. Education also has not described how it will coordinate crosscutting teacher quality improvement activities intended to support its goal of improving student achievement in its annual performance plan. Our previous work has identified the use of strategic and annual plans as a practice that can help enhance and sustain collaboration. Without clear strategies for sustained coordination, Education may be missing key opportunities to leverage and align its resources, activities, and processes to assist states, school districts, and institutions of higher education improve teacher quality.

Education has conducted evaluations for some of its teacher quality programs and has awarded grants to researchers for a variety of research on teacher quality interventions, which are intended to inform policymakers and educators about program operations and which programs or interventions are having an impact. While evaluations have been done or are under way for about two-fifths of these programs, little is known about whether most of the programs are achieving their desired results. Education provides information from evaluations and also from research through the Internet and a system of regional and national providers. These providers also either conduct or synthesize research and provide assistance mainly to states and school districts. These providers coordinate among themselves and with one another in various ways.

State agency officials reported through our surveys that limited resources and incompatible data systems were the greatest challenges to their collaborative efforts to improve teacher quality. State officials reported that data systems could be used to inform teacher quality policy efforts by linking student and teacher data, or linking data from kindergarten through 12th grade and the postsecondary education systems. To help address these challenges, Education provides some financial support and other assistance. For example, one $65 million program that helps states develop statewide data systems also received another $250 million in the American Recovery and Reinvestment Act of 2009. Also, the act requires states to report on the progress they are making toward linking statewide data systems that allow matching of individual student achievement to individual teachers. This additional funding could help states defray costs associated with these efforts.

ABBREVIATIONS

ESEA   Elementary and Secondary Education Act of 1965
GPRA   Government Performance and Results Act

HEA	Higher Education Act
IES	Institute of Education Sciences
IHE	Institution of higher education
K-12	Kindergarten through 12th grade
NCLBA	No Child Left Behind Act
OIG	Office of Inspector General
Recover Act	American Recovery and Reinvestment Act of 2009
REL	Regional Educational Laboratories
SAHE	State agency for higher education
SEA	State education agency
STEM	Science, technology, engineering, and mathematics

July 6, 2009

The Honorable Rubén Hinojosa
Chairman
Subcommittee on Higher Education,
Lifelong Learning, and Competitiveness
Committee on Education and Labor
House of Representatives

Dear Mr. Chairman:

Nationwide there are about 3 million teachers employed in approximately 14,000 public school districts with about 89,000 schools. Policymakers, researchers, and educators have focused on improving the quality of our nation's teachers in an attempt to raise the achievement of students in key academic areas, such as reading and mathematics. A variety of approaches have been taken to improve the quality of teachers, including focusing on instructional practices. Among these approaches, improving the qualifications of teachers is a focus of federal policy. Specifically, the No Child Left Behind Act of 2001 (NCLBA), which amended and reauthorized the Elementary and Secondary Education Act of 1965 (ESEA), established federal requirements that all teachers of core academic subjects be "highly qualified." This means teachers must generally have a bachelor's degree, be fully certified, and demonstrate their knowledge of the subjects they teach. According to the U.S. Department of Education (Education), most teachers meet their states' requirements to be considered highly qualified under ESEA. However, the percentage of teachers who are not highly qualified is higher for certain populations of teachers, such as special education teachers and teachers in high-poverty and high-minority schools.[1]

ESEA as well as several other federal statutes, such as the Higher Education Act and the Education Sciences Reform Act, authorize various grant programs and other forms of assistance, like research, for states, school districts, and institutions of higher education to help individuals meet the teacher qualification requirements as well as other efforts aimed at improving teacher quality. This funding and assistance are administered by Education, either directly or indirectly through state and local entities.

Student access to high-quality teachers may be affected, in part, by the extent to which the kindergarten through 12th grade (K-12) and higher education systems work together at the federal, state, and local levels. However, it is unclear how conducive the current configuration of entities is to these complementary relationships. Given the importance of teacher quality to student achievement and the role that the federal and state governments play in this area, you asked us to address the following questions: (1) To what extent does Education fund and coordinate teacher quality programs? (2) How does Education target monitoring of its teacher quality program grantees and coordinate these efforts? (3) What evaluation and research does Education conduct on teacher quality, and how does it provide and coordinate research-related assistance to states and school districts? (4) What are the challenges to collaboration within states and how does Education address these challenges?

To conduct our work, we used a variety of methods, including interviews with Education officials, surveys of states and the District of Columbia, and site visits in three states. To learn about the major federal programs supporting teacher quality efforts, we selected programs from the *Guide to U.S. Department of Education Programs 2008* and verified that these were the relevant programs with Education officials. For each grant program, we reviewed federal laws, nonregulatory guidance, policies, procedure manuals, and other documentation, and interviewed officials from a range of Education offices overseeing teacher quality programs to determine how they coordinate program efforts as well as how they monitor grantees. We also interviewed officials from a selection of relevant Education-funded research organizations and related assistance providers at the regional and national levels to understand how Education funds and supports efforts to improve teacher quality. To learn about the specific areas of teacher quality that state agencies are focusing on and the challenges to collaboration within their states,[2] we administered two surveys between August and November 2008—one to heads of state educational agencies and another to heads of state agencies for higher education in states and the District of Columbia using self-administered, electronic questionnaires posted on the Internet.[3] We received a 94 percent response rate for the state educational agency survey and a 96 percent response rate for the state agency for higher education survey. We also conducted site visits to three states—Louisiana, New Jersey, and Oregon—that were selected based on their having initiatives that focus on teacher quality, such as coordinating bodies that are intended to bridge the K-12 and higher education systems,[4] and on diversity in terms of geographic location, population, and amount of federal teacher quality program funding. We met with state officials in each state and, to understand the local perspective, we met with officials in at least one school district and two universities in each state. A more detailed explanation of our scope and methodology can be found in appendix I. The surveys and a more complete tabulation of aggregated results can be viewed at GAO-09-594SP.

We conducted our work from February 2008 through July 2009 in accordance with generally accepted government auditing standards. Those standards require that we plan and perform the audit to obtain sufficient, appropriate evidence to provide a reasonable basis for our findings and conclusions based on our audit objectives. We believe that the evidence obtained provides a reasonable basis for our findings and conclusions based on our audit objectives.

BACKGROUND

Research points to teacher quality as an important school-level factor influencing student learning and ultimately preparing children for their futures as citizens and workers in a knowledge-based economy. However, efforts to improve the quality of teachers face several challenges. One challenge is a lack of consensus about what makes teachers effective. Even though research demonstrates that some teachers affect their students' academic growth more than other teachers, research has not categorically identified the specific indicators of teacher quality, such as the characteristics, classroom practices, and qualifications that are most likely to improve student learning.[5] Some researchers have shown that with the exception of a few factors, they cannot state, with a strong degree of certainty and consistency, which aspects of teacher quality matter most for student learning. Another challenge is the high attrition rates and shortages of teachers, especially in high-poverty areas. For example, almost half of teachers leave the profession in the first 5 years of teaching, and there is an anticipated surge in retirements of teachers from the baby boom generation. Moreover, research has shown that many students, especially those in high-poverty and high-minority schools, have teachers who have limited knowledge of the subjects they teach. In addition, there are concerns that graduates of teacher education programs are inadequately prepared to teach to high standards and that once teachers are in the classroom, training to help remedy this situation is sporadic and uncoordinated.

While many teachers follow a traditional career path of preparation followed by ongoing professional development, there are also alternative career paths. Many prospective teachers receive their undergraduate degrees through teacher preparation programs administered by institutions of higher education. Traditional teaching preparation programs typically include field-based experience, courses in specific subject matter, and strategies of instruction or pedagogy. Within institutions of higher education, these prospective teachers generally learn subject matter content in schools of arts and sciences and learn pedagogy in schools of education. Under this traditional approach, prospective teachers must complete all their certification requirements before beginning to teach. Teachers may also gain certification through alternative routes designed for prospective teachers who have been out of the job market (e.g., stay-at-home mothers) or have a career in a different field and who hold at least an undergraduate degree. Alternative route candidates receive training needed to meet the certification requirements of other teachers while teaching in the classroom. Generally, after completing a traditional or alternative teacher preparation program, teachers in the classroom participate in ongoing training or professional development. Training for new and veteran teachers may differ, with some states and school districts providing mentoring or induction programs for new teachers. Induction for new teachers may include district- or school- level orientation sessions, special in-service training, mentoring by an experienced teacher, and classroom observation. See figure 1 for an illustration of the various steps in the career path for teachers.

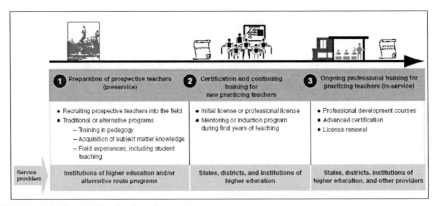

Source: GAO analysis, Art Explosion (images).

Figure 1. Career Path of Teachers

Table 1. Roles and Responsibilities of State and Local Education Institutions

Education activity	State educational agency	State agency for higher education[b]	Institution of higher education	School district	School
Legal and administrative responsibility for state education system	•	•		•	
Recruitment	•		•	•	•
Hiring				•	
Compensation				•	
Retention	•			•	•
Certification	•				
Classroom teacher training	•	•	•	•	•
Teacher assignments				•	•
Teacher evaluations					•
Alternative routes to certification	•		•	•	
Traditional routes to certification	•		•		
Mentoring or induction	•			•	•
Academic program approval at public institutions of higher education		•			

Responsible entity for each activity[a]

Sources. Education, Congressional Research Service, and state education sources.

[a] The roles and responsibilities of each entity may vary from state to state depending on the school governance system; for example, some states delegate more control to the local level than others do.

[b] State agencies for higher education have varied levels of formal authority, such as authority for academic programs and budget, over public institutions of higher education.

Entities at the local, state, and federal levels each play a role in the preparation and ongoing professional development training of teachers. The roles and responsibilities of these entities sometimes overlap (see table 1). For example, about half of alternative teacher certification programs are administered by institutions of higher education, and school districts, state educational agencies (SEA), and other entities can also offer alternative routes to certification.

State agencies for higher education (SAHE)—also referred to as the board of regents or the department, commission, or council for postsecondary or higher education—can also play a role in teacher quality. These agencies oversee state institutions of higher education where most teachers are trained. SAHEs generally approve of new academic programs at institutions of higher education and some may have budgetary authority.

School districts, institutions of higher education, and states collect and report data, which include tracking teachers' professional development hours, maintaining records of certified teachers, tracking student test scores and graduation rates, as well as producing teacher supply and demand studies. These and other data are intended to inform efforts such as improving schools, reducing student achievement gaps, and tracking the highly qualified status of all teachers. To make better use of these data, many states are putting in place longitudinal data systems that link data, such as student test scores and enrollment patterns, of individuals or groups of students over time. In addition, many states are using or have interest in using growth models—a term that refers to a variety of methods for tracking changes in a variable over time—to measure progress for schools and for student groups or individual students. For example, one type of model (known as a value-added model) measures students' gains from previous test scores. GAO has reported that states with a longitudinal data system will be better positioned to implement a growth model than they would have been without it.[6]

The federal government plays an important role in education. Education's mission is, among other things, to ensure equal access to education and promote educational excellence throughout the nation by supporting state and local educational improvement efforts, as well as improving coordination and management of federal education programs. For example, Education provides financial assistance through various formula and competitive grant programs. Formula grants allocate federal funds to states or school districts in accordance with a distribution formula prescribed by statute or administrative regulation. Competitive grants are awarded through a competitive process, whereby grant applications are reviewed according to published selection criteria and legislative and regulatory requirements established for the program. Education has discretion to determine which applications best address the program requirements and are thus worthy of funding. In addition, Education monitors and conducts activities related to the particular program and grantees receiving these funds. Education has eight principal offices responsible for specific program areas. These principal offices award and manage all grant programs for that program area. In addition, each principal office contains several program offices that administer the day- to-day activities of one or more grant programs, such as those authorized in Title I of ESEA (see table 2). Thirty-two program offices manage about 150 grant programs departmentwide.

A goal of ESEA is improving student achievement so that all students will be proficient in math and reading by 2014. To accomplish this goal, Education has established a series of strategic objectives that include improving teacher quality.[7] To assess its progress in meeting this objective, Education has established performance measures in its strategic plan. These measures all relate to having highly qualified teachers in core academic classes at elementary and secondary schools, including low- and high-poverty schools. These measures are also included in Education's annual performance plan. These plans are intended to provide a direct linkage between an agency's longer-term goals (as defined in the strategic plan) and what its managers and staff are doing on a day-to-day basis.

Table. 2. Principal and Program Offices within Education

Principal office	Program offices
Office of English Language Acquisition	• Continuation and Professional Grants Division
Institute of Education Sciences	• National Center for Education Research
	• National Center for Special Education Research
	• National Center for Education Statistics
Office of Elementary and Secondary Education	• Academic Improvement and Teacher Quality Programs
	• School Support and Technology Programs
	• Impact Aid Programs
	• Student Achievement and School Accountability
	• Office of Migrant Education
	• Office of Indian Education
Office of Safe and Drug Free Schools	• Center for School Preparedness
	• Drug-Violence Prevention-State Programs
	• Drug-Violence Prevention-National Programs
	• Health, Mental Health, Environmental Health and Physical Education
	• Character and Civic Education
	• Policy and Cross-Cutting Programs
Office of Innovation and Improvement	• Improvement Programs
	• Fund for the Improvement in Education
	• Parental Options and Information
	• Teacher Quality Programs
	• Technology in Education Programs
Office of Postsecondary Education	• Higher Education Preparation and Support Service
	• Institutional Development and Undergraduate Education Service
	• International Education Programs Service
	• Teacher and Student Development Programs Service
	• Fund for the Improvement of Postsecondary Education
Office of Special Education and Rehabilitative Services	•National Institute on Disability and Rehabilitation Research
	• Rehabilitation Services Administration
	• Office of Special Education Programs
Office of Vocational and Adult Education	• Adult Education and Literacy Division
	• Academic and Technical Education Division
	• Policy Research and Evaluation Staff

Source: Education.

A number of federal laws govern teacher quality. With the 2001 reauthorization of ESEA, which requires public school teachers to be highly qualified in every core academic subject they teach, the federal government established specific criteria for teachers.[8] Title I of ESEA requires every state and school district receiving Title I funds to develop and submit a plan for how it intends to meet the teacher qualification requirements, which is part of a broader plan outlining how it will meet other requirements of the act such as those requiring challenging academic content and student achievement standards. In addition, the state plan must establish each district's and school's annual measurable objectives for increasing the number of teachers meeting qualification requirements and receiving high-quality professional development with the goal of ensuring that all teachers met the requirements by the end of the 2005-2006 school year. While there is evidence that most teachers meet their states' requirements to be considered highly qualified, schools and school districts with high student poverty rates have generally had particular difficulty attracting and retaining highly qualified teachers; as a result, their students are often assigned to teachers with less experience, education, and skills than those who teach other students.

As GAO has reported, Title II of ESEA provides states and districts with funding to help them implement various initiatives for raising teacher and principal qualifications.[9] In addition, other federal laws that authorize programs intended to influence teacher quality include the following:

- The Individuals with Disabilities Education Act is the primary federal law addressing the educational needs of students with disabilities. The act, as amended, cross-references the ESEA "highly qualified" teacher definition, but unlike ESEA, this act requires that all special education teachers—not just those teaching core subjects—must meet certain requirements.
- The Higher Education Act (HEA), as amended by the Higher Education Opportunity Act, authorizes most of Education's programs targeted to postsecondary education. Specifically, the act established discretionary grants to prepare prospective teachers and accountability requirements for teacher preparation programs and states.[10] For example, it requires annual reporting on the quality of traditional and alternative teacher preparation programs, including the efforts of institutions of higher education to increase the number of prospective teachers teaching in high-need areas and being responsive to the needs of school districts.[11]
- The Education Sciences Reform Act is intended to strengthen the principal education research, statistics, and evaluation activities of Education. Within Education, it established the Institute of Education Sciences, which has a mission to provide reliable information about the condition and progress of education in the United States, educational practices that support learning and improve achievement, and the effectiveness of federal and other education programs.

EDUCATION FUNDS A WIDE ARRAY OF PROGRAMS INTENDED TO IMPROVE TEACHER QUALITY AND HAS TAKEN SOME STEPS TO COORDINATE THESE PROGRAMS ON OCCASION

Over a third of the programs that Education administers support efforts to improve teacher quality. Many of these statutorily authorized programs supporting teacher quality are intended to specifically support teacher quality activities, such as professional development training for teachers already serving in the classroom; the remaining programs support teacher quality activities but do so in pursuit of other program purposes or goals. Education officials said they have taken some steps to share information among the multiple offices administering these programs and have established and completed broader collaborative efforts on occasion.

Education Administers 56 Programs Supporting Efforts to Improve Teacher Quality, Especially for Local Efforts to Train Existing Teachers

In fiscal year 2009, Education administered 56 statutorily authorized programs that support efforts to improve teacher quality. Of these 56 programs, Education allocated about $4.1 billion to 23 programs that have, as a specific purpose, improving teacher quality, including increasing the number of highly qualified teachers in the classroom. The remaining 33 programs do not have the primary purpose of improving teacher quality and focus on other program goals or purposes, such as increasing student access to institutions of higher education. Nevertheless, these programs allow or require some portion of program funding to be used for teacher quality activities. Education officials said that they do not collect specific data on the amount of funding going to teacher quality activities for most of these programs. Appendixes II and III provide information about each of the programs.

Twenty-three Programs Specifically Focus on Teacher Quality
Of the 23 programs that specifically focus on improving teacher quality, a majority of the funds (approximately $3 billion) are concentrated in one program, the Improving Teacher Quality State Grant program. This formula grant is allocated primarily to school districts and may be used for a wide variety of activities to improve teacher quality, such as providing funding for teacher preparation, training for teachers already in the classroom, and recruitment.[12] In addition, states may retain approximately 5 percent of these program funds to support teacher quality efforts—generally split evenly between state educational agencies (to support state-level teacher initiatives) and state agencies for higher education (to support partnerships between institutions of higher education and high- need school districts that work to provide training to teachers already teaching in the classroom).

As shown in figure 2, 16 of the 23 programs specifically focused on teacher quality each received less than $50 million. Nearly all of these programs are competitive grants, and each has its own policies, applications, award competitions, reporting requirements, and, in some cases, federal evaluations. Furthermore, these programs are focused to support specific activities, such as improving teachers' knowledge and understanding of American history, recruiting midcareer professionals to teaching, or training existing teachers in music, dance, and drama.

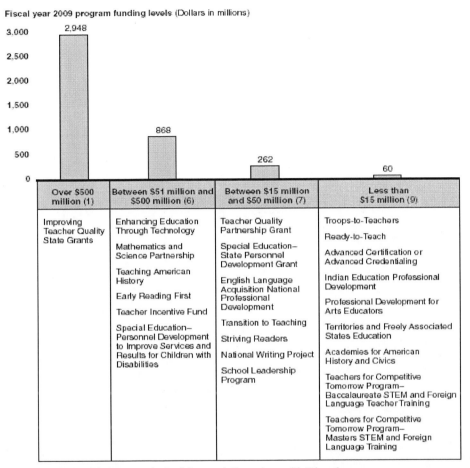

Sources: GAO analysis of documents obtained from and discussions with Education.

Note: Education's fiscal year 2010 budget request proposes eliminating 2 of these 23 programs: the Ready-to-Teach program and the Academies for American History and Civics program. In fiscal year 2009, both programs are funded at less than $15 million. Education proposes eliminating the Readyto-Teach program because it limits eligibility only to telecommunications providers and not additional professional development providers that utilize other delivery methods, such as the Internet and other digital media platforms. Education proposes eliminating the American History and Civics program because the program is considered too small to leverage funding effectively and Education has minimal evidence that the program has a positive impact on participating students and teachers. Further, Education states that school districts and other entities that wish to implement history and civics training programs can use funds provided under other federal programs, such as the Teaching American History program.

Figure 2. Funding Levels of the 23 Programs Specifically Focused on Teacher Quality

As illustrated in table 3, most of the 23 programs allow funds to be used for professional development training for teachers already in the classroom, but many allow grantees to use funding for a range of activities throughout a teacher's career path, such as teacher preparation, teacher recruitment or retention, certification or licensure, and induction or mentoring.

Table 3. Activities Funded by Programs Specifically Focused on Teacher Quality Program

Program	Recruitment or retention	Teacher preparation[a]	Certification or licensure	Induction or mentoring[b]	Professional development	Compensation
Improving Teacher Quality State Grants	●	●	●	●	●	●
Mathematics and Science Partnerships	●				●	
Enhancing Education Through Technology Program					●	
National Writing Project					●	
Advanced Certification or Advanced Credentialing	●		●			
Troops-to-Teachers	●	●	●			
Early Reading First					●	
Striving Readers					●	
Teacher Incentive Fund						●
Territories and Freely Associated States Education Grant Program					●	
Indian Education Professional Development Grants[c]	●	●	●	●	●	
School Leadership Program	●			●	●	●
Teaching American History					●	
Transition to Teaching Program	●	●	●	●		
Professional Development for Arts Educators					●	
Ready-to-Teach Grant Program					●	
Academies for American History and Civics					●	
English Language Acquisition Professional Development Program			●		●	
Special Education–Personnel Development to Improve Services and Results for Children with Disabilities	●	●		●	●	
Special Education–State Personnel Development Grant Program		●			●	
Teacher Quality Partnership Grants	●	●		●	●	
Teachers for a Competitive Tomorrow Program: Masters STEM and Foreign Language Teacher Training		●			●	
Teachers for a Competitive Tomorrow Program: Baccalaureate STEM and Foreign Language Teacher Training		●	●	●	●	

Source: Analysis of statutes authorizing these programs and Education documents.

[a] The category "teacher preparation" may include teaching residency programs. A teaching residency program for prospective teachers is a school-based teacher preparation program for recent college graduates and midcareer professional s who are not teaching. These prospective teachers teach alongside a mentor teacher and receive concurrent instruction in the teaching of a content area in which the teacher will become certified.

[b] Induction for new teachers might include district- or school-level orientation sessions, special in- service training, mentoring by an experienced teacher, classroom observation, and formative assessment.

[c] Although one of the purposes stated in the statute authorizing the Indian Education Professional Development Grants program is to provide professional development, the focus of the fiscal year 2009 grant competition is on preservice or teacher preparation.

Thirty-three Programs Allow or Require Portions of Funds to Be Used for Teacher Quality Activities but Have Other Program Goals or Purposes

The remaining 33 programs allow or require portions of their funds to be used for teacher quality activities, but their primary focus is not on improving the quality of teachers. Education does not routinely track spending on teacher quality activities for nearly all of these programs.[13] Specifically, only 3 of these 33 programs have collected information about the portion of funds spent on teacher-related activities. For example, according to Education, ESEA Title I, Part A, which provides support to programs designed to address the needs of educationally disadvantaged children, also provided approximately $1.9 billion (or about 8 percent of Title I, Part A funds) for spending on training for existing teachers in fiscal year 2009.[14] According to Education, between fiscal years 2000 and 2008, the Fund for the Improvement of Postsecondary Education-Comprehensive Program—a program supporting innovative reform projects for improving the quality of postsecondary education and increasing student access—awarded about $82 million in grants for teacher quality-related activities. For example, in fiscal year 2007 Western Oregon University received a grant totaling $685,685 to support a statewide collaboration of institutions of higher education to build the capacity of elementary grades math and science instruction. Education officials said the department does not collect data on expenditures for most other programs in this category.

In addition to the funds provided through the regular fiscal year 2009 appropriations for Education, the American Recovery and Reinvestment Act of 2009 (the Recovery Act) provides additional funds to several of these 56 teacher quality programs for fiscal year 2009. For example, $200 million in Recovery Act funds was provided to the Teacher Incentive Fund, which is a competitive grant program intended to help states and school districts design performance-based teacher compensation systems that incorporate student performance as a factor in assessing the effectiveness of practicing teachers.[15] Moreover, the Recovery Act requires that the Secretary of Education set aside $5 billion for State Incentive Grants, referred to by Education as the Reach for the Top program, and the establishment of an Innovation Fund. Education is providing most of this $5 billion of funding to states for efforts that could include making improvements in evaluating teacher effectiveness as well as ensuring that all students have access to highly qualified and effective teachers. Appendix II contains information on the 23 programs receiving Recovery Act funds.

Education Has Taken Some Steps to Coordinate These Programs and Completed Broader Collaborative Efforts on Occasion

According to Education officials, the multiple offices administering the 23 programs specifically focused on teacher quality coordinate with one another, and on occasion the department has established and completed broader collaborative efforts. Federal support for teacher quality is dispersed across a wide array of grant programs in Education, with nine program offices responsible for administering them (see table 4). Education's program office officials said their offices take some steps to coordinate with one another, such as participating in informal discussions to share ideas, attending and presenting at one another's conferences, and reviewing one another's draft grant announcements. In addition, officials said that they have formed task groups to address broader issues and phase them out once their tasks are complete. For example, in early 2003, Education formed a teacher quality policy group under the auspices of the Office of the Undersecretary of Education to coordinate multiple offices' efforts related to ESEA implementation of the highly qualified teacher requirements. Nevertheless, in the past, GAO's and Education's Inspector General's findings have shown that Education's programs could better plan and coordinate to, among other things, leverage expertise and resources as well as guide consideration of different options for addressing potential problems among the current configuration of programs.[16] While Education's collaborative efforts have occurred intermittently, several Education officials told us that they see value in routinely working together to exchange information across the program offices. Officials we spoke with noted that this type of sustained coordination required support and attention from senior departmental officials, such as formalizing the responsibilities and roles of a working group and its members. Given that the Recovery Act provides funds to improve teacher effectiveness, Education officials said that this presents an opportunity to coordinate Education's resources to improve teacher quality. Specifically, Education officials said that they recently have initiated coordination efforts to address the Recovery Act requirements related to teachers by forming a team made up of representatives from several program offices and led by the Secretary's advisors.

Education officials said that although several teacher quality programs support similar activities, differing statutory requirements can hamper coordination among the programs. Specifically, some officials said that statutory barriers, such as programs with differing definitions for similar populations of grantees, create an impediment to coordination. For example, Education officials told us that the Mathematics and Science Partnerships grant and the Improving Teacher Quality State (Title II, Part A) Grant to institutions of higher education both require partnerships that include a "high-need" school district. However, while the Title II, Part A program's authorizing legislation contains a specific statutory definition of a high-need school district, the Mathematics and Science Partnerships program allows states to define this term. This may hinder states' ability to coordinate resources among these initiatives because in most states far fewer school districts meet the Title II, Part A definition than meet the definition that the state develops for the Mathematics and Science Partnerships program.

Education has not described in its annual performance plan how it will coordinate various crosscutting teacher quality activities supporting its goal of improving student achievement. Our previous work has identified using strategic and annual plans as a practice that can help enhance and sustain collaboration.[17] As indicated in Education's strategic plan required by the Government Performance and Results Act (GPRA), one of Education's primary goals is improving student achievement so that all students will be proficient in math and reading by 2014. To accomplish this goal, it has established improving teacher quality as a strategic objective. However, the annual performance plan neither describes how Education coordinates or will coordinate its teacher quality efforts nor identifies barriers to such coordination. GPRA offers a structured means for identifying multiple programs—within and outside the agency—that are to contribute to the same or similar goals and for describing coordination efforts to ensure that goals are consistent and program efforts are mutually reinforcing. As GAO has previously reported, agencies can strengthen their commitment to work collaboratively by articulating their efforts in formal documents, such as in a planning document.[18] We have also reported that uncoordinated program efforts can waste scarce funds, confuse and frustrate program customers, and limit the overall effectiveness of the federal effort.[19]

Table 4. Offices That Administer the 23 Programs Focused Primarily on Teacher Quality

Principal offices[a]	Program offices	Teacher quality programs
Office of Elementary and Secondary Education	School Support and Technology Programs	• Territories and Freely Associated States Education GrantProgram • Enhancing Education Through Technology Program
	Academic Improvement and Teacher Quality	• Striving Readers • Improving Teacher Quality State Grants • Mathematics and Science Partnerships • Teacher Incentive Fund • Early Reading First
	Office of Indian Education	• Indian Education Professional Development Grants
Office of Innovation and Improvement	Teacher Quality Programs	• Advanced Certification or Advanced Credentialing • School Leadership Program • Teaching American History • National Writing Project • Transition to Teaching Program • Troops-to-Teachers • Academies for American History and Civics • Teacher Quality Partnership Grants[b]
	Improvement Programs	• Professional Development for Arts Educators
	Technology in Education Programs	• Ready-to-Teach Grant Program
Office of Postsecondary Education	Teacher and Student Development Programs Service	• Teachers for a Competitive Tomorrow Program: Baccalaureate STEM and Foreign Language Teacher Training • Teachers for a Competitive Tomorrow Program: Masters STEM and Foreign Language Teacher Training
Office of English Language Acquisition	Continuation and Professional Grants Division	• English Language Acquisition Professional Development Program
Office of Special Education and Rehabilitative Services	Office of Special Education Programs	• Special Education-State Personnel Development Grant Program • Special Education-Personnel Development to Improve Services and Results for Children with Disabilities

Source: GAO analysis of Education documentation.

[a] A principal office is an organizational unit of Education responsible for administering grant programs. A program office is a subunit of a principal office that conducts the daily work of administering grant programs.

[b] As of fiscal year 2009, the Teacher Quality Partnership Program was moved from the Office of Postsecondary Education to the Office of Innovation and Improvement. However, the Office of Postsecondary Education will continue overseeing all grants awarded prior to fiscal year 2009.

OFFICES ADMINISTERING EDUCATION'S TEACHER IMPROVEMENT PROGRAMS USE A VARIETY OF METHODS TO TARGET MONITORING, AND EDUCATION IS BEGINNING TO IMPLEMENT MECHANISMS INTENDED TO IMPROVE AND COORDINATE THESE EFFORTS

Officials we spoke with in four principal offices overseeing some of the teacher quality improvement programs said that they use a variety of methods and sources of information throughout the life of the grant process to gain insight into the performance of grantees and to target monitoring assistance accordingly. To help ensure grantee accountability for using teacher quality program resources, monitoring begins with pre- award planning, training, and guidance to potential grantees and continues through all phases of the award and postaward processes (i.e., a so-called cradle-to-grave approach). For example, for the Teaching American History program, program officials said they provide guidance to applicants and grantees about how to develop performance measures related to program goals so that Education can obtain credible information on funded project outcomes from grantees. For competitive grant programs, officials in the relevant principal offices we spoke with said they review grantees' annual performance reports to assess whether grantees' activities are consistent with planned objectives, with Office of Innovation and Improvement officials saying they use a standard form to guide their review.

Furthermore, staff from the Office of Elementary and Secondary Education visit each state at least once every 3 years to monitor state efforts to meet the teacher qualification requirements and states' administration of ESEA Title II, Part A Improving Teacher Quality State Grants. In 2008, the Office of Elementary and Secondary Education conducted monitoring visits to 18 states and Puerto Rico, including 2 of our 3 site visit states and provided written monitoring reports on Education's Web site about these states' implementation of the ESEA teacher qualification requirements. For example, Education found instances in 2 of our site visit states of grants being awarded by state agencies for higher education that included an ineligible partnership. In 2009 Education officials said they plan to conduct monitoring visits to 15 other states through June as part of the department's goal to monitor each state every 3 years. In addition, Office of Special Education and Rehabilitative Services officials said they use the results of telephone conversations with grantees, technical assistance meetings, and conferences to understand grantee activities.

In addition to these methods of targeting teacher quality program grantees, senior Education officials said that Education is beginning to implement risk management mechanisms to help program offices, including those administering teacher quality programs, better identify and target grantees not in compliance with grant requirements or not meeting performance goals. Senior Education officials said that applying risk management in Education is a relatively new endeavor and that responsibility rests with individual program offices for identifying risks confronting each program and for using risk indicators. These officials said Education's risk management approaches will continue to evolve as processes mature and lessons are learned.

Given that this endeavor is relatively new and that principal and program offices tailor their monitoring to the particular teacher quality program or grantee involved, we found that some of the program offices are further along in developing risk indicators than others. For example, the Office of Postsecondary Education has developed an electronic grants monitoring system using risk-based criteria for its competitive grants. Officials we spoke with in some of the other program offices that administer teacher quality programs had not developed formal risk-based criteria or electronic systems; however, as described previously, they have a means for identifying and targeting grantees that may be at risk of noncompliance with grant requirements or not meeting performance goals.

Education is beginning to implement mechanisms intended to enhance as well as coordinate these efforts, such as sharing information about grantees. To coordinate a departmentwide risk-based management strategy, as well as assist program offices with their monitoring efforts, Education created the Risk Management Service. This office provides services to program offices, such as responding to their inquiries about policy interpretations and monitoring grants. Some program office officials we spoke with said that the Risk Management Service alerts them about grantees that are having problems managing other Education grants.

As part of this effort, senior Education officials described plans for standardizing departmentwide systems for sharing information about grantees' management of federal funds and performance. For example, Education is developing an automated process for enhancing its review of the findings of financial audits, called single audits, within their programs.[20] As has been done in the past, this information is shared with teacher quality program managers and others in the department. Education officials we spoke with who are in several of the offices overseeing teacher quality programs said they review single-audit results, as required, to determine whether entities receiving an Education grant may have compliance or financial management issues. In addition, officials also said that Education is in the process of developing a departmentwide electronic tool to help program offices improve efforts to quantify, evaluate, and report on grantee risk.

EDUCATION CONDUCTS A VARIETY OF TEACHER QUALITY IMPROVEMENT STUDIES AND PROVIDES ASSISTANCE TO STATES AND DISTRICTS THROUGH REGIONAL AND NATIONAL SERVICE PROVIDERS, WHICH COORDINATE IN VARIOUS WAYS

In addition to providing grants for teacher quality, Education has conducted evaluations for some of its 23 teacher quality programs, although little is known about the effectiveness of these programs. Moreover, Education awards grants to researchers for original research on teacher quality programs and interventions. Information from the evaluation and research is provided mainly through various vehicles on the Internet, and Education directs research and assistance to states and school districts through a system of regional and national providers. Education officials reported that these regional and national providers coordinate to provide this assistance to states and school districts.

Education Conducts a Variety of Evaluations of Program Operations and Their Outcomes, but Evaluations Have Been Done or Are under Way for about Two-fifths of the Teacher Quality Programs

Education conducts various types of evaluations, such as process or implementation, outcome, and impact, which are intended to inform policymakers, program managers, and educators about program operations, how well programs are working, and which programs or interventions are having the greatest impact.[21] Officials said that these evaluations are done in response to congressional mandates, requests from Education's program offices or management, or proposals developed by the Institute of Education Sciences.

While evaluations have been done or are under way for about two-fifths of the teacher quality programs, little is known about the extent to which most programs are achieving their desired results. Among the 23 programs focusing specifically on teacher quality, Education reported that it has awarded contracts, totaling about $36.5 million, to evaluate 9 federal programs, of which 6 have been completed (see table 5). Three of the completed evaluations—those for the Early Reading First program, Teacher Quality Partnership Grants, and one of two evaluations of the Mathematics and Science Partnerships program—provide information about how a program focused on teacher quality is directly affecting student achievement or how program outcomes could be indirectly affecting student achievement through their effect on teacher quality. For example, the impact evaluation of the Early Reading First program found that providing scientifically based materials and professional development to teachers had a statistically significant impact on children's ability to recognize letters of the alphabet and to associate letters with their sounds, but it did not have a statistically discernable impact on other aspects of children's reading or listening skills.[22] The outcome evaluation of the Teacher Quality Partnership Grants found that funded partnerships that included colleges of education, schools of arts and sciences, and school districts led to changes in teacher preparation programs and the development of professional development programs for veteran teachers.[23] The three remaining completed evaluations, which include a second evaluation for the Mathematics and Science Partnerships program, are process evaluations that provide information about program operations, but they do not directly address how the program is affecting student achievement through improved teacher quality.

The three evaluations under way are impact or outcome evaluations. Education officials said that for the remaining 14 programs that do not have an evaluation under way, evaluations are not planned over the next 3 years. Of these 14 programs, 2 were initially funded in fiscal year 2008 and another 1 in 2005, but the other 11 have been operating for at least 7 years and have never been evaluated.

According to Education officials, some programs may be difficult to evaluate. In some cases federal funds are combined with state and local funds, such as under the Improving Teacher Quality State Grants (Title II, Part A) program, making it difficult to isolate the impact of federal funds. While the Improving Teacher Quality State Grants program has not been evaluated, Education has examined the implementation of teacher quality provisions in the ESEA, primarily those related to the teacher qualification requirements. Moreover, Education officials said that several of the teacher quality programs are small in terms of their funding levels and as a result, have few program-associated funds for evaluation. However, as we have reported in the past, evaluations can be designed to consider the size of the program and the costs associated with measuring outcomes and collecting data.[24]

Table 5. Evaluations of the 23 Programs Specifically Focused on Teacher Quality

Programs that have a completed evaluation	Focus of evaluation
Teaching American History[a]	To identify (1) the types of activities that grantees implemented; (2) the content of the activities, including specific subjects and areas of American history on which projects focused; and (3) the characteristics and qualifications of teachers participating in the activities for the first 2 years of the program.
Transition to Teaching[b]	Interim report examines whether grantees are (1) increasing the pool of highly qualified teachers by recruiting nontraditional candidates into teaching; (2) bringing increased flexibility to the teacher preparation system by encouraging the creation and expansion of alternative routes or pathways to teacher certification and lowering barriers of time and cost of preparations while raising standards and program rigor; and (3) improving the retention rate of new teachers by supporting mentoring and induction programs, including a 3-year commitment to high-need schools in high-need districts.
Teacher Quality Partnership Grants	To determine if partnerships encouraged colleges and universities to (1) partner with and address the teacher preparation needs of high-need districts, (2) implement activities to improve the academic content knowledge of new or veteran teachers, (3) change student internship component associated with a partnership effort to improve teacher preparation, and (4) institute accountability for teacher preparation programs.
Enhancing Education Through Technology	To determine the role that the Enhancing Education Through Technology program plays, the state priorities and programs that it supports, and the relationship between state programs that the program supports, and the relationship between state educational technology activities and the goals and the purposes of ESEA.
Early Reading First	To determine the effects of providing preschools with funds to provide teachers with focused professional development and scientifically based methods and materials on children's language development and emergent literacy.
Mathematics and Science Partnerships	This evaluation describes the participants and activities of the Mathematics and Science Partnerships projects for 2003-2004 as they began the initial year of program implementation.
	A second evaluation summarizes information submitted by Mathematics and Science Partnership participants for 2005, which included (1) characteristics of the projects and participants, (2) professional development models and activities, and (3) outcomes of the programs.
Programs currently being evaluated	**Focus of evaluation**
Striving Readers	To examine the extent that (1) targeted interventions improve reading proficiency among struggling adolescent readers, and (2) schoolwide literacy-throughout-the-curriculum interventions to improve reading proficiency among secondary students.

United States Government Accountability Office

Table 5. (Continued)

Programs that have a completed evaluation	Focus of evaluation
Special Education-Personnel Development to Improve Services and Results for Children with Disabilities	This evaluation will (1) examine the quality of materials developed and the services provided by national centers with funds provided by the program, and (2) examine the use of the grant funds, qualifications of the faculty hired, and the quality of the study materials created using the funds. Also it will estimate how many new students enrolled and how many completed the course.
Teacher Incentive Fund	To determine the degree of success and challenges to implementing the variety of pay-for-performance systems in the program and, given adequate implementation, any increases in effective principal and teacher recruitment and retention in high-need schools and hard-to-staff subjects.
Programs that have not been evaluated	
English Language Acquisition National Professional Development Project	
Troops-to-Teachers	
Ready-to-Teach	
Territories and Freely Associated States Education Grant Program	
Special Education-State Personnel Development Grant Program	
Teachers for a Competitive Tomorrow: Baccalaureate STEM and Foreign Language Teacher Training	
Professional Development for Arts Educators	
School Leadership Program	
Indian Education Professional Development Grants	
Advanced Certification or Advanced Credentialing	
National Writing Project	
Programs that have not been evaluated	
Academies for American History and Civics	
Teachers for a Competitive Tomorrow Program: Masters STEM and Foreign Language Teacher Training	
Improving Teacher Quality State Grants	

Source: GAO analysis of Education data.

[a] Another evaluation of Teaching American History is currently under way.

[b] Transition to Teaching is an interim evaluation.

In addition to the federal program evaluations shown in table 5, Education evaluates specific interventions intended to improve teacher quality. For example, Education has conducted or has under way evaluations on teacher induction programs, teacher preparation programs, and reading and mathematics professional development and software programs. Specifically, Education completed studies on the impact of professional development on teacher practices and student achievement in early reading as well as on teachers trained through different routes to certification.[25] Moreover, Education and the National Academy of Sciences completed another study on the National Board for Professional Standards, which offers advanced-level certification to teachers.[26] Further, Education officials said that they have 5 other studies under way, such as a study on moving high-performing teachers to low-performing schools. Interventions such as teacher induction programs and professional development are funded under a broad array of teacher quality programs, such as the

Improving Teacher Quality State Grants, the Teacher Quality Partnership Grants, the Transition to Teaching program, and Mathematics and Science Partnerships. Education officials overseeing evaluations said that to inform staff in program offices working on related issues, they provide briefings on the results of pertinent evaluations. These briefings include discussions about how the evaluation might be useful for program improvement.

Education Awards Grants to Researchers to Study Interventions Related to Teacher Quality to Inform Policymakers and Educators about Their Impact

In addition to evaluating federal programs, Education also awards grants to researchers to conduct studies related to teacher quality ranging from assessing the effectiveness of reading and mathematics programs to measuring the relationship between teacher content knowledge and student achievement. For example, Education sponsors scientifically rigorous research on strategies for improving the performance of classroom teachers, 1 of 13 research areas established by Education's Institute of Education Sciences (IES).[27] Between 2003 and 2009, Education awarded almost $160 million in grants to research institutions for 69 studies focused on teacher quality. (See app. IV more information about these studies.)

Education Provides Research and Related Assistance to States and School Districts through the Internet and a System of Regional and National Providers

Education disseminates results from its research to educators and policymakers mainly through the Internet and a system of regional and national providers. Overall, while SEAs reported that the assistance was more useful than SAHEs reported, the results of our survey and discussions with state officials suggest that most of these services are targeted to SEAs and school districts rather than higher education entities. For example, one of the primary Internet vehicles for disseminating research—the What Works Clearinghouse—was identified by officials in 24 of the 48 SEAs as moderately to extremely useful, but only by officials in 15 of the 47 SAHEs that responded to our survey as moderately to extremely useful, as shown in figure 3. Overseen by IES, the What Works Clearinghouse provides educators, policymakers, researchers, and other users with information on what IES considers the best evidence on the effectiveness of specific interventions. For example, IES officials told us that the results of research are synthesized into Practice Guides to make them more usable to practitioners. Current Practice Guides provide information in areas such as reducing behavior problems in the classroom and encouraging girls in math and science.[28]

Education also disseminates research through another Internet vehicle, the Doing What Works Web site, which is intended to help teachers make use of effective teaching practices. Most of the content of Doing What Works is based on information provided through the What Works Clearinghouse, such as classroom practices that are distilled from research contained in the Practice Guides; the site is overseen by the Office of Planning, Evaluation and Policy Development. Only 16 of the 48 SEA and 10 of 47 SAHE officials who responded to our respective surveys identified the Doing What Works Internet site as moderately to extremely useful. According to an Education official, these views may reflect the fact that the site is relatively new, and Education has not widely publicized it.

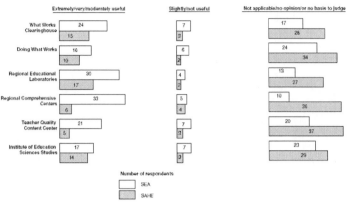

Source: GAO surveys.
Note: In some cases, respondents do not total 48 for the SEAs and 47 for the SAHEs because not all SEA and SAHE officials responding to the surveys answered every question.

Figure 3. SEA and SAHE Views of the Usefulness of Education Assistance Vary

Education provides research and research-related assistance on teacher quality through regional and national service providers, which work directly with states and school districts. Regional services are provided through the 10 Regional Educational Laboratories (REL) and 16 Regional Comprehensive Centers; national services are provided through the National Comprehensive Center for Teacher Quality. The RELs provide policymakers and educators with technical assistance, training, and research that are based on findings from scientifically valid research. The RELs distill and explain research as well as conduct research to identify effective programs and to address classroom issues facing the states, school districts, schools, and policymakers within their respective regions.[29] Among the 48 SEA officials who responded to our survey, 30 reported that the RELs are moderately to extremely useful, and 17 of the 47 SAHE officials who responded to our survey reported that the RELs are moderately to extremely useful.

Education's 16 Regional Comprehensive Centers assist SEAs within their regions to implement ESEA and to build SEA capacity to help their districts and schools meet student achievement goals. Unlike the RELs, the Regional Comprehensive Centers do not conduct research, but they do identify and synthesize existing research to help SEA officials understand what information is available to improve their schools and student achievement, according to Education officials. Among the 48 SEA officials who responded to our survey, 33 reported Regional Comprehensive Centers' assistance as moderately to extremely useful, while only 6 of the 47 SAHE officials who responded to our survey said that the Regional Comprehensive Centers were moderately to extremely useful.

The National Comprehensive Center for Teacher Quality (one of five National Content Centers supported by the Office of Elementary and Secondary Education) assists the 16 Regional Comprehensive Centers by providing technical assistance in conjunction with their work with the states.[30] Like the Regional Comprehensive Centers, the National Comprehensive Center for Teacher Quality does not conduct original research but provides technical assistance as well as synthesizes and disseminates scientifically based research on effective practice and research-based products on teacher quality.

Regional and National Providers Coordinate in Various Ways to Assist States and Districts

Regional and national providers coordinate among themselves and with each other to assist states and districts to improve teacher quality. For example, REL officials said that RELs coordinate among themselves to prevent unnecessary duplication of activities among the regions, as required by their funding agreements with Education. The REL Mid- Atlantic is responsible for ensuring that there is coordination among the 10 RELs. In this role, it manages a REL Web site, which includes information on past and ongoing projects, and it holds regular meetings among the RELs. Regional Comprehensive Center officials also reported that they share information among themselves but on a more informal basis than the RELs.[31] One comprehensive center director reported that the comprehensive center network has several mechanisms for discussing work with states, including semiannual director meetings and conferences that are attended by the staff and directors from the various Regional Comprehensive Centers.

RELs, Regional Comprehensive Centers, and the National Comprehensive Center on Teacher Quality also coordinate with each other as needed. For example, an official with the National Comprehensive Center on Teacher Quality told us that officials often coordinate with the Regional Comprehensive Centers and the SEAs to provide expertise on teacher quality issues. In addition, Education officials said that RELs and the Regional Comprehensive Centers coordinate as needed to address common concerns as well. For example, in one region the Regional Comprehensive Center brought together the REL and the National Comprehensive Center for Teacher Quality to conduct a study of the distribution of highly qualified teachers in one state, as well as the policies, practices, and conditions that affect that distribution. In this effort, the REL used its expertise in research to provide support on research design and data analysis; the National Comprehensive Center for Teacher Quality, while not involved directly with the research, developed surveys and interview protocols for the study; and the Regional Comprehensive Center coordinated the project and piloted the data collection instruments.

STATES FACE SEVERAL CHALLENGES IN COLLABORATING INTERNALLY TO IMPROVE TEACHER QUALITY; EDUCATION PROVIDES SOME ASSISTANCE TO HELP ADDRESS THESE CHALLENGES

State agency officials cited limited resources and incompatible data systems as the greatest challenges to their collaborative efforts within the state to improve teacher quality. Resistance to change, sustained commitment, and state governance structure also affected their efforts to collaborate. While state officials reported some challenges, they also reported successes in their efforts to collaborate within their states across a wide array of teacher quality areas. Nevertheless, they also cite a need for more collaboration, specifically to address training for existing teachers. To help address some of these challenges, Education provides financial support and other forms of assistance to some states.

State Officials Cite Limited Funding, Available Staff and Time, as well as Incompatible K-12 and Postsecondary Data Systems, as the Greatest Challenges, among Other Factors

State officials reported through our surveys (see figure 4) and state site visits that state budget cuts and reduced staff levels at their agencies inhibit teacher quality collaborative efforts. Collaborative efforts require a commitment of resources, staff, and time, and state officials report that reduced staffing levels have limited the available time that they can commit to collaborating, and it is difficult to be continuously involved. One state official told us that staff are focused on fulfilling state and federal requirements and have little time to address other teacher quality initiatives.

State officials also reported that incompatible data systems across the educational information system, such as those containing student-level, teacher-level, and postsecondary data, pose challenges to collaboration on teacher quality efforts. State officials said that some of their objectives for data systems are to link student and teacher data, or to link data from the K-12 education system and the postsecondary education system, to inform and measure teacher quality policy efforts. For example, state officials and experts we spoke with said longitudinal data systems can be used to measure teacher effectiveness through value-added models that estimate existing teachers' contributions to student learning, and that these models may also allow states to determine which teacher preparation programs produce graduates whose students have the strongest academic growth. For example, Louisiana officials said that although it has taken several years, they have developed a value-added model, based on longitudinal data, that allows them to evaluate the extent to which graduates from teacher preparation programs improve student learning in the classroom. However, experts, a state official, and an Education report cautioned about using student and teacher data in value-added models for reasons such as methodological concerns and an overemphasis on student test scores to the exclusion of other teacher factors that may positively affect students and schools. Moreover, senior officials from Education and state agencies we spoke with said that some key education stakeholders have reservations about linking student and teacher data to measure teacher effectiveness and/or the implications for privacy. Nevertheless, several states reported that statewide longitudinal data for the K-12 through higher education systems can increase collaboration by enhancing feedback loops between the K-12 and higher education systems. This information could, for example, help state agencies address professional development for teachers in the classroom as well as the effectiveness of teacher preparation programs for prospective teachers.

In addition to citing limited resources and incompatible data systems, state agency officials reported that several other factors, such as resistance to change, sustaining commitment, and state governance structures pose challenges to their collaborative efforts to improve teacher quality in their states. For example, state officials reported that different agencies and institutions are resistant to change as a result of long-held beliefs or difficulty in valuing new approaches to improving teacher quality. In one instance, state officials also told us that it is hard to maintain a sustained commitment to address teacher preparation issues because of the volume of state initiatives focused on improving student achievement. Another state official reported that the K-12 and postsecondary systems have separate governance systems, a factor that, given the different missions of each agency, limits how the two interact on education policy. Other state officials said the number of entities playing a role in teacher quality policy limits the state agencies' ability to collaborate on statewide teacher quality initiatives because the state agency must facilitate feedback from a multitude of stakeholders, which can be a time consuming process.

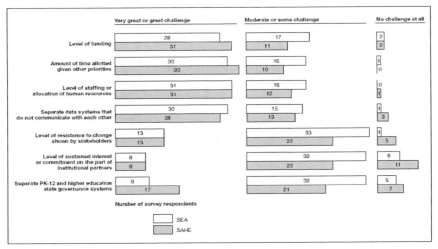

Source: GAO survey.
Note: In some cases, respondents do not total 48 for the SEAs and 47 for the SAHEs because not all SEA and SAHE officials responding to the surveys answered every question.

Figure 4. Challenges to Collaborative Efforts within States to Improve Teacher Quality

Although states face challenges to collaboration, state officials responding to our surveys and during site visits stressed the importance of these efforts and said that more collaboration is needed, especially to improve professional development training for existing teachers. Our survey results illustrate that states' teacher quality policy efforts cut across many interrelated areas within the K-12 and postsecondary systems, such as preservice preparation, recruitment, mentoring and induction, teacher assessments for licensure/certification, and continued learning for veteran teachers. State officials reported that improving teacher quality is best achieved through several interrelated initiatives that involve the various stakeholders within the two systems. In our survey, 22 of 48 SEA officials and 34 of 47 SAHE officials cited a great to very great need for more collaboration on teacher quality issues. Although state officials who provided written responses cited a range of teacher quality issues for which more collaboration was needed, including teacher preparation and retention, 16 SEA officials and 21 SAHE officials specifically cited training for existing teachers as a need.

In an effort to further enhance collaboration within the education system, several states have established coordinating bodies to address state education issues, including teacher quality improvement. According to our survey results, these coordinating bodies (often referred to as P-16 or P-20 bodies)—which are intended to create a seamless education system from prekindergarten through the postsecondary system through comprehensive education initiatives—have been generally effective at fostering an integrated approach to teacher quality within states that reported having a coordinating body. For example, one state official reported that the state coordinating body facilitates open communication among state agencies. Nevertheless, state officials reported through our surveys that these coordinating bodies also face challenges to enhancing collaboration, including having limited resources and needing to set priorities and allocate roles and responsibilities. In their review of state coordinating bodies, the Education Commission of the States reported that for these coordinating bodies to be successful, they must commit to long-term reform, include representatives from key stakeholder groups, coordinate initiatives at the state level, and integrate reform into other ongoing efforts. [32]

Education Provides Some Financial Support and Other Assistance That May Help Address State- Reported Challenges as well as Enhance Other Collaborative Efforts, Especially for Local-Level Activities

Education administers a grant program designed to help states develop longitudinal data systems and provides some assistance related to these efforts.[33] The State Longitudinal Data Systems grant program is aimed at enhancing SEAs' ability to develop statewide longitudinal data systems. These systems are intended to efficiently manage and analyze education data (including individual student records) to address federal reporting, accountability, and other requirements such as those related to ESEA. One of the program's allowable activities is to expand existing data systems to include teacher data and to link K-12 and higher education data systems. (As shown in app. III, the State Longitudinal Data Systems grant program is 1 of 33 programs that allow or require portions of funding to be used for teacher quality activities, but does so in pursuit of other program purposes or goals.) In our review of applications of states that received grant awards in 2006 or 2007, we found that most states are seeking to link student and teacher data or to link the K-12 and higher education data systems. For fiscal years 2006, 2007, and 2009, 41 states and the District of Columbia were awarded at least one grant ranging from about $1.5 million to $9.0 million.[34] In fiscal year 2009, Congress appropriated $65 million to support the State Longitudinal Data Systems grant program, about a $17 million increase over the fiscal year 2008 level.

Establishing a longitudinal data system that links prekindergarten through 12th grade and higher education data systems is one of the assurances that states must make to be eligible to receive their portion of the Recovery Act's State Fiscal Stabilization Fund.[35] Specifically, Education is asking states to report their progress toward implementing a statewide data system that includes the 12 elements described in the America COMPETES Act (Pub. L. No. 110-69), one of which is the matching of student data with individual teacher data. Education has provided preliminary guidance on the specific information that states must provide in their applications for funding through the State Fiscal Stabilization Fund.[36] Another $250 million is provided for the State Longitudinal Data Systems grant program in the Recovery Act that could help states defray costs associated with these efforts.

Education also facilitates information sharing and provides assistance with and research results on state data systems to state officials through technical assistance related to the State Longitudinal Data Systems grant program as well as through a network of regional and national providers that we described previously. Education's Web site contains information on a variety of topics related to data system development and management. Further, Education has hosted grantee conferences that have included panels on topics ranging from data privacy to how states can leverage one another's experiences with these data systems. In addition, a 2007 REL Midwest report outlined how states within its region use data systems and the promising practices of and challenges confronting these states, concluding that opportunities exist to capitalize on states' commitment to developing longitudinal data systems by thinking about these issues more comprehensively and systematically.[37] In March 2009, the REL Midwest and National Comprehensive Center on Teacher Quality cosponsored a live webcast to discuss and disseminate ongoing research on utilizing data systems in teacher evaluation models. In addition to grant funds provided by the State Longitudinal Data System Grant program, state officials told us that conferences, training, and technical assistance from the REL network would assist states in addressing their data system challenges.

In addition to providing the specific funding and assistance for data systems, Education also provides funding to support partnerships within states to address teacher quality. Some of these programs are intended to support accountability for teacher preparation programs at institutions of higher education or to improve teacher preparation programs by requiring partnerships, mainly between school districts and institutions of higher education. Of the 23 programs directed at improving teacher quality that we discussed previously, 8 fund projects specifically requiring partnerships. For example, according to state and university officials in New Jersey, Teacher Quality Enhancement grants have funded efforts to recruit high school students who are interested in pursing teaching in high- need school districts and designing teacher preparation programs for middle school students based on strong content knowledge. These types of efforts are accomplished through consortia, such as partnerships among universities and their respective teacher preparation programs and liberal arts and sciences departments as well as school districts. State and university officials in our site visit states said that these partnership grants generally facilitate useful collaboration among the grant partners. However, one state official told us that outside of federal- and state-funded partnerships between some school districts and institutions of higher education, there are limited opportunities for collaboration between K-12 and higher education. These officials also said the partnerships are sometimes difficult to sustain after the grants have expired. Moreover, another state official and an expert we spoke with explained that these partnership grants do not support a systemic collaboration between the K12 and higher education systems because the grants involve only a select few institutions in partnerships.

CONCLUSION

Providing all children with qualified teachers is a focus of federal policy, and this goal is reflected in Education's strategic and annual performance plans. To help accomplish this goal, Education distributes billions of federal dollars and provides research and other

104 United States Government Accountability Office

assistance for teacher quality activities through multiple offices and statutorily authorized programs. While Education has engaged in some coordination to share information and expertise within the department, and from time to time has established and completed broader collaborative efforts, coordination among all the relevant offices does not occur on a regular basis.

The success of Education's mission and the achievement of its goals for improving teacher quality and ultimately for increasing student achievement depend in part on how well it manages its wide array of programs and initiatives with regard to funding, assistance, and other priorities, as well as its evaluation and research efforts. Also, the Recovery Act, with its large infusion of onetime funds, as well as its provisions encouraging states, school districts, and institutions of higher education to make improvements in assessing teacher effectiveness and in distributing qualified and effective teachers equitably, creates an opportunity for the department to leverage new resources with existing structures in a way to improve teacher quality and effectiveness. However, this wide array of programs, initiatives, and structures also creates a challenge for the department. In the absence of a written departmentwide strategy for integrating its wide array of teacher quality programs and efforts, Education's offices may not be aligned in their actions to achieve Education's long-term goal of improving teacher quality. A departmental strategy for collaboration could help states overcome their barriers to improving teacher quality through facilitating compatible data systems as well as encouraging systemic collaboration between state K-12 and higher education institutions and detailing the role each plays in the success of the other. Without clearly articulated strategies and sustained collaborative activities, Education may be missing important opportunities to leverage its financial and other resources, align its activities and processes, as well as develop joint strategies to assist states, districts, and institutions of higher education in improving teacher quality.

RECOMMENDATION FOR EXECUTIVE ACTION

To ensure that departmental goals to improve teacher quality are achieved and that the department's many related efforts are mutually reinforcing, we recommend that the Secretary of Education establish and implement a strategy for sustained coordination among existing departmental offices and programs. A key purpose of this coordination would be to facilitate information and resource sharing as well as strengthening linkages among teacher quality improvement efforts to help states, school districts, and institutions of higher education in their initiatives to improve teacher quality.

AGENCY COMMENTS AND OUR EVALUATION

We provided a draft of this report to Education for review and comment. Education's comments are reproduced in appendix V. In its comments, Education agreed that coordination is beneficial, but it favors short-term coordination focused on discrete issues or problems. Education will review the advisability of forming a cross-program committee, but it would first want to ensure that such a group would lead to improvements in the way Education coordinates its approach to teacher quality and the way states and school districts promote teacher quality. Education officials pointed out that these efforts do not always prove useful and said that efforts to coordinate program implementation cannot fully eliminate barriers to program alignment.

While we agree with Education that these efforts have not always been useful and they face numerous barriers and challenges, we nonetheless believe that it is important for the department to develop a strategy for sustained coordination. As it develops a coordination strategy, Education should use its knowledge of past efforts and existing barriers to put in place the conditions necessary for addressing these and other challenges. For example, in their comments Education officials highlighted a barrier from this report of some teacher quality programs having inconsistent legislative definitions and requirements. As part of establishing and implementing a strategy for sustained coordination, Education could consider identifying these specific definitional barriers and others and develop a strategy for addressing them. Successful strategic and annual planning involve identifying goals and challenges facing an agency and detailing how an agency intends to achieve these goals and address these challenges. As we mention in the report, these efforts should include information on how program officials will coordinate and plan crosscutting efforts with other related programs. We encourage Education to formalize its coordination efforts by incorporating them into its planning efforts. Because responsibilities for improving teacher quality are shared among multiple offices, we believe taking a more systematic approach than what has occurred will ensure that different offices routinely become involved in sharing information and resources as well as facilitating linkages among teacher quality improvement efforts.

We acknowledged Education's effort to bring together different offices to work together on discrete issues or problems related to teacher quality and we modified the report to reflect Education's recent coordination effort to address the Recovery Act requirements related to teachers. Education also provided technical comments that we incorporated into the report as appropriate.

Sincerely yours,

Cornelia M. Ashby

Cornelia M. Ashby
Director, Education, Workforce,
and Income Security

APPENDIX I. SCOPE AND METHODOLOGY

To address the objectives of this study, we used a variety of methods. To document the extent to which Education funds and coordinates teacher quality programs, we interviewed Education officials as well as reviewed Education documents and relevant laws. To understand how Education funds and supports research efforts to improve teacher quality, we interviewed officials from a selection of relevant Education-funded research and related assistance providers and at the regional and national levels. To understand the challenges to collaboration within states, we conducted two national surveys—one was sent to state educational agency (SEA) officials in the 50 states and the District of Columbia and a separate survey was sent to state agency for higher education (SAHE) officials in 48 states plus the District of Columbia.[38] We did not send a SAHE survey to New York or Michigan because (1) in New York the executive official of higher education is also responsible for directing kindergarten through 12th grade education and (2) in Michigan there is no state agency or officer with governance authority over higher education. In addition, we conducted site visits in 3 states to understand further the state perspective as well as that of school districts and institutions of higher education. In addition, we interviewed national experts on the various areas of teacher quality. We conducted our work between February 2008 and July 2009 in accordance with generally accepted government auditing standards. Those standards require that we plan and perform the audit to obtain sufficient, appropriate evidence to provide a reasonable basis for our findings and conclusions based on our audit objectives. We believe that the evidence obtained provides a reasonable basis for our findings and conclusions based on our audit objectives.

Objectives 1 and 2. Extent of Education Funding and Coordination of Teacher Quality Programs as well as Education's Monitoring of these Programs

To determine the extent that Education funds and coordinates teacher quality programs, we first identified relevant programs from the *Guide to U.S. Department of Education Programs 2008* and classified these programs into two groups based on these differences:[39] (1) programs designed to support teacher quality improvement, and (2) programs that may support teacher quality improvement but do so in pursuit of other goals or purposes. For the first group, or "primary programs," we reviewed the program description for each program, identifying those with a purpose of improving teaching in the classroom for elementary and secondary schools. The description statement of these programs included terms such as *professional development, teacher training, teacher preparation, teacher retention, teacher certification, improving teaching through scientifically based research* and *curriculum development*. In addition, we identified the second group of programs—which have a purpose other than improving teacher quality—through a review of the descriptions of the types of projects funded in Education's Program Guide to determine that training teachers or improving instructional programs was an allowable activity. After identifying the respective group of programs, Education officials reviewed the list of programs to verify that we had identified the relevant programs and categorized each program correctly. To understand Education's efforts and requirements for coordinating the 23 programs that we identified as primarily focusing on teacher quality, we reviewed relevant federal laws, performance and accountability reports, and other documentation to identify requirements for coordinating its programs. In addition, we interviewed officials for the offices that oversee these programs to determine whether and how they coordinate their programs to improve teacher quality. These interviews included officials from the Office of Elementary and Secondary Education, the

Office of Innovation and Improvement, the Office of Postsecondary Education, the Office of Special Education and Rehabilitative Services, and the Office of English Language Acquisition. We also interviewed officials in Education's Office of Inspector General (OIG) and reviewed relevant OIG reports on Education's efforts to coordinate programs.

To understand how Education monitors states and districts that receive formula and discretionary grants on teacher quality we reviewed relevant federal laws, nonregulatory guidance, policy and procedure manuals, monitoring checklists, and monitoring reports or letters to grantees, as well as outside evaluations or audits such as OIG and GAO reports. In addition, to determine the process and procedures for monitoring these programs, we conducted interviews with the relevant officials from each of the five program offices overseeing each of these programs, including officials from the Office of Elementary and Secondary Education, Office of Innovation and Improvement, Office of Postsecondary Education, and Office of Special Education and Rehabilitation Services as well as OIG, and the Office of Risk Management Service in the Secretary of Education's office. Finally, to gather information about Education's monitoring, we interviewed state and district officials during our site visits.

Objective 3. Evaluation and Research as well as Related Assistance Pertaining to Teacher Quality

To gather information on Education's evaluation of federal programs, research on teacher quality, and research-related assistance provided to states and districts, we interviewed relevant Education officials as well as state and district officials during our site visits, and reviewed documents and responses to questions on research-related assistance in the survey. To obtain information on Education's evaluation and research efforts as well as dissemination practices, we interviewed relevant officials from Education's Institute of Education Sciences, the Office of Elementary and Secondary Education, and the Office of Planning Evaluation and Policy Development, as well as submitted written follow-up questions to these offices. In addition, we reviewed documented information available on the evaluations conducted on federal programs on teacher quality and on completed and ongoing research on teacher quality practices and interventions. To learn about the research-related assistance provided directly to states, we interviewed officials from the three Regional Educational Laboratories and Regional Comprehensive Centers that provide assistance to our three site visit states.[40] We also interviewed officials from the National Comprehensive Center on Teacher Quality. In addition, during our site visits we asked state and district officials about the kinds of assistance that they receive directly from Education, the Regional Educational Laboratories, Regional Comprehensive Centers, and the National Comprehensive Center on Teacher Quality. Finally, in our surveys, we asked state respondents about the usefulness of the Regional Educational Laboratories, the Regional Comprehensive Centers, the National Comprehensive Center on Teacher Quality, the Institute of Education Sciences studies, as well as the What Works Clearinghouse and Doing What Works Internet sites.

Objective 4. Challenges to Collaboration within States and Education Efforts to Address these Challenges

To understand the challenges facing state agencies' in their efforts to collaborate within their states on efforts to improve teacher quality, we used two approaches—two state surveys and site visits to three states. First we designed and administered two identical Web-based surveys— one that was sent to SEA officials in all 50 states and the District of Columbia and a second to SAHE officials in 48 states and the District of Columbia. We did not send a SAHE survey to New York or Michigan because (1) in New York the executive official of higher education is also responsible for directing kindergarten through 12th grade education and in Michigan there is no state agency or officer with governance authority over higher education. The surveys were conducted between August and November 2008. Questionnaires were completed by SEA officials in 48 states for a response rate of 94 percent, and SAHE officials in 47 states for a response rate of 96 percent.

The surveys posed a combination of questions that allowed for open- ended and closed-ended responses. They included questions about state efforts including (1) state agency initiatives across a wide range of teacher quality areas, (2) state agencies' collaborative activities within their state, the role of a state coordinating body (where applicable) in teacher quality initiatives, and (4) the usefulness of grant funds and technical assistance provided by Education.

The surveys were conducted using self-administered electronic questionnaires posted on the World Wide Web. We sent e-mail notifications to all 51 SEA officials and 49 SAHE officials beginning on September 15, 2008. To encourage respondents to complete the questionnaire, we sent an e-mail message to prompt each nonrespondent each week after the initial e-mail, on September 22, 2008, and October 1, 2008. We also contacted officials by telephone to further increase our response rate. We closed both surveys on November 23, 2008.

Some of the survey questions were open-ended, allowing respondents an opportunity to provide thoughts and opinions in their own words. To categorize and summarize these responses, we performed a systematic content analysis of a select number of open-ended questions. Two GAO staff independently coded the responses. All initial disagreements regarding placement into categories were discussed and reconciled. Agreement regarding each placement was reached again between at least two analysts. The numbers of responses in each content category were then summarized and tallied.

Because this was not a sample survey, there are no sampling errors. However, the practical difficulties of conducting any survey may introduce nonsampling errors, such as variations in how respondents interpret questions and their willingness to offer accurate responses. We took a number of steps to minimize nonsampling errors. For example, a social science survey specialist designed the questionnaires in collaboration with GAO staff with subject matter expertise. During survey development, we received feedback from three external peer reviewers and Education officials. The questionnaires also underwent a peer review by a second GAO survey specialist. Each draft instrument was then pretested two times with appropriate officials in New Mexico, Wisconsin, and West Virginia to ensure that the questions and information provided to respondents were relevant, clearly stated, and easy to comprehend. The pretesting took place during July and August 2008. Since these were

Web- based surveys, respondents entered their answers directly into electronic questionnaires. This eliminated the need to have data keyed into databases, thus removing an additional source of error. Finally, to further minimize errors, computer programs used to analyze the survey data were independently verified by a second GAO data analyst to ensure the accuracy of this work.

While we did not fully validate specific information that states reported through our survey, we took several steps to ensure that the information was sufficiently reliable for the purposes of this report. For example, we contacted state officials via phone and e-mail to follow up on obvious inconsistencies, errors, or incomplete answers. We also performed computer analyses to identify inconsistencies in responses and other indications of error. On the basis of our checks, we believe our survey data are sufficient for the purposes of this report. The surveys and a complete tabulation of aggregated results can be viewed at GAO-09-594SP.

We also conducted site visits to three states—Louisiana, New Jersey, and Oregon. These states were selected based on their having initiatives that focus on teacher quality, such as coordinating bodies that are intended to bridge the K-12 and higher education systems,[41] and on diversity in terms of geographic location, population, and amount of federal teacher quality program funding. In each state we met with SEA and SAHE officials, and to understand the local perspective, we met with officials in at least one school district and two universities. In addition, we interviewed experts on teacher quality, including those at the American Institutes for Research, Education Trust, Congressional Research Service, and the University of Pennsylvania. We also reviewed several studies on teacher quality funding and activities.

APPENDIX II. PRIMARY PROGRAMS: TWENTY-THREE PROGRAMS PROVIDING FUNDING SPECIFICALLY TO IMPROVE THE QUALITY OF TEACHERS

Program name	Grant design	Eligible recipients	Purpose	Fiscal year 2009 appropriations (Dollars in thousands)
Elementary and Secondary Education Act				
Improving Teacher Quality State Grants (also known as Title II, Part A)	Formula	Awards made to state educational agencies (SEA) that, in turn, make formula subgrants to school districts. State agencies for higher education (SAHE) also receive a formula grant that, in turn, is awarded competitively to partnerships that must include at least one institution of higher education (IHE) and its division that prepares teachers and principals, a school of arts and sciences, and a high-need school district.	To increase academic achievement by improving teacher and principal quality.	$2,947,749
Enhancing Education Through Technology Program	Formula	SEAs.	To improve student achievement through use of technology in elementary and secondary schools and to help all students become technologically literate by the end of the eighth grade and, through the integration of technology with both teacher training and curriculum development, establishing research-based instructional methods that can be widely implemented.	269,872
Mathematics and Science Partnerships	Formula	Awards are made to SEAs. Partnerships of school districts and IHEs may apply to states for subgrants. Partnership must include, at a minimum, an engineering, mathematics, or science department of an IHE, and a high-need school district.	To increase the academic achievement of students in mathematics and science by enhancing the content knowledge, teaching skills, and instruction practices of classroom teachers.	178,978

Program name	Grant design	Eligible recipients	Purpose	Fiscal year 2009 appropriations (Dollars in thousands)
Teaching American History	Competitive	School districts applying in partnership with one or more of the following: IHEs, nonprofit history or humanities organizations, libraries, or museums.	To raise student achievement by improving teachers' knowledge and under-standing of and appreciation for traditional U.S. history.	118,952
Early Reading First	Competitive	School districts eligible for a Reading First subgrant and public or private organizations or agencies located in a community served by an eligible district may apply.	Supports local efforts to enhance the early language, literacy, and prereading development of preschool-age children, particularly those from low-income families, through strategies and professional development that are based on scientifically based reading research.	112,549
Teacher Incentive Fund	Competitive	School districts, including charter schools that are districts in their state, SEAs, or partnerships of (1) a district, SEA, or both, and (2) at least one nonprofit organization may apply.	To support efforts to develop and implement performance-based teacher and principal compensation systems in high-need schools.	97,270[a]
Transition to Teaching	Competitive	High-need school districts, SEAs, for-profit or nonprofit organizations, IHEs, regional consortia of SEAs, or consortia of high-need districts may apply. IHEs, for-profits, and nonprofits must be in partnership with a high-need district or an SEA.	To support the recruitment and retention of highly qualified mid-career professionals, including qualified paraprofessionals, and recent college graduates who have not majored in education to teach in high-need schools and districts through the development of new or enhanced alternative routes to certification.	43,707
English Language Acquisition National Professional Deve-Lopment Project	Competitive	IHEs as well as consortia of these institutions and SEAs or school districts.	To support professional development activities for education personnel working with English language learners.	41,800

Table. (Continued)

Program name	Grant design	Eligible recipients	Purpose	Fiscal year 2009 appropriations (Dollars in thousands)
Striving Readers	Competitive	(1) School district that (a) are eligible to receive funds under the Elementary and Secondary Education Act (ESEA), Title I, Part A, pursuant to Sec. 1113 of ESEA and (b) serve students in one or more of grades 6 through 12. Eligible districts may apply individually, with other eligible districts, or in partnership with one or more of the following entities: SEAs; intermediate service agencies; public or private IHEs; and public or private organizations with expertise in adolescent literacy, rigorous evaluation, or both. (2) SEAs on behalf of one or more districts that meet the requirements above. SEAs must apply on behalf of one or more eligible districts and also may partner with one or more of the following entities: inter-mediate service agencies; public or private IHEs; and public or private organizations with expertise in adolescent literacy, rigorous evaluation, or both. For any application, the fiscal agent must be an eligible district or an SEA.	To raise student achievement in middle- and high-school-aged students who are reading below grade level, and serve schools by improving the literacy skills of struggling adolescent readers and to help build a strong, scientific research base around specific strategies that improve adolescent literacy skills.	35,371
School Leadership Program	Competitive	High-need school districts, consortia of high-need districts, or partnerships that consist of at least one high-need school district and at least one nonprofit organization (which may be a community- or faith-based organization) or institutions of higher education may apply.	To support the development, enhancement, or expansion of innovative programs to recruit, train, and mentor principals (including assistant principals) for high-need districts.	19,220

Program name	Grant design	Eligible recipients	Purpose	Fiscal year 2009 appropriations (Dollars in thousands)
Troops-to-Teachers	Non-competitive	Current and former members of the U.S. armed forces, including members of the Armed Forces Reserves.	Provides financial assistance and counseling to help military personnel obtain their teacher licenses, especially in shortage areas, such as math, science, and special education, and find employment in high-need districts and schools, as well as charter schools.	14,389
Indian Education Professional Development Grants	Competitive	(1) IHEs, including Indian IHEs; (2) SEAs or school districts, in consortium with these institutions; (3) Indian tribes or organizations, in consortium with IHEs; and (4) the U.S. Department of the Interior's Bureau of Indian Education-funded schools in consortium with IHEs.	To prepare and train Indian individuals to serve as teachers and education professionals. Professional development grants are awarded to increase the number of qualified Indian individuals in professions that serve Indians; provide training to qualified Indians to become teachers, administrators, teacher aides, social workers, and ancillary education personnel; and improve the skills of those qualified Indians who serve currently in those capacities.	8,211
Ready-to-Teach	Competitive	For National Telecommunications Grants, nonprofit telecommunication entities or a partnership of such entities may apply.	Supports two types of grants to nonprofit telecommunications entities: (1) grants to carry out a national telecommunications-based program to improve teaching in core curriculum areas and (2) digital educational programming grants that enable eligible entities to develop, produce, and distribute educational and instructional video programming.	10,700
Advanced Certification or Advanced Credentialing	Non-competitive	SEAs; school districts; the National Board for Professional Teaching Standards, in partnership with a high-need school district or SEA; the National Council on Teacher Quality, in partnership with a high-need SEA or district; or another recognized entity, including another recognized certification or credentialing organization, in partnership with a high-need SEA or district.	Supports activities to encourage and sup-port teachers seeking advanced certification or advanced credentialing through high-quality professional teacher enhancement programs designed to improve teaching and learning.	10,649

Table. (Continued)

Program name	Grant design	Eligible recipients	Purpose	Fiscal year 2009 appropriations (Dollars in thousands)
Indian Education Professional Development Grants	Competitive	(1) IHEs, including Indian IHEs; (2) SEAs or school districts, in consortium with these institutions; (3) Indian tribes or organizations, in consortium with IHEs; and (4) the U.S. Department of the Interior's Bureau of Indian Education-funded schools in consortium with IHEs.	To prepare and train Indian individuals to serve as teachers and education professionals. Professional development grants are awarded to increase the number of qualified Indian individuals in profess-ions that serve Indians; provide training to qualified Indians to become teachers, administrators, teacher aides, social workers, and ancillary education personnel; and improve the skills of those qualified Indians who serve currently in those capacities.	8,211
Ready-to-Teach	Competitive	For National Telecommunications Grants, nonprofit telecommunication entities or a partnership of such entities may apply.	Supports two types of grants to nonprofit telecommunications entities: (1) grants to carry out a national telecommunications-based program to improve teaching in core curriculum areas and (2) digital educational programming grants that enable eligible entities to develop, produce, and distribute educational and instructional video programming	10,700
Advanced Certification or Advanced Credentialing	Non-competitive	SEAs; school districts; the National Board for Professional Teaching Standards, in partnership with a high-need school district or SEA; the National Council on Teacher Quality, in partnership with a high-need SEA or district; or another recognized entity, including another recognized certification or credentialing organization, in partnership with a high-need SEA or district.	Supports activities to encourage and sup-port teachers seeking advanced certification or advanced credentialing through high-quality professional teacher enhancement programs designed to improve teaching and learning.	10,649

Program name	Grant design	Eligible recipients	Purpose	Fiscal year 2009 appropriations (Dollars in thousands)
Professional Development for Arts Educators	Competitive	(1) A school district acting on behalf of a school or schools where at least 50 percent of the children are from low-income families; and (2) must work in partnership with at least one of the following: a state or local nonprofit or governmental arts organization; an institution of higher education; a SEA or regional education service agency; a public or private agency, institution, or organization including a museum, arts education association, library, theater, or community- or faith-based organization.	Supports the implementation of high-quality professional development model programs in elementary and secondary education in music, dance, drama, media arts, and visual arts for arts educators and other instructional staff of K-12 students in high-poverty schools.	7,464
Territories and Freely Associated States Education Grant Program	Competitive, but limited to outlying areas	School districts in the outlying areas (American Samoa, Guam, the Commonwealth of the Northern Mariana Islands, the U.S. Virgin Islands) and the Republic of Palau.	To support teacher training, curriculum development, instructional materials or general school improvement and reform, and direct educational services. The Pacific Regional Educational Laboratory provides technical assistance and makes recommendations for funding to the Secretary of Education, who conducts a grants competition.	5,000
National Writing Project	Non-competitive	Only the National Writing Project is eligible.	The National Writing Project is a nation-wide nonprofit education organization that promotes K-16 teacher training programs in the effective teaching of writing.	24,291
Higher Education Act				
Teacher Quality Partnership Grants	Competitive	Partnership of institution of higher education, including a teacher preparation program and a school or department of arts and science, at least one high-need school district, and either a high-need school or a consortium of high-need schools served by the high-need school district; or as applicable, a high-need early childhood education program.	Through collaborative efforts, to support the prebaccalaureate preparation of teachers or a teaching residency program, or a combination of such programs. Grants may also be used to carry out a leadership development program.	50,000[b]

Program name	Grant design	Eligible recipients	Purpose	Fiscal year 2009 appropriations (Dollars in thousands)
Individuals with Disabilities Education Act				
Special Education—Personnel Development to Improve Services and Results for Children with Disabilities	Competitive	Institutions of higher education, school districts, nonprofit organizations, and other organizations and/or SEAs.	To improve the quality of K-12 special education teacher preparation programs to ensure that program graduates are able to meet the highly qualified teacher requirements and are well prepared to serve children with a high incidence of disabilities.	90,653
Special Education—State Personnel Development Grant Program	Competitive	SEA.	To assist SEAs in reforming and improving their systems for personnel preparation and professional development in early intervention, education, and transition services in order to improve results for children with disabilities	48,000
America COMPETES Act				
Teachers for a Competitive Tomorrow Program: Baccalaureate Science, Technology, Engineering and Mathematics (STEM) and Foreign Language Teacher Training	Competitive	Institutions of higher education.	To develop and implement programs providing courses of study in science, technology, engineering, and mathematics fields or critical foreign languages that are integrated with teacher education. Graduates receive baccalaureate degrees in STEM fields or critical foreign languages, concurrent with teacher certification.	1,092
Teachers for a Competitive Tomorrow Program: Masters STEM and Foreign Language Teacher Training	Competitive	Institutions of higher education.	To offer a master's degree in a STEM field or critical foreign language content areas to current teachers and to enable professionals in these fields to pursue a 1-year master's degree that leads to teacher certification.	1,092

American History and Civics Education Act of 2004				
Academies for American History and Civics	Competitive	IHEs, museums, libraries, and other public and private agencies, organizations, and institutions (including for-profit organizations) or a consortium of such agencies, organizations, and institutions may apply. Applicants must demonstrate expertise in historical methodology or the teaching of history.	Supports the establishment of Presidential Academies for Teachers of American History and Civics that offer workshops for both veteran and new teachers of American history and civics to strengthen their knowledge and preparation for teaching these subjects. The program also supports establishment of Congressional Academies for Students of American History and Civics for high school students to develop a broader and deeper understanding of these subjects.	$1,945

Source: GAO analysis of Department of Education data.

aThe Teacher Incentive Fund also received $200 million in funding through the American Recovery and Reinvestment Act of 2009 (Recovery Act).

bThe Teacher Quality Enhancement grant received an additional $100 million through the Recovery Act.

APPENDIX III. PROGRAMS THAT SUPPORT BROAD OBJECTIVES BUT ALLOW OR REQUIRE SOME FUNDS TO BE USED FOR TEACHER QUALITY

Program	Purpose	Grant recipient
Grant design: formula grants		
Improving Basic Academic Achievement Programs for the Disadvantaged	To ensure that all children have a fair, equal opportunity to obtain a high-quality education and reach, at a minimum, proficiency on challenging state academic achievement standards and state academic assessments.	SEAs and school districts.
Tech Prep Education	Program provides assistance to states to award grants to consortia of school districts and postsecondary education institutions for the development and operation of programs consisting of the last 2 years of secondary education and at least 2 years of postsecondary education, designed to provide Tech Prep education to the student leading to an associate degree or a 2-year certificate.	Awards are made to eligible state agencies for career and technical education, which award funds on the basis of a formula or competition to consortia. Eligible consortia must include at least one member in each of the two following categories: (1) A school district, an intermediate education agency, education service agency, or an area career and technical education school serving secondary school students, or a secondary school funded by Bureau

Table. (Continued)

Program	Purpose	Grant recipient
		of Indian Affairs; or (2) either (a) a nonprofit institution of higher education (IHE) that offers a 2-year associate degree, 2-year certificate, or 2-year postsecondary apprenticeship program, or (b) a proprietary institution of higher education that offers a 2-year associate degree program.
Career and Technical Education—Basic Grants to States	To develop the academic, career, and technical skills of secondary and postsecondary students who enroll in career and technical programs. This program provides states with support for leadership activities, administration of the state plan for career and technical education, and subgrants to eligible recipients to improve career and technical education programs.	State agencies for career and technical education.
Indian Education— Formula Grants to Local Education Agencies	Program designed to address the unique education and culturally related academic needs of American Indian and Alaska Native students, including preschool children, so that these students can achieve the same challenging state performance standards expected of all students. This is Education's principal vehicle for addressing the particular needs of Indian children. Grant funds supplement the regular school programs and support such activities as after-school programs, early childhood education, tutoring, and dropout prevention.	Districts that enroll a threshold number of eligible Indian children and certain schools funded by the Bureau of Indian Affairs; Indian tribes, and under certain conditions, may also apply.
Migrant Education— Basic State Formula Grants	Supports high-quality education programs for migratory children and helps ensure that migratory children who move among the states are not penalized by disparities among states in curriculum, graduation requirements, or state academic content and student academic achievement standards. States use program funds to identify eligible children and provide education and support services. These may include academic instruction, bilingual and multicultural instruction, career education services, advocacy services, counseling and testing services, health services, and preschool services.	SEAs, which in turn make subgrants to local operating agencies that serve migrant students. Local operating agencies may be school districts, institutions of higher education, and other public and nonprofit agencies.

Program	Purpose	Grant recipient
Even Start	Program offers grants to support local family literacy projects that integrate early childhood education, and adult literacy. Five percent of funds are is aside for family literacy grants for migratory worker families, the outlying areas, and Indian tribes and tribal organizations; one grant must be awarded to a women's prison and up to 3 percent is for evaluation activities. Remaining funds are allocated to SEAs based on their Title I, Part A allocation and SEAs make competitive subgrants to partnerships of school districts and other organizations. Projects include providing staff training and support services.	SEAs and subgrants to school district partnerships.
Small Rural School Achievement	To provide financial assistance to rural school districts to assist them in meeting their state's definition of adequate yearly progress. Note: a school district that is eligible for this program is not eligible for the Rural and Low-Income Schools program (see below).	Primarily to districts that (1) have a total average daily attendance of fewer than 600 students or only serve schools located in counties of fewer than 10 persons per square mile, and (2) serve schools with Education's National Center for Education Sciences locale code of 7 or 8 or located in an area defined as rural by state.
Rural and Low-Income Schools	To provide financial assistance to rural districts to assist them in meeting their state's definition of adequate yearly progress. This program provides grant funds to rural districts that serve concentrations of children from low-income families.	SEAs receive grants and provide subgrants to school districts in which (1) 20 percent or more of the children age 5-17 served by the school district are from families with incomes below the poverty line, (2) all schools served by the district have a school locale code of 6,7, or 8; and are (3) not eligible to participate in the Small Rural School Achievement program.
Preschool Grants for Children with Disabilities	To provide special education services to children with disabilities, ages 3-5. Permitted expenditures include the salaries of special education teachers and costs associated with related services.	SEAs.
Special Education Grants to States	Assists states including the District of Columbia and Puerto Rico in meeting the costs of providing special education and related services to children with disabilities. States may use funds to provide a free appropriate public education to children with disabilities. Permitted expenditures include the salaries of special education teachers and costs associated with related services personnel, such as speech therapists and psychologists.	SEAs and school districts.

Table. (Continued)

Program	Purpose	Grant recipient
English Language Acquisition State Grants	To improve the education of limited English proficient children and youths by helping them to learn English and meet state academic content and student academic achievement standards.	SEAs and subgrants to school districts.
Grant design: competitive grants		
Career and Technical Education—Grants to Native Americans and Alaska Natives	To improve the career and technical education skills of Native Americans and Alaska Natives. Projects make improvements in career and technical education programs for Native American and Alaska Native youths.	Federally recognized Indian tribes, tribal organizations, Alaska Native entities, and consortia of any of the previously mentioned entities may apply.
Career and Technical Education—Native Hawaiians	Provides assistance to plan, conduct, and administer programs or portions of programs that provide career and technical training and related activities to Native Hawaiians. Program supports career and technical education and training projects for the benefit of Native Hawaiians.	Community-based organizations primarily serving and representing Native Hawaiians.
Advanced Placement Incentive Program	Enables grantees to increase the participation of low-income students in both pre-advanced placement and advanced placement courses and tests. Allowable activities include professional development for teachers, curriculum development, the purchase of books and supplies, and other activities directly related to expanding access to and participation in advanced placement courses and tests for low-income students.	School districts, SEAs, and nonprofit organizations.
Improving Literacy Through School Libraries	Program helps school districts improve reading achievement by providing students with increased access to up-to-date school library materials; well-equipped, technologically advanced school library media centers; and professionally certified school library media specialists. School districts may use funds for a variety of activities such as providing professional development for school library media specialists and providing activities that foster increased collaboration among library specialists, teachers, and administrators.	School districts in which at least 20 percent of students served are from families with incomes below the poverty line.

Program	Purpose	Grant recipient
Indian Education Demonstration Grants for Indian Children	Designed to improve the education opportunities and achievement of preschool, elementary, and secondary Indian children by developing, testing, and demonstrating effective services and programs. Funding priorities in 2008 were for (1) school readiness projects that provide age-appropriate educational programs and language skills to 3- and 4-year-old Indian students to prepare them for successful entry into school at the kindergarten level and (2) college preparatory programs for secondary school students designed to increase competency and skills in challenging subject matter, such as mathematics and science.	SEAs, school districts, Indian tribes, Indian organizations, federally supported elementary and secondary schools for Indian students, and Indian institutions, including Indian institutions of higher education, or consortia of such entities.
Migrant Education Program—Even Start	Designed to help break the cycle of poverty and improve the literacy of participating migrant families by integrating early childhood education, adult literacy or adult basic education, and parenting education into a unified family literacy program. Funds support projects such as early childhood education, adult education; Head Start programs, training for staff, and support services.	Institutions of higher education, school districts, SEAs, and nonprofit and other organizations and agencies.
Carol M. White Physical Education Program	Provides grants to initiate, expand, and improve physical education programs for K-12 students to help them make progress toward meeting state standards for physical education. Funds may be used to provide equipment and support and to enable students to participate actively in physical education activities. Funds also may support staff and teacher training and education.	School districts and community-based organizations.
Magnet Schools Assistance	Grants assist in the desegregation of public schools by supporting the elimination, reduction, and prevention of minority group isolation in elementary and secondary schools with substantial numbers of minority group students. Projects must support the development and implementation of magnet schools that assist in the achievement of systemic reforms and provide all students with the opportunity to meet challenging academic content and achievement standards. Projects support the development and design of innovative education methods and practices that	School districts or consortia of districts that are implementing court-ordered or federally approved voluntary desegregation plans that include magnet schools are eligible to apply.

Table. (Continued)

Program	Purpose	Grant recipient
	promote diversity and increase choices in public education programs. The program supports capacity development through professional development and other activities, such as the implementation of courses of instruction in magnet schools that strengthen students' knowledge of core academic subjects. Program supports the implementation of courses of instruction in magnet schools that strengthen students' knowledge of core academic subjects.	
Arts in Education— Model Development and Dissemination Grants Program	Supports the enhancement, expansion, documentation, evaluation, and dissemination of innovative, cohesive models that demonstrate effectiveness in (1) integrating into and strengthening arts in the core elementary and middle school curricula, (2) strengthening arts instruction, and (3) improving students' academic performance, including their skills in creating, performing, and responding to the arts. Funds must be used to (1) further the development of programs designed to improve or expand the integration of arts education, (2) develop materials designed to help replicate or adapt arts programs, (3) document and assess the results and benefits of arts programs, and (4) develop products and services that can be used to replicate arts programs in other settings.	School districts and nonprofit organizations.
Women's Educational Equity	Promotes education equity for women and girls through competitive grants. Allowable activities include training for teachers and other school personnel to encourage gender equity in the classroom, evaluating exemplary model programs, school-to-work transition programs, guidance and counseling activities to increase opportunities for women in technologically demanding workplaces, and developing strategies to assist districts in evaluating, disseminating, and replicating gender-equity programs.	Institutions of higher education, school districts, SEAs, nonprofit organizations, other organizations and agencies.
Native American and Alaska Native Children in School	Provides grants to support language instruction education projects for Limited English Proficient children from Native American, Alaska Native, Native Hawaiian, and Pacific Islander	Indian tribes; tribally sanctioned education authorities; Native Hawaiian or Native American Pacific Islander native language education organizations; and elementary, secondary, or

Program	Purpose	Grant recipient
	backgrounds to ensure that they meet the same rigorous standards for academic achievement that all children are expected to meet.	postsecondary schools operated or funded by the Bureau of Indian Affairs Education, or a consortium of such schools and an institution of higher education.
Fund for the Improvement of Education—Programs of National Significance	This program provides authority for the Secretary of Education to support nationally significant programs to improve the quality of elementary and secondary education at the state and local levels and to help all students meet challenging state academic standards.	Institutions of higher education, school districts, SEAs, and nonprofit and other organizations and agencies.
Jacob K. Javits Gifted and Talented Student Education	To carry out a coordinated program of scientifically based research, demonstration projects, innovative strategies, and similar activities designed to enhance the ability of K-12 schools to meet the education needs of gifted and talented students.	Institutions of higher education, school districts, SEAs, nonprofit organizations, other organizations and agencies.
Foreign Language Assistance Program (Districts)	Provides grants to establish, improve, or expand innovative foreign language programs for elementary and secondary school students. In awarding grants under this program, the Secretary of Education supports projects that (1) show the promise of being continued beyond their project period and (2) demonstrate approaches that can be disseminated and duplicated by other school districts.	School districts.
Foreign Language Assistance Program (SEAs)	Provides grants to establish, improve, or expand innovative foreign language programs for elementary and secondary school students. In awarding grants under this program, the Secretary of Education supports projects that promote systemic approaches to improving foreign language learning in the state.	SEAs.
Native Hawaiian Education Program	To develop innovative educational programs to assist Native Hawaiians and to supplement and expand programs and authorities in the area of education.	School districts, SEAs, and IHEs with experience in developing or operating Native Hawaiian programs or programs of instruction in the Native Hawaiian language, and Native Hawaiian education organizations; public and private nonprofit organizations, agencies, and institutions; and consortia thereof.
Alaska Native Education Equity	To meet the unique education needs of Alaska Natives and support supplemental programs to benefit Alaska Natives. Activities include, but are not limited to, the development of curricula and education programs that address student needs and the development and operation of student enrichment programs in science and mathematics.	An SEA or school district may apply as part of a consortium involving an Alaska Native organization. Also Alaska Native organizations, education entities with experience in developing or operating Alaska Native programs or programs of instruction conducted in Alaska Native languages, cultural and community-based organizations with experience in developing or operating

Table. (Continued)

	Eligible activities also include professional development for educators, activities carried out through Even Start and Head Start programs, family literacy services, and dropout prevention programs.	programs to benefit Alaska Natives, and consortia or organizations.
Special Education— National Activities- Technology and Media Services	To (1) improve results for children with disabilities by promoting the development, demonstration, and use of technology; (2) support educational media services activities designed to be of value in the classroom setting for children with disabilities; and (3) provide support for captioning and video description that and appropriate for use in the classroom setting. Program supports technology development, demonstration, and utilization. Educational media activities, such as video descriptions and captioning of educational materials, also are supported.	Institutions of higher education, school districts, SEAs, nonprofit organizations, or other organizations.
Special Education— National Activities— Technical Assistance and Dissemination	To promote academic achievement and improve results for children with disabilities by providing technical assistance, model demonstration projects, dissemination of useful information, and implementation activities that are supported by scientifically based research.	Institutions of higher education, school districts, SEAs, nonprofit organizations, and other organizations and/or agencies.
Excellence in Economic Education	This program promotes economic and financial literacy among all students in kindergarten through grade 12 through the award of one grant to a national nonprofit education organization that has as its primary purpose the improvement of the quality of student understanding of personal finance and economics.	The National Council on Economic Education, SEAs, school districts.
Fund for the Improvement of Postsecondary Education— Comprehensive Program	A program supporting innovative reform projects for improving the quality of postsecondary education and increasing student access.	Institutions of higher education, and other organizations and agencies.
Statewide Longitu-dinal Data Systems	To enable SEAs to design, develop, and implement statewide longitudinal data systems to efficiently and accurately manage, analyze, disaggregate, and use individual student data, consistent with the Elementary and Secondary Education Act of 1965, as amended (20 U.S.C. 6301 et seq.).	SEAs.

Source: GAO analysis of Department of Education data.

APPENDIX IV. INSTITUTE OF EDUCATION SCIENCES' SPONSORED RESEARCH ON TEACHER QUALITY, 2003–2009

Year	Research recipient	Teacher quality project	Grant award
2009	University of California, Berkeley	Teacher Quality: The Role of Teacher Study Groups as a Model of Professional Development in Early Literacy for Preschool Teachers	$1,339,403
2009	Education Development Center, Inc.	Assessing the Efficacy of a Comprehensive Intervention in Physical Science on Head Start Teachers and Children	2,999,841
2009	University of Texas Health Science Center at Houston	Improving School Readiness of High Risk Preschoolers: Combining High Quality Instructional Strategies with Responsive Training for Teachers	2,653,503
2009	University of Cincinnati	INSPIRE Urban Teaching Fellows Program	1,500,000
2009	The Pennsylvania State University	Improving Classroom Learning Environments by Cultivating Awareness and Resilience in Education	932,424
2009	University of Illinois at Chicago	Enhancing Effectiveness and Connectedness Among Early Career Teachers in Urban Schools	1,012,701
2008	University of California, San Diego	Education Research: BioBridge Teacher Quality—The BioBridge Teacher Professional Development	948,447
2008	University of South Florida	Leadership for Integrated Middle-School Science	1,444,403
2008	University of Michigan	Development of an Interactive, Multimedia Assessment of Teachers' Knowledge of Early Reading	1,770,582
2008	National Bureau of Economic Research	Value-Added Models and the Measurement of Teacher Quality: Tracking or Causal Effects	294,295
2008	University of Pittsburgh	The Iterative Design of Modules to Support Reading Comprehension Instruction	1,386,901
2008	Ohio State University	Efficacy of Read It Again! In Rural Preschool Settings	3,073,485
2008	Rutgers, the State University of New Jersey	Development and Validation of a Teacher Progress Monitoring Scale for Elementary School Teachers	1,438,905
2008	Iris Media Inc.	Online Teacher Training: Promoting Student Social Competence to Improve Academic and Behavioral Outcomes in Grades K-3	2,293,415
2008	Mid-Continent Regional Educational Laboratory	Visualizing Science with Adapted Curriculum Enhancements	1,489,399

Table. (Continued)

Year	Research recipient	Teacher quality project	Grant award
2007	Mills College	Improving the Mathematical Content Base of Lesson Study Design and Test of a Research-Based Toolkit	1,997,590
2007	WestEd	Understanding Science: Improving Achievement of Middle School Students in Science	1,990,754
2007	University of Virginia	The Efficacy of the Responsive Classroom Approach for Improving Teacher Quality and Children's Academic Performance	2,814,668
2007	Milwaukee School of Engineering	Effect of the SUN Teacher Workshop on Student Achievement	1,262,083
2007	Purdue University	Classroom Links to Vocabulary and Phonological Sensitivity Skills	1,738,508
2007	University of Virginia	Pre-K Mathematics and Science for At-Risk Children: Outcomes-Focused Curricula and Support for Teaching Quality	1,949,854
2007	University of Oregon	Reading Intervention with Spanish Speaking Students: Maximizing Instructional Effectiveness in English and Spanish	3,498,216
2007	University of Michigan	Modeling Situation Awareness in Teachers	816,936
2007	University of Illinois, Chicago	Collaborative Teacher Network	1,207,516
2007	University of Kansas	Improving Instruction Through Implementation of the Partnership Instructional Coaching Model	1,919,577
2007	Florida State University	The Effects of Teacher Preparation and Professional Development on Special Education Teacher Quality	640,044
2007	University of Florida	The Influence of Collaborative Professional Development Groups & Coaching on the Literacy Instruction of Upper Elementary Special Education Teachers	2,293,415
2007	University of Florida	Impact of Professional Development on Preschool Teachers' Use of Embedded-Instruction Practices	1,288,510
2006	University of California, Berkeley	Integrating Science and Diversity Education: A Model of Pre-Service Elementary Teacher Preparation	1,473,522
2006	LessonLab, Inc.	Using Video Clips of Classroom Instruction as Item Prompts to Measure Teacher Knowledge of Teaching Mathematics: Instrument Development and Validation	1,413,121

Year	Research recipient	Teacher quality project	Grant award
2006	California State University, Long Beach	Standards-Based Differentiated ELD Instruction to Improve English Language Arts Achievement for English Language Learners	991,630
2006	University at Albany, State University of New York	Enhancing Knowledge Related to Research-Based Early Literacy Instruction Among Pre-Service Teachers	1,440,551
2006	University of California, Irvine	The Pathway Project: A Cognitive Strategies Approach to Reading and Writing Instruction for Teachers of Secondary English Language Learners	2,942,842
2006	University of Pittsburgh	Content-Focused Coaching for High Quality Reading Instruction	5,946,864
2006	Research Foundation of the State University of New York	Do Lower Barriers to Entry Affect Achievement and Teacher Retention: The Case of New York City Math Immersion	429,500
2006	Miami Museum of Science	Early Childhood Hands-On Science Curriculum Development and Demonstration Project	1,415,652
2006	University of Virginia	National Center for Research on Early Childhood Education (NCRECE): Preschool Teacher Professional Development Study	11,016,009
2006	Vanderbilt University	National Center for Performance Incentives	10,835,509
2006	Urban Institute	Center for the Analysis of Longitudinal Data in Education Research (CALDER)	10,000,000
2006	University of Hawaii	I in the IEP [IEP is the acronym for Individual Education Program.]	1,500,000
2005	Allegheny Singer Research Institute	Mentoring Teachers Through Pedagogical Content Knowledge Development	957,825
2005	Education Development Center, Inc.	Assessing the Potential Impact of a Professional Development Program in Science on Head Start Teachers and Children	1,367,500
2005	University of Nebraska-Lincoln	Evolving Inquiry: An Experimental Test of a Science Instruction Model for Teachers in Rural, Culturally Diverse Schools	1,261,684
2005	University of Toledo	Utah's Improving Science Teacher Quality Initiative	913,620
2005	South Carolina Department of Education	Investigating the Efficacy of a Professional Development Program in Classroom Assessment for Middle School Reading and Mathematics	1,680,625
2005	SRI International	Comparing the Efficacy of Three Approaches to Improving Teaching Quality in Science Education: Curriculum Implementation, Design, and Adaptation	1,864,415

Table. (Continued)

Year	Research recipient	Teacher quality project	Grant award
2005	University of South Florida	Replication and Outcomes of the Teaching SMART Program in Elementary Science Classrooms	2,408,168
2005	Florida State University	Identifying the Conditions Under Which Large Scale Professional Development Policy Initiatives are Related to Teacher Knowledge Instructional Practices, and Student Reading Outcomes	500,000
2005	Success for All Foundation	Embedded Classroom Multimedia: Improving Implementation Quality and Student Achievement in a Cooperative Writing Program	1,498,045
2005	Texas A&M University	Enhancing the Quality of Expository Text Instruction Through Content and Case-Situated Professional Development	1,498,530
2005	University of Texas at San Antonio	Teaching Teachers to Teach Critical Reading Strategies (CREST) Through an Intensive Professional Development Model	926,814
2005	Education Development Center Inc.	Examining the Efficacy of Two Models of Preschool Professional Development in Language and Literacy	2,834,272
2005	WestEd	A Randomized Controlled Study of the Efficacy of Reading Apprenticeship Professional Development for High School History and Science Teaching and Learning	2,997,972
2005	University of Michigan	Assessment of Pedagogical Knowledge of Teachers of Reading	1,677,575
2005	Utah State University	Connecting Primary Grade Teacher Knowledge to Primary Grade Student Achievement: Developing the Evidence-Based Reading/Writing Teacher Knowledge Assessment System	926,814
2004	DePaul University	Algebra Connections: Teacher Education in Clear Instruction and Responsive Assessment of Algebra Patterns and Problem Solving	1,052,822
2004	Educational Testing Service	The Relationship Between Mathematics Teachers' Content Knowledge and Students' Mathematics Achievement: Exploring the Predictive Validity of the Praxis Series Middle School Mathematics Test	1,573,623
2004	Purdue University	Professional Development in Early Reading	1,418,091
2004	University of North Carolina at Chapel Hill	Improving Teacher Quality to Address the Language and Literacy Skills of Latino Children in Pre-Kindergarten Programs	1,467,046

Year	Research recipient	Teacher quality project	Grant award
2004	University of Chicago	Can Literacy Professional Development be Improved With Web-Based Collaborative Learning Tools? A Randomized Field Trial	3,046,054
2004	Florida State University	Assessing Teacher Effectiveness: How Can We Predict Who Will Be a High Quality Teacher?	978,698
2004	RAND Corporation	Teacher Licensure Tests and Student Achievement	1,590,967
2004	Vanderbilt University	Opening the Black Box in Choice and Regular Public Schools (a research project within the National Research & Development Center on School Choice)	3,262,563
2004	University of North Carolina at Chapel Hill	National Research Center on Rural Education Support (estimated amount of total award devoted to teacher quality research)	11,200,000
2004	Vanderbilt University	Scaling Up Peer Assisted Learning Strategies to Strengthen Reading Achievement	5,618,237
2003	LessonLab Inc.	Improving Achievement by Maintaining the Learning Potential of Rich Mathematics Problems: An Experimental Study of a Video- and Internet-Based Professional Development Program	1,594,021
2003	Haskins Laboratories	Mastering Reading Instruction: A Professional Development Project for First Grade Teachers	2,912,063
2003	Instructional Research Group	Teacher Quality Study: An Investigation of the Impact of Teacher Study Groups as a Means to Enhance The Quality of Reading Instruction for First Graders in High Poverty Schools in Two States	2,820,670
2003	University of Michigan	Identifying Key Components of Effective Professional Development in Reading for First Grade Teachers and Their Students	1,677,575
Total grants			$159,393,859

Source: GAO analysis of IES research projects.

APPENDIX V. COMMENTS FROM THE U.S. DEPARTMENT OF EDUCATION

UNITED STATES DEPARTMENT OF EDUCATION
WASHINGTON, D.C. 20202-

June 9, 2009

Ms. Cornelia M. Ashby
Director
Education, Workforce, and
 Income Security Issues
U.S. Government Accountability Office
441 G Street, NW
Washington, DC 20548

Dear Ms. Ashby:

I am writing in response to the recommendation made in the Government Accountability Office (GAO) report, "Teacher Quality: Sustained Coordination among Key Federal Education Programs Could Enhance State Efforts to Improve Teacher Quality" (GAO-09-593).

This report had one recommendation for the Secretary of Education. Following is the Department's response.

Recommendation: To ensure that departmental goals to improve teacher quality are achieved and that its many related efforts are mutually reinforcing, we recommend that the Secretary of Education establish and implement a strategy for sustained coordination among existing departmental offices and programs. A key purpose of this coordination would be to facilitate information and resource sharing as well as to strengthen linkages among teacher quality improvement efforts to help states, school districts, and institutions of higher education in their initiatives to improve teacher quality.

Response: While the Department agrees that coordination is beneficial, the Department's experience indicates that creating interdepartmental committees solely for the purpose of coordinating agency activities or sharing information across offices is not always a useful exercise. While the Department will review the advisability of forming a cross-program committee, it would first want to ensure that such a group would truly lead to improvements in the way the Department coordinates its approach to teacher quality and the way States and school districts promote teacher quality.

The Department has effectively brought together individuals from different offices to work together on discrete issues or problems related to teacher quality when such action is needed. Good examples are the coordination that occurred on the implementation of the highly qualified teacher (HQT) requirements of the Elementary and Secondary Education Act, as amended, (ESEA) and on the development of common performance measures for teacher professional development programs.

Teacher Quality: Sustained Coordination Among Key Federal Education ...   131

In recent months, the Department has taken additional actions to coordinate activities in response to new demands and needs. The Department has initiated a number of coordination efforts to address the American Recovery and Reinvestment Act of 2009 (ARRA) requirements. One team, which is led by the Secretary's advisors on teacher issues and made up of representatives from several program offices, focuses on teachers and school leadership. As additional needs arise, such as those that may emanate from the implementation of the ARRA or the development of proposals for the reauthorization of the ESEA or other legislation, the Department can create additional inter-office working groups or coordinating bodies to address them.

Efforts to coordinate program implementation cannot fully eliminate barriers to program alignment. Individual programs have unique, and often inconsistent, legislative definitions and requirements. While increased internal coordination may alleviate some problems, it is unlikely to completely resolve them. The draft report identifies a cogent example: on page 19, the authors note that the Improving Teacher Quality State Grants (ITQ) program has a statutory definition of "high-need local educational agency," while the Mathematics and Science Partnerships program does not have a statutory definition of that term. The authors claim that this inconsistency may hinder States' ability to coordinate their implementation of the two programs, but intra-agency coordination could not eliminate this inconsistency.

The enclosed document includes the Department's suggested technical changes to the report.

We appreciate the opportunity to share our comments on the draft report.

Sincerely,

Joseph C. Conaty
Delegated Authority to Perform the Functions and
Duties of the Assistant Secretary for Elementary and
Secondary Education

Enclosure

End Notes

[1] U.S. Department of Education, Office of Policy and Program Studies Services, *State and Local Implementation of the No Child Left Behind Act: Volume VII—Teacher Quality Under NCLB: Final Report* (U.S. Department of Education, 2009). High-poverty and low-poverty schools are respectively those in the top and bottom quartiles when schools in a state are ranked by level of poverty in descending order; most states based level of poverty on the percentage of students eligible for free or reduced lunch in the school.

[2] "Collaboration" is a broad term that can include activities that others have variously defined as "cooperation," "coordination," and "integration," and previous GAO work has identified various practices that can enhance collaboration, such as establishing compatible policies and procedures to operate across organizational boundaries. See GAO, *Results Oriented Government: Practices that Can Help Enhance and Sustain Collaboration among Federal Agencies*, GAO-06-15 (Washington, D.C.: Oct. 21, 2005).

[3] Because of differences in higher education governance among states, state agencies for higher education include offices, commissions, boards, committees, departments, or organizations with governing authority over higher education in the state.

[4] Coordinating bodies work to integrate a student's education from kindergarten through a 4-year college degree by coordinating statewide education initiatives and reforms. Examples of such coordinating bodies include what are commonly referred to as P-16/20 councils, or prekindergarten through college/master's, though some states

132   United States Government Accountability Office

refer to them differently (e.g., commission, roundtable, committee, initiative, etc.). On the basis of our review of the literature, we found that a large number of these bodies address some aspect of teacher quality.

[5] Laura Goe and Leslie M. Stickler, *Teacher Quality and Student Achievement: Making the Most of Recent Research* (Washington, D.C.: National Comprehensive Center for Teacher Quality, 2008).

[6] GAO, *No Child Left Behind: States Face Challenges in Measuring Academic Growth that Education's Initiatives May Help Address*, GAO-06-661 (Washington, D.C.: July 17, 2006).

[7] Under the Government Performance and Results Act (Pub. L. No. 103-62 (1993)), federal agencies are required to develop strategic plans, performance plans, and performance reports. The plans are to include long-term and annual goals, respectively, along with the means for accomplishing the goals. The performance report is to include the extent to which the goals have been achieved.

[8] Core subjects include English, reading or language arts, mathematics, science, foreign languages, civics and government, economics, arts, history, and geography.

[9] GAO, *No Child Left Behind Act: Improved Accessibility to Education's Information Could Help States Further Implement Teacher Qualification Requirements*, GAO-06-25 (Washington, D.C.: Nov. 21, 2005).

[10] GAO has reported that in general, HEA provisions tend to focus on the preparation of prospective teachers, while ESEA provisions tend to focus on training for teachers already in the classroom and are funded at a higher level than HEA programs. See GAO, *Teacher Quality: Approaches, Implementation, and Evaluations of Key Federal Efforts*, GAO-07-861T (Washington, D.C.: May 17, 2007).

[11] Title II, section 205 of the HEA, as amended by the Higher Education Opportunity Act, Pub. L. No. 110-315, requires the annual preparation and submission of reports on teacher preparation and qualifications from institutions of higher education that conduct a traditional teacher preparation program or alternative route to state certification or licensure. Section 206 requires these institutions of higher education to set annual quantifiable goals for increasing the number of prospective teachers trained in teacher shortage areas and to provide specific assurances to the Secretary of Education that include being responsive to the needs of school districts in which the institution's graduates are likely to teach.

[12] According to Education, during the 2007-2008 school year, districts used most of the funding for hiring highly qualified teachers to reduce classroom size and professional development training for teachers already teaching in the classroom.

[13] These 33 programs have other primary goals or purposes, such as providing assistance to rural school districts to help them meet state academic goals, supporting career and technical skills of secondary or postsecondary students, or paying the salaries of teachers serving certain student populations.

[14] This total includes an estimated $1.15 billion from the fiscal year 2009 appropriation and about $800 million from the American Recovery and Reinvestment Act of 2009 (Pub. L. No. 111-5).

[15] Other teacher quality programs that received Recovery Act funds and that are specifically focused on teacher quality include the Enhancing Education Through Technology Program and the Teacher Quality Partnership Grant Program.

[16] GAO, *Troops to Teachers: Program Brings More Men and Minorities into Teaching Workforce, but Education Could Improve Management to Enhance Results*, GAO-06-265 (Washington, D.C.: Mar. 1, 2006); *Special Education: Additional Assistance and Better Coordination Needed among Education Offices to Help States Meet the NCLBA Teacher Requirements*, GAO-04-659 (Washington, D.C.: July 15, 2004); and U.S. Department of Education, Office of the Inspector General, *Overlapping Services in the Department of Education's Office of Postsecondary Education Programs*, Audit Report No. ED-OIG/X07F0002 (Washington, D.C.: Feb. 27, 2006).

[17] GAO, *Results Oriented Government: Practices that Can Help Enhance and Sustain Collaboration among Federal Agencies*, GAO-06-15 (Washington, D.C.: Oct. 21, 2005).

[18] GAO-06-15.

[19] GAO, *Managing for Results: Building on Agencies' Strategic Plans to Improve Federal Management*, GAO/T-GGD/AIMD-98-29 (Washington, D.C.: Oct. 30, 1997).

[20] All nonfederal entities that expend $500,000 or more in federal awards in a year are required to obtain an annual audit in accordance with the Single Audit Act, as amended, and Office of Management and Budget Circular A-133, "Audits of States, Local Governments and Non-Profit Organizations."

[21] Process studies are conducted to evaluate the extent to which a program is operating as it was intended. These studies typically use methodologies such as case studies and surveys to assess whether program activities conform to statutory and regulatory requirements, program design, and professional standards or customer expectations. Outcome evaluations assess the extent to which a program achieves its outcome-oriented objectives, but may also assess program processes to understand how outcomes are produced. Impact evaluations use scientific research methods to assess the net effect of a program by comparing program outcomes with an estimate of what would have happened in the absence of the program.

[22] U.S. Department of Education, Institute of Education Sciences, *National Evaluation of Early Reading First, Final Report to Congress* (Washington, D.C.: May 2007).

[23] U.S. Department of Education, Office of Planning, Evaluation, and Policy Development, *Partnerships for Reform: Changing Teacher Preparation Through the Title II HEA Partnership Program: Final Report* (Washington, D.C.: May 2006).

[24] GAO, *Higher Education: Federal Science, Technology, Engineering, and Mathematics Programs and Related Trends*, GAO-06-114 (Washington, D.C.: Oct. 12, 2005).

[25] U.S. Department of Education, Institute of Education Sciences, *The Impact of Professional Development Models and Strategies on Teacher Practice and Student Achievement in Early Reading* (Washington, D.C.: September 2008); and *An Evaluation of Teachers Trained Through Different Routes to Certification* (Washington, D.C.: February 2009).

[26] National Research Council, *Assessing Accomplished Teaching: Advanced-Level Certification Programs* (Washington, D.C.: 2008).

[27] IES also includes the National Center for Education Statistics, which is the primary federal entity for collecting, analyzing, and reporting data on the condition of education in the United States and other nations. IES maintains large data sets, such as the Schools and Staffing Survey, which are available to the public and researchers.

[28] Research information is also provided in other products, including Topic Reports, which compile information from intervention reports in specific topics such as reading and mathematics, and Intervention Reports, which examine all studies for a specific intervention within a topic area, rating each study based on evidence standards.

[29] REL research that meet IES standards is presented on the What Works Clearinghouse.

[30] Each of the five National Content Centers focuses on and provides expertise, analysis, and research in one of the following areas: accountability, instruction, teacher quality, innovation and improvement, or high schools.

[31] The Educational Technical Assistance Act of 2002 (Pub. L. No. 107-279, Title II) requires that each comprehensive center coordinate its activities, collaborate, and regularly exchange information with the REL in the region in which the center is located as well as with other technical assistance providers in the region.

[32] Carl Krueger, *The Progress of P-16 Collaboration in the States* (Denver, Colo.: Education Commission of the States, April 2006).

[33] Education also provides some funding for the Center for Analysis of Longitudinal Data in Education Research (CALDER), housed at the Urban Institute. CALDER's mission is to inform education policy development through analyses of data on individual students and teachers over time.

[34] According to Education, new grant awards were not made in fiscal year 2008. Most of the funding available in fiscal year 2008 supported 13 continuation awards; the remainder was combined with fiscal year 2009 funding for a new competition. In fiscal year 2009, the 12 states that were awarded a second grant were Arkansas, California, Connecticut, Florida, Kansas, Kentucky, Maryland, Michigan, Ohio, Oregon, Pennsylvania, and Wisconsin.

[35] The State Fiscal Stabilization Fund is designed, in part, to help stabilize state and local budgets to minimize and avoid reductions in education and other essential services.

[36] Included in this guidance is information on specific data metrics that states would use to make transparent their status in the education reform areas. The data metrics include teacher effectiveness and ensuring that all schools have highly qualified teachers, higher standards and rigorous assessments that will improve both teaching and learning, and better information to educators and the public to address the individual needs of students and improve teacher performance. For each metric, a state would need to demonstrate that it collects the required data and that it will make the data easily accessible to the public.

[37] Sarah-Kathryn McDonald, Jolynne Andal, Kevin Brown, and Barbara Schneider, *Getting the Evidence for Evidence-based Initiatives: How the Midwest States Use Data Systems to Improve Education Processes and Outcomes* (Washington, D.C.: REL Midwest, 2007).

[38] Because of differences in higher education governance among states, state agencies for higher education include offices, commissions, boards, committees, departments, or organizations with governing authority over higher education in the state.

[39] This guide is a subset of the *Catalog of Federal Domestic Assistance*, which includes the federal programs from all federal agencies. We updated fiscal year 2008 funding levels with fiscal year 2009 funding levels based on information in the fiscal year 2009 Omnibus Appropriations Act, Education budget documents, and a review of these figures by Education officials.

[40] The Regional Educational Laboratories included the Northwest Regional Educational Laboratory, the Mid-Atlantic Regional Educational Laboratory, and the Southwest Regional Educational Laboratory; the Regional Comprehensive Centers included the Northwest Regional Comprehensive Center, the Mid-Atlantic Regional Comprehensive Center, and the Southeast Regional Comprehensive Center.

[41] Coordinating bodies work to integrate a student's education from kindergarten through a four-year college degree by coordinating statewide education initiatives and reforms. Examples of such coordinating bodies include what are commonly referred to as P-16/20 councils, though some states refer to them differently (e.g., commissions, roundtables, committees, initiatives, etc.). On the basis of our review of the literature, we found that a large number of these bodies address some aspect of teacher quality.

In: Teacher Quality and Student Achievement
Editor: Katherine E. Westley

ISBN: 978-1-61728-274-4
© 2010 Nova Science Publishers, Inc.

Chapter 5

STUDENT ACHIEVEMENT: SCHOOLS USE MULTIPLE STRATEGIES TO HELP STUDENTS MEET ACADEMIC STANDARDS, ESPECIALLY SCHOOLS WITH HIGH PROPORTIONS OF LOW-INCOME AND MINORITY STUDENTS[*]

United States Government Accountability Office

WHY GAO DID THIS STUDY

The federal government has invested billions of dollars to improve student academic performance, and many schools, teachers, and researchers are trying to determine the most effective instructional practices with which to accomplish this. The Conference Report for the Consolidated Appropriations Act for Fiscal Year 2008 directed GAO to study strategies used to prepare students to meet state academic achievement standards. To do this, GAO answered: (1) What types of instructional practices are schools and teachers most frequently using to help students achieve state academic standards, and do those instructional practices differ by school characteristics? (2) What is known about how standards-based accountability systems have affected instructional practices? (3) What is known about instructional practices that are effective in improving student achievement? GAO analyzed data from a 2006-2007 national survey of principals and 2005-2006 survey of teachers in three states, conducted a literature review of the impact of standardsbased accountability systems on instructional practices and of practices that are effective in improving student achievement, and interviewed experts.

---

[*] This is an edited, reformatted and augmented version of a U. S. Government Accountability Office publication dated November 2009.

What GAO Recommends

GAO makes no recommendations in this report. Education provided comments about issues pertaining to the study's approach that it believes should be considered. GAO clarified the report as appropriate.

What GAO Found

Nationwide, most principals focused on multiple strategies to help students meet academic standards, such as using student data to inform instruction and increasing professional development for teachers, according to our analysis of data from a U.S. Department of Education survey. Many of these strategies were used more often at high-poverty schools—those where 75 percent or more of the students were eligible for the free and reduced-price lunch program—and high-minority schools—those where 75 percent or more of students were identified as part of a minority population, than at lower poverty and minority schools. Likewise, math teachers in California, Georgia, and Pennsylvania increased their use of certain instructional practices in response to their state tests, such as focusing more on topics emphasized on assessments and searching for more effective teaching methods, and teachers at high-poverty and high-minority schools were more likely than teachers at lower-poverty schools and lower-minority schools to have made these changes, according to GAO's analysis of survey data collected by the RAND Corporation. Some researchers suggested that differences exist in the use of these practices because schools with lower poverty or lower minority student populations might generally be meeting accountability requirements and therefore would need to try these strategies less frequently.

Research shows that standards-based accountability systems can influence instructional practices in both positive and negative ways. For example, some research notes that using a standards-based curriculum that is aligned with corresponding instructional guidelines can facilitate the development of higher order thinking skills in students. But, in some cases, teacher practices did not always reflect the principles of standards-based instruction, and the difficulties in aligning practice with standards were attributed, in part, to current accountability requirements. Other research noted that assessments can be powerful tools for improving the learning process and evaluating student achievement, but assessments can also have some unintended negative consequences on instruction, including narrowing the curriculum to only material that is tested.

Many experts stated that methodological issues constrain knowing more definitively the specific instructional practices that improve student learning and achievement. Nevertheless, some studies and experts pointed to instructional practices that are considered to be effective in raising student achievement, such as differentiated instruction. Professional development for teachers was also highlighted as important for giving teachers the skills and knowledge necessary to implement effective teaching practices.

ABBREVIATIONS

AYP	adequate yearly progress
ESEA	Elementary and Secondary Education Act of 1965
IASA	Improving America's Schools Act of 1994
NCLBA	No Child Left Behind Act of 2001
NLS-NCLB	National Longitudinal Study of No Child Left Behind
NSF	National Science Foundation
RAND	The RAND Corporation

November 16, 2009

Congressional Committees

The federal government has invested billions of dollars to help schools meet requirements of the No Child Left Behind Act of 2001 (NCLBA) to improve student academic performance in reading, math, and science.[1] To this end, many schools, teachers, and researchers are trying to determine the most effective instructional practices to improve student achievement. Instructional practices refer to school or district-level improvement strategies, such as aligning curriculum with academic standards, restructuring the school day, or providing additional professional development to teachers.[2] Instructional practices can also refer to classroom teaching practices like assigning more homework or searching for more effective teaching methods. Little is known about the extent to which instructional practices have changed in response to NCLBA's accountability requirements, whether these practices vary by type of school, and the extent to which some practices have proven to be more effective than others.

Under NCLBA, states are required to develop challenging student academic achievement standards, administer tests based on those standards (standards-based assessments) to measure student proficiency, and develop targets for performance on these tests. Specifically, NCLBA requires states to develop a plan to ensure that their students are making adequate yearly progress (AYP) toward proficiency in reading, math, and science by 2014 for students collectively and in key student subgroups, including low-income and minority students.

While NCLBA creates requirements for student proficiency, it generally allows states to determine how best to meet those requirements. The Conference Report accompanying the Consolidated Appropriations Act for Fiscal Year 2008 directed that GAO conduct a study of strategies used to prepare students to meet state academic achievement standards. In response, we agreed with the Senate and House Appropriations Committees, the Senate Committee on Health, Education, Labor and Pensions, and the House Committee on Education and Labor to address the following questions:

1. What types of instructional practices are schools and teachers most frequently using to help students achieve state academic standards, and do those instructional practices differ by school characteristics?
2. What is known about how standards-based accountability systems such as that in NCLBA have affected instructional practices?

3. What is known about instructional practices that are effective in improving student achievement?

To answer these questions, we analyzed data from two recent surveys of principals and teachers that were conducted by the RAND Corporation (RAND). The first survey, the nationally representative National Longitudinal Study of No Child Left Behind (NLS-NCLB), was sponsored by the U.S. Department of Education (Education) and asked principals the extent to which their schools were focusing on certain strategies in their school improvement efforts.[3] We conducted an analysis of the school year 2006-2007 survey data on school improvement strategies by controlling for school characteristic variables, such as the percentage of a school's students receiving free or reduced price lunch (poverty); the percentage of students who are a racial minority (minority); whether the school is in an urban, urban fringe or large town, or rural area (school location); and the school's AYP performance status. The second survey, a three-state survey sponsored by the National Science Foundation (NSF), asked elementary and middle school teachers in California, Georgia, and Pennsylvania how their classroom teaching strategies differed due to a state math test.[4]

RAND selected these states to represent a range of approaches to standards-based accountability and to provide some geographic and demographic diversity. Using school year 2005-2006 data from the three- state survey, which is representative only of those three states individually, we measured associations between the teacher responses and the school characteristic variables. As part of these survey analyses, we reviewed documentation and performed electronic testing of the data obtained through the surveys and conducted interviews with the primary RAND researchers responsible for the data collection and analysis. We determined the survey data were sufficiently reliable for the purposes of our study. To answer questions two and three, we conducted a literature review and synthesis.[5] We supplemented our synthesis by interviewing prominent education researchers identified in frequently cited articles and through discussions with other knowledgeable individuals.[6] We also reviewed relevant federal laws and regulations.

We conducted our work from July 2008 to November 2009 in accordance with all sections of GAO's Quality Assurance Framework that are relevant to our objectives. The framework requires that we plan and perform the engagement to obtain sufficient and appropriate evidence to meet our stated objectives and to discuss any limitations in our work. We believe that the information and data obtained, and the analysis conducted, provide a reasonable basis for any findings and conclusions in this product.

BACKGROUND

NCLBA reauthorized the Elementary and Secondary Education Act of 1965 (ESEA)[7] and built upon accountability requirements created under a previous reauthorization, the Improving America's Schools Act of 1994 (IASA).[8] Under ESEA, as amended, Congress sought to improve student learning by incorporating academic standards and assessments in the requirements placed on states. Academic standards, which describe what students should know and be able to do at different grade levels in different subjects, help guide school systems in their choice of curriculum and help teachers plan for classroom instruction.

Assessments, which states use to measure student progress in achieving the standards, are required to be administered by states.

NCLBA further strengthened some of the accountability requirements contained in ESEA, as amended. Specifically, NCLBA's accountability provisions require states to develop education plans that establish academic standards and performance goals for schools to meet AYP and lead to 100 percent of their students being proficient in reading, math, and science by 2014. This proficiency must be assessed annually in reading and math in grades 3 through 8 and periodically in science, whereas assessments were required less frequently under the IASA.[9] Under NCLBA, schools' assessment data generally must be disaggregated to assess progress toward state proficiency targets for students in certain designated groups, including low-income students, minority students, students with disabilities, and those with limited English proficiency. Each of these groups must make AYP in order for the school to make AYP. Schools that fail to make AYP for 2 or more consecutive years are required to implement various improvement measures identified in NCLBA, and these measures are more extensive than those required under IASA. Education, which has responsibility for general oversight of NCLBA, reviews and approves state plans for meeting AYP requirements. As we have previously reported, Education had approved all states' plans—fully or conditionally—by June 2003.[10]

NCLBA also recognizes the role of teachers in providing a quality education by requiring states to ensure that all teachers in core academic subjects are "highly qualified." Under this requirement, teachers generally must have a bachelor's degree, be fully certified, and demonstrate their knowledge of the subjects they teach. Previously, there were no specific requirements regarding teacher quality under ESEA, as amended.[11]

Principals and Teachers Used a Variety of Instructional Practices to Help Students Meet Standards, and Many of These Practices Were Used More Frequently at Schools with Higher Proportions of Low- Income and Minority Students

According to our analysis of NLS-NCLB data from Education, most principals reported their schools focused on multiple instructional practices in their voluntary school improvement efforts.[12] These strategies were used more often at schools with higher proportions of low-income students ("high-poverty schools") and schools with higher proportions of minority students ("high-minority schools") than at schools with lower proportions of low-income students ("low-poverty schools") and schools with lower proportions of minority students ("low-minority schools").[13] Likewise, the survey of math teachers in California, Georgia, and Pennsylvania indicates teachers were using many different instructional practices in response to their state tests, and teachers at high-poverty and high-minority schools were more likely than teachers at low-poverty and low-minority schools to have been increasing their use of some of these practices. Some researchers we spoke with suggested that differences in the use of these instructional practices exist because

140   United States Government Accountability Office

schools with low- poverty or low-minority student populations might generally be meeting accountability standards and, therefore, would need to try these strategies less frequently.

Principals at High-Poverty and High-Minority Schools Emphasized Certain School Improvement Strategies More Than Principals at Other Schools

According to nationally representative data from Education's NLS-NCLB, in school year 2006-2007 most principals focused on multiple strategies in their school improvement efforts. The survey asked principals the extent to which their schools were focusing on ten different strategies in their voluntary school improvement initiatives. The three most common strategies were: (1) using student achievement data to inform instruction and school improvement; (2) providing additional instruction to low- achieving students; and (3) aligning curriculum and instruction with standards and/or assessments. (See figure 1.) Nearly all school principals placed a major or moderate focus on three or more surveyed strategies in their school improvement efforts, and over 80 percent of principals placed a major or moderate focus on six or more strategies. However, as Education's report on the survey data cautioned, the number of improvement strategies emphasized was not necessarily an indication of the intensity or quality of the improvement efforts.

While nearly all principals responded that they used multiple improvement strategies, there were statistically significant differences in principals' responses across a range of school characteristics, including percentage of the school's students receiving free or reduced price lunch (poverty), percentage of minority students, the school's location, and AYP status.[14] For example, when comparing schools across poverty levels, we found that principals at high-poverty schools were two to three times more likely than principals at low-poverty schools to focus on five particular strategies in their school improvement efforts:

- Restructuring the school day to teach core content areas in greater depth;[15]
- Increasing instructional time for all students (e.g., by lengthening the school day or year, shortening recess);
- Providing extended-time instructional programs (e.g., before-school, after- school, or weekend instructional programs);
- Implementing strategies for increasing parents' involvement in their children's education; and
- Increasing the intensity, focus, and effectiveness of professional development.[16]

Likewise, when comparing schools across minority levels, we found that principals at high- and moderate-minority schools were approximately two to three times more likely than principals at low-minority schools to make six particular school improvement strategies a major or moderate focus of their school improvement efforts.[17] For instance, principals at schools with a high percentage of minority students were more than three times as likely as principals at schools with a low percentage of minority students to provide extended-time instruction such as after-school programs. A school's location was associated with differences in principals' responses about the strategies they used as well: principals at rural schools were only about one-third to one-half as likely as central city schools to make five of these school improvement strategies a moderate or major focus of their school improvement efforts.[18]

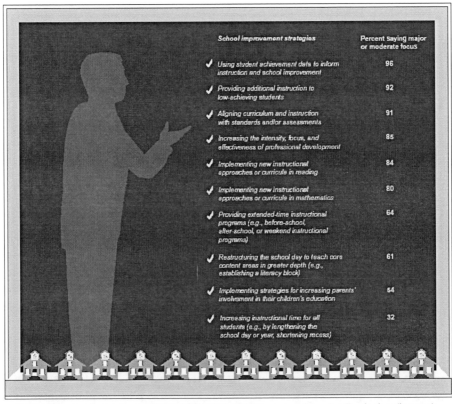

Sources: GAO analysis of school year 2006-2007 NLS-NCLB survey data, Art Explosion (images).
Note: Some of the voluntary school improvement strategies identified above are similar to the corrective actions and restructuring options schools identified for improvement under NCLBA are required to choose from in preparing their school improvement plan. For example, implementing a new curriculum and extending the school day are both voluntary improvement strategies and possible strategies for improvement under the law.

Figure 1. Principals' Responses Indicating That a School Improvement Strategy Was a Major or Moderate Focus of the School Improvement Efforts.

When we compared principal responses based on AYP status, there was some evidence of a statistically significant association between AYP status and the extent to which principals focused these strategies in their school improvement efforts, but it was limited when the other variables such as poverty and minority were taken into account. AYP status had some correlation with the demographic characteristics of poverty and minority, and those characteristics explained the patterns of principals' responses more fully than the AYP characteristic. However, our analysis generally showed that schools that had not made AYP were more likely to make six of these school improvement strategies a moderate or major focus of their school improvement plan than schools that had made AYP. Additionally, Education reported that schools identified for improvement under NCLBA—that is, schools that have not made AYP for two or more consecutive years—were engaged in a greater number of improvement efforts than non-identified schools. Therefore, principals of the non-identified schools may have been less likely than principals of identified schools to view specific strategies as a major or moderate focus.

We spoke with several researchers about the results of our analysis of the principals' responses, especially at high-poverty and high-minority schools. While the researchers could not say with certainty the reasons for the patterns, they noted that high-poverty and high-minority schools tend to be most at risk of not meeting their states' standards, so that principals at those schools might be more willing to try different approaches. Conversely, the researchers noted that principals at schools meeting standards would not have the same incentives to adopt as many school improvement strategies.

Most Math Teachers in Three Surveyed States Have Increased Their Use of Certain Instructional Practices in Response to State Tests, especially in High-Poverty and High- Minority Schools

The RAND survey of elementary and middle school math teachers in California, Georgia and Pennsylvania showed that in each of the three states at least half of the teachers reported increasing their use of certain instructional practices in at least five areas as a result of the statewide math test (see figure 2). For example, most teachers in Pennsylvania responded that due to the state math test they: (1) focused more on standards, (2) emphasized assessment styles and formats, (3) focused more on subjects tested, (4) searched for more effective teaching methods, and (5) spent more time teaching content.

As we did with the survey responses of principals, we analyzed the teacher survey data to determine whether math teachers' responses differed by school characteristics for poverty, minority, location, and AYP status. As with the principals' responses, we found that elementary and middle school math teachers in high-poverty and high-minority schools were more likely than teachers in low-poverty and low-minority schools to report increasing their use of certain instructional practices, and this pattern was consistent across the three states (see figure 3). For example, 69 percent of math teachers at high-poverty schools in California indicated they spent more time teaching test-taking strategies as opposed to 38 percent of math teachers in low-poverty schools. In Georgia, 50 percent of math teachers in high-poverty schools reported offering more outside assistance to non- proficient students in contrast to 26 percent of math teachers in low- poverty schools. Fifty-one percent of math teachers at high-poverty schools in Pennsylvania reported focusing more attention on students close to proficiency compared to 23 percent of math teachers doing so in low poverty schools.[19]

Similar to what our poverty analysis showed, survey responses provided some evidence that math teachers in high-minority schools were more likely than those in low-minority schools to change their instructional practices. Math teachers at high-minority schools in each of the three states, as compared to those at low-minority schools, were more likely to:

- rely on open-ended tests in their own classroom assessments;
- increase the amount of time spent teaching mathematics by replacing non-instructional activities with mathematics instruction;

- focus on topics emphasized in the state math test; and
- teach general test-taking strategies.

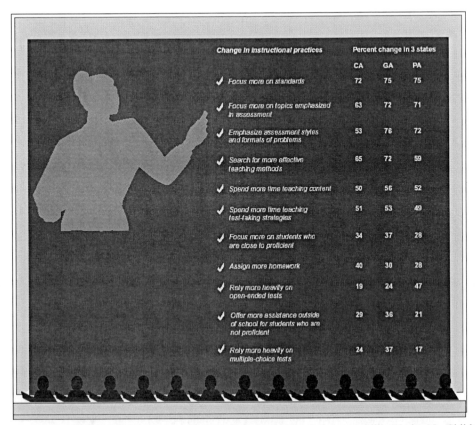

Sources: GAO analysis of 2005 survey data from Standards-Based Accountability Under No Child Left Behind: Experiences of Teachers and Administrators in Three States. Hamilton et al. Art Explosion (images).

Figure 2. Percent of Elementary and Middle School Math Teachers Who Reported Increasing Their Use of Certain Instructional Practices as a Result of State Test.

We also analyzed the RAND data with regard to school location and a school's AYP status, but results from these characteristics were not significant for as many instructional practices.[20]

As we did regarding the survey responses of principals, we spoke to several researchers, including the authors of the three-state teacher study, regarding possible reasons for the patterns we saw in the teacher survey data. The researchers we spoke with provided similar possible reasons for the patterns in the teacher survey as they did for patterns in the principal survey. For instance, the researchers noted that high-poverty and high- minority schools are more likely to be at risk of failing to meet the state standards, which might prompt teachers to try different approaches. On the other hand, the researchers stated that teachers at those schools meeting the standards would not have the same incentives to change their instructional practices.

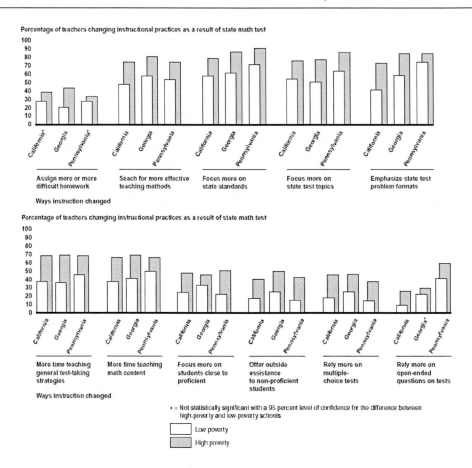

Sources: GAO analysis of school year 2005-2006 survey data from Standards-Based Accountability Under No Child Left Behind: Experiences of Teachers and Administrators in Three States. Hamilton et al.

Figure 3. How Survey Responses Differed between Math Teachers at High-Poverty and Low-Poverty Schools in Three States.

RESEARCH SHOWS THAT STANDARDS-BASED ACCOUNTABILITY SYSTEMS CAN INFLUENCE INSTRUCTIONAL PRACTICES THROUGH STANDARDS AND ASSESSMENTS IN BOTH POSITIVE AND NEGATIVE WAYS

Research shows that using a standards-based curriculum that is aligned with corresponding instructional guidelines can positively influence teaching practices. Specifically, some studies reported changes by teachers who facilitated their students developing higher-order thinking skills, such as interpreting meaning, understanding implied reasoning, and developing conceptual knowledge, through practices such as multiple answer problem solving, less lecture and more small group work. Additionally, a few researchers we interviewed stated that a positive effect of NCLBA's accountability provisions has been a renewed focus on standards and curriculum.[21]

Student Achievement: Schools Use Multiple Strategies to Help Students Meet... 145

However, some studies indicated that teachers' practices did not always reflect the principles of standards-based instruction and that current accountability policies help contribute to the difficulty in aligning practice with standards. Some research shows that, while teachers may be changing their instructional practices in response to standards-based reform, these changes may not be fully aligned with the principles of the reform. That research also notes that the reliability in implementing standards in the classroom varied in accordance with teachers' different beliefs in and support for standards-based reform as well as the limitations in their instructional capabilities. For example, one observational study of math teachers showed that, while teachers implemented practices envisioned by standards-based reform, such as getting students to work in small groups or using manipulatives (e.g., cubes or tiles), their approaches did not go far enough in that students were not engaged in conversations about mathematical or scientific concepts and ideas.[22] To overcome these challenges, studies point to the need for teachers to have opportunities to learn, practice, and reflect on instructional practices that incorporate the standards, and then to observe their effects on student learning. However, some researchers have raised concerns that current accountability systems' focus on test scores and mandated timelines for achieving proficiency levels for students do not give teachers enough time to learn, practice, and reflect on instructional practices and may discourage some teachers from trying ambitious teaching practices envisioned by standards-based reform.

Another key element of a standards-based accountability system is assessments, which help measure the extent to which schools are improving student learning through assessing student performance against the standards. Some researchers note that assessments are powerful tools for managing and improving the learning process by providing information for monitoring student progress, making instructional decisions, evaluating student achievement, and evaluating programs. In addition, assessments can also influence instructional content and help teachers use or adjust specific classroom practices. As one synthesis concluded, assessments can influence whether teachers broaden or narrow the curriculum, focus on concepts and problem solving—or emphasize test preparation over subject matter content.[23]

In contrast, some of the research and a few experts we interviewed raised concerns about testing formats that do not encourage challenging teaching practices and instructional practices that narrow the curriculum as a result of current assessment practices.[24] For example, depending on the test used, research has shown that teachers may be influenced to use teaching approaches that reflect the skills and knowledge to be tested. Multiple choice tests tend to focus on recognizing facts and information while open-ended formats are more likely to require students to apply critical thinking skills. Conclusions from a literature synthesis conducted by the Department of Education stated that " teachers respond to assessment formats used, so testing programs must be designed and administered with this influence in mind. Tests that emphasize inquiry, provide extended writing opportunities, and use open-ended response formats or a portfolio approach tend to influence instruction in ways quite different from tests that use closed-ended response formats and which emphasize procedures."[25] We recently reported that states have most often chosen multiple choice items over other item types of assessments because they are cost effective and can be scored within tight time frames. While multiple choice tests provide cost and time saving benefits to states, the use of multiple choice items make it difficult, if not impossible, to measure highly complex content. [26] Other research has raised concerns that, to avoid potential consequences from low-scoring assessment results under NCLBA, teachers are narrowing the curriculum being taught—sometimes referred to as "teaching to the test"—either by spending more classroom time on tested subjects at the expense of other non-tested subjects, restricting the breadth of content covered to focus only on the content covered by the test, or focusing more time on test-taking strategies than on subject content.[27]

RESEARCH HIGHLIGHTS SOME POTENTIALLY SUCCESSFUL PRACTICES FOR IMPROVING STUDENT ACHIEVEMENT, ALTHOUGH EXPERTS CONTEND THAT METHODOLOGICAL ISSUES CONSTRAIN REACHING DEFINITIVE CONCLUSIONS ABOUT WHAT WORKS

Our literature review found some studies that pointed to instructional practices that appear to be effective in raising student achievement. But, in discussing the broader implications of these studies with the experts that we interviewed, many commented that, taken overall, the research is not conclusive about which specific instructional practices improve student learning and achievement.

Some researchers stated that this was due to methodological issues in conducting the research. For example, one researcher explained that, while smaller research studies on very specific strategies in reading and math have sometimes shown powerful relationships between the strategy used and positive changes in student achievement, results from meta- analyses of smaller studies have been inconclusive in pointing to similar patterns in the aggregate. A few other researchers stated that the lack of empirical data about how instruction unfolds in the classroom hampers the understanding about what works in raising student performance.

A few researchers also noted that conducting research in a way that would yield more conclusive results is difficult. One of the main difficulties, as explained by one researcher, is the number of variables a study may need to examine or control for in order to understand the effectiveness of a particular strategy, especially given the number of interactions these variables could have with each other. One researcher mentioned cost as a challenge when attempting to gather empirical data at the classroom level, stating "teaching takes place in the classroom, but the expense of conducting classroom-specific evaluations is a serious barrier to collecting this type of data." Finally, even when research supports the efficacy of a strategy, it may not work with different students or under varying conditions. In raising this point, one researcher stated that "educating a child is not like making a car" whereby a production process is developed and can simply be repeated again and again. Each child learns differently, creating a challenge for teachers in determining the instructional practices that will work best for each student.

Some of the practices identified by both the studies and a few experts as those with potential for improving student achievement were:

- *Differentiated instruction.* In this type of instruction, teaching practices and plans are adjusted to accommodate each student's skill level for the task at hand. Differentiated instruction requires teachers to be flexible in their teaching approach by adjusting the curriculum and presentation of information for students, thereby providing multiple options for students to take in and process information. As one researcher described it, effective teachers understand the strategies and practices that work for each student and in this way can move all students forward in their learning and achievement.

- *More guiding, less telling.* Researchers have identified two general approaches to teaching: didactic and interactive. Didactic instruction relies more on lecturing and demonstrations, asking short answer questions, and assessing whether answers are correct. Interactive instruction focuses more on listening and guiding students, asking questions with more than one correct answer, and giving students choices during learning. As one researcher explained, both teaching approaches are important, but some research has shown that giving students more guidance and less direction helps students become critical and independent thinkers, learn how to work independently, and assess several potential solutions and apply the best one. These kinds of learning processes are important for higher-order thinking. However, implementing "less instruction" techniques requires a high level of skill and creativity on the part of the teacher. [28]

- *Promoting effective discourse.* An important corollary to the teacher practice of guiding students versus directing them is effective classroom discussion. Research highlights the importance of developing students' understanding not only of the basic concepts of a subject, but higher-order thinking and skills as well. To help students achieve understanding, it is necessary to have effective classroom discussion in which students test and revise their ideas, and elaborate on and clarify their thinking. In guiding students to an effective classroom discussion, teachers must ask engaging and challenging questions, be able to get all students to participate, and know when to provide information or allow students to discover it for themselves.

Additionally, one synthesis of several experimental studies examining practices in elementary math classrooms identified two instructional approaches that showed positive effects on student learning. The first was cooperative learning in which students work in pairs or small teams and are rewarded based on how well the group learns. The other approach included programs that helped teachers introduce math concepts and improve skills in classroom management, time management, and motivation. This analysis also found that using computer-assisted instruction had moderate to substantial effects on student learning, although this type of instruction was always supplementary to other approaches or programs being used.

We found through our literature review and interviews with researchers that the issue of effective instructional practices is intertwined with professional development. To enable all students to achieve the high standards of learning envisioned by standards-based accountability systems, teachers need extensive skills and knowledge in order to use effective teaching practices in the classroom. Given this, professional development is critical to supporting teachers' learning of new skills and their application. Specifically, the research concludes that professional development will more likely have positive impacts on both teacher learning and student achievement if it:

- Focuses on a content area with direct links to the curriculum;
- Challenges teachers intellectually through reflection and critical problem solving;
- Aligns with goals and standards for student learning;

- Lasts long enough so that teachers can practice and revise their techniques;
- Occurs collaboratively within a teacher learning community—ongoing teams of teachers that meet regularly for the purposes of learning, joint lesson planning, and problem solving;
- Involves all the teachers within a school or department;
- Provides active learning opportunities with direct applications to the classroom; and
- Is based on teachers' input regarding their learning needs.

Some researchers have raised concerns about the quality and intensity of professional development currently received by many teachers nationwide. One researcher summarized these issues by stating that professional development training for teachers is often too short, provides no classroom follow up, and models more "telling than guiding" practices. Given the decentralized nature of the U.S. education system, the support and opportunity for professional development services for teachers varies among states and school districts, and there are notable examples of states that have focused resources on various aspects of professional development. Nevertheless, shortcomings in teachers' professional development experiences overall are especially evident when compared to professional development requirements for teachers in countries whose students perform well on international tests, such as the Trends in International Mathematics and Science Study and the Program for International Student Assessment. For example, one study showed that fewer than 10 percent of U.S. math teachers in school year 2003-04 experienced more than 24 hours of professional development in mathematics content or pedagogy during the year; conversely, teachers in Sweden, Singapore, and the Netherlands are required to complete 100 hours of professional development per year.[29]

AGENCY COMMENTS AND OUR EVALUATION

We provided a copy of our draft report to the Secretary of Education for review and comment. Education's written comments, which are contained in appendix V, expressed support for the important questions that the report addresses and noted that the American Recovery and Reinvestment Act of 2009 included $250 million to improve assessment and accountability systems. The department specifically stated that the money is for statewide data systems to provide information on individual student outcomes that could help enable schools to strengthen instructional practices and improve student achievement. However, the department raised several issues about the report's approach. Specifically, the department commented that we (1) did not provide the specific research citations throughout the report for each of our findings or clearly explain how we selected our studies; (2) mixed the opinions of education experts with our findings gleaned from the review of the literature; (3) did not present data on the extent to which test formats had changed or on the relationship between test format and teaching practices when discussing our assessment findings; and (4) did not provide complete information from an Education survey regarding increases and decreases in instructional time.

As stated in the beginning of our report, the list of studies we reviewed and used for our findings are contained in appendix IV. We provide a description in appendix I of our criteria, the types of databases searched, the types of studies examined (e.g., experimental and nonexperimental) and the process by which we evaluated them. We relied heavily on two literature syntheses conducted by the Department of Education— *Standards in Classroom Practice: Research Synthesis* and *The Influence of Standards on K-12 Teaching and Student Learning: A Research Synthesis*, which are included in the list. These two syntheses covered, in a more comprehensive way than many of the other studies that we reviewed, the breadth of the topics that we were interested in and included numerous research studies in their reviews. Many of the findings in this report about the research are taken from the conclusions reached in these syntheses. However, to make this fact clearer and more prominent, we added this explanation to our abbreviated scope and methodology section on page 5 of the report.

Regarding the use of expert opinion, we determined that obtaining the views of experts about the research we were reviewing would be critical to our understanding its broader implications. This was particularly important given the breadth and scope of our objectives. The experts we interviewed, whose names and affiliations are listed in appendix III, are prominent researchers who conduct, review, and reflect on the current research in the field, and whose work is included in some of the studies we reviewed, including the two literature syntheses written by the Department of Education and used by us in this study. We did not consider their opinions "conjecture" but grounded in and informed by their many years of respected work on the topic. We have been clear in the report as to when we are citing expert opinion, the research studies, or both.

Regarding the report section discussing the research on assessments, it was our intent to highlight that, according to the research, assessments have both positive and negative influences on classroom teaching practices, not to conclude that NCLBA was the cause of either. Our findings in this section of the report are, in large part, based on conclusions from the department's syntheses mentioned earlier. For example, *The Influence of Standards on K-12 Teaching and Student Learning: A Research Synthesis* states "... tests matter—the content covered, the format used, and the application of their results—all influence teacher behavior." Furthermore, we previously reported that states most often have chosen multiple choice assessments over other types because they can be scored inexpensively and their scores can be released prior to the next school year as required by NCLBA.[30] That report also notes that state officials and alignment experts said that multiple choice assessments have limited the content of what can be tested, stating that highly complex content is "difficult if not impossible to include with multiple choice items." However, we have revised this paragraph to clarify our point and provide additional information.

Concerning the topic of narrowing the curriculum, we agree with the Department of Education that this report should include a fuller description of the data results from the cited Education survey in order to help the reader put the data in an appropriate context. Hence, we have added information to that section of the report. However, one limitation of the survey data we cite is that it covers changes in instructional time for a short time period—from school year 2004-05 to 2006-07. In the its technical comments, the Department refers to its recent report, *Title I Implementation: Update on Recent Evaluation Findings* for a fuller discussion of this issue. The Title I report, while noting that most elementary teachers reported no change from 2004–05 to 2006–07 in the amount of instructional time that they spent on various subjects, also provides data over a longer, albeit earlier period time period, from 1987–88 to 2003–04, from the National Center on Education Statistics Schools and Staffing Survey. In analyzing this data, the report states that elementary teachers had increased instructional time on reading and mathematics and decreased the amount of time spent on science and social studies during this period. We have added this information as well. Taken together, we believe these data further reinforce our point that assessments under current accountability systems can have, in addition to positive influences on teaching, some negative ones as well, such as the curriculum changes noted in the report, even if the extent of these changes is not fully known.

Education also provided technical comments that we incorporated as appropriate.

Cornelia M. Ashby
Director, Education, Workforce, and
Income Security Issues

List of Congressional Committees

The Honorable Tom Harkin
Chairman
The Honorable Thad Cochran
Ranking Member
Subcommittee on Labor, Health and Human Services, Education
and Related Agencies
Committee on Appropriations
United States Senate

The Honorable Dave Obey
Chairman
The Honorable Todd Tiahrt
Ranking Member
Subcommittee on Labor, Health and Human Services, Education
and Related Agencies
Committee on Appropriations
House of Representatives

APPENDIX I. SCOPE AND METHODOLOGY

To address the objectives of this study, we used a variety of methods. To determine the types of instructional practices schools and teachers are using to help students achieve state academic standards and whether those practices differ by school characteristics, we used two recent surveys of principals and teachers. The first survey, a nationally- representative survey from the Department of Education's (Education) National Longitudinal Study of No Child Left Behind (NLS-NCLB) conducted by the RAND Corporation (RAND), asked principals the extent to which their schools were focusing on certain strategies in their voluntary school improvement efforts. Education's *State and Local Implementation of the No Child Left Behind Act Volume III— Accountability Under NCLB: Interim Report* included information about the strategies emphasized by principals as a whole, and we obtained from Education the NLS-NCLB database to determine the extent to which principals' responses differed by school characteristic variables. We conducted this analysis on school year 2006-2007 data by controlling for four school characteristic variables: (1) the percentage of a school's students receiving free or reduced price lunch (poverty); (2) the percentage of students who are a racial minority (minority); (3) whether the school is in an urban, urban fringe (suburban), or rural area (school location); and (4) the school's adequate yearly performance (AYP) status.

We analyzed data from a second RAND survey, which was a three-state survey sponsored by the National Science Foundation that asked math teachers in California, Georgia, and Pennsylvania how their classroom teaching strategies differed due to a state math test.[31] RAND selected these states to represent a range of approaches to standards-based accountability and to provide some geographic and demographic diversity; the survey data is representative only for those three states individually. RAND's report on the three-state survey data included information about how teachers within each of the three states had changed their teaching practices due to a state accountability test.[32] RAND provided us with descriptive data tables based on its school year 2005-2006 survey data; we analyzed the data to measure associations between the strategies used and the school characteristic variables.[33] We requested tables that showed this information for teachers in all schools, and separately for teachers in different categories of schools (elementary and middle schools) and by the school characteristics of poverty, minority, school location and AYP status. We obtained from RAND standard error information associated with the estimates from the different types of schools and thus were able to test the statistical significance of differences in likelihood between what teachers from different types of schools reported.

As part of our analyses for both surveys, we reviewed documentation and performed electronic testing of the data obtained through the surveys. We also conducted several interviews with several researchers responsible for the data collection and analyses and obtained information about the measures they took to ensure data reliability. On the basis of our efforts to determine the reliability of the data, we determined the data from each of these surveys were sufficiently reliable for the purposes of our study.

We reviewed existing literature to determine what researchers have found regarding the effect of standards-based accountability systems on instructional practices, and practices that work in raising student achievement. To identify existing studies, we conducted searches of various databases, such as the Education Resources Information Center, Proquest, Dialog EDUCAT, and Education Abstracts. We also asked all of the education researchers that we interviewed to recommend additional studies. From these sources, we identified 251 studies that were relevant to our study objectives about the effect of standards-based accountability systems on instructional practices and instructional practices there are effective in raising student achievement. We selected them according to the following criteria: covered the years 2001 through 2008 and were either experimental or quasi-experimental studies, literature syntheses, or studied multiple sites.[34] We selected the studies for our review based on their methodological strength, given the limitations of the methods used, and not necessarily on whether the results could be generalized. We performed our searches from August 2008 to January 2009.

152 United States Government Accountability Office

To assess the methodological quality of the selected studies, we developed a data collection instrument to obtain information systematically about each study being evaluated and about the features of the evaluation methodology. We based our data collection and assessments on generally accepted social science standards. We examined factors related to the use of comparison and control groups; the appropriateness of sampling and data collection methods; and for syntheses, the process and criteria used to identify studies. A senior social scientist with training and experience in evaluation research and methodology read and coded the methodological discussion for each evaluation. A second senior social scientist reviewed each completed data collection instrument and the relevant documentation to verify the accuracy of every coded item. This review identified 20 selected studies that met GAO's criteria for methodological quality.

We supplemented our synthesis by interviewing prominent education researchers identified in frequently cited articles and through discussions with knowledgeable individuals. We also conducted interviews with officials at the U.S. Department of Education, including the Center on Innovation and Improvement, and the Institute on Education Sciences' National Center for Education Evaluation and Regional Assistance, as well as other educational organizations. We also reviewed relevant federal laws and regulations.

APPENDIX II. ANALYSES OF THE RELATIONSHIP BETWEEN SCHOOL CHARACTERISTICS AND PRINCIPALS' FOCUS ON SCHOOL IMPROVEMENT STRATEGIES

In order to analyze the National Longitudinal Study of No Child Left Behind (NLS-NCLB) principal survey conducted by the RAND Corporation, we analyzed strategies on which principals most often focused, taking into account the percentage of a school's students receiving free or reduced price lunch (poverty), the percentage of students who are a racial minority (minority), whether the school is in an urban, suburban, or rural area (school location), and the school's adequate yearly performance (AYP) status (see table 1).[35] Our analyses used "odds ratios," generally defined as the ratio of the odds of an event occurring in one group compared to the odds of it occurring in another group, to express differences in the likelihoods of schools with different characteristics using these strategies. We used odds ratios rather than percentages because they are more appropriate for statistical modeling and multivariate analysis. Odds ratios indicate how much higher (when they are greater than 1.0) or lower (when they are less than 1.0) the odds were that principals would respond that a given strategy was a major or moderate focus. We included a reference category for the school characteristics (low minority, low poverty, and central city) in the top row of table 1, and put comparison groups beneath those reference categories, as indicated by the column heading in the second row (high-minority, high- poverty, or rural schools). As an example, the third cell in the "high- minority schools" column indicates that principals in high-minority schools were 2.65 times more likely to make "implementing new instructional approaches or curricula in reading/language arts/English" a focus of their school improvement efforts. In another example, the odds that principals would "restructure the school day to teach core content areas in greater depth (e.g., establishing a literacy block)" were 2.8 times higher for high-poverty schools than low poverty schools, as seen in the sixth cell under "high-poverty schools." Those cells with an asterisk indicate statistically significant results; that is, we have a high degree of confidence that the differences we see are not just due to chance but show an actual difference in the survey responses. See appendix I for further explanation of our methodology.

Table 1. Odds Ratios Indicating the Difference in Likelihood of Principals to Make School Improvement Strategies a Moderate or Major Focus after Controlling for Different Factors

School demographic School Improvement Strategy	(Compared to low-minority schools)		(Compared to low-poverty schools)		(Compared to central city schools)	
	High-minority schools	Middle minority schools	High-poverty schools	Middle poverty schools	Rural schools	Suburban/ fringe schools
Using student achievement data to inform instruction and school improvement	1.24	3.01*	2.51	1.34	0.46	0.98
Aligning curriculum and instruction with standards and/or assessments	1.24	2.09*	1.81	0.92	0.58	0.79
Implementing new instructional approaches or curricula in reading/language arts/English	2.65*	1.66	0.99	1.24	0.80	0.97
Implementing new instructional approaches or curricula in mathematics	1.78	1.79*	1.68	1.39	0.56*	0.85
Providing additional instruction to low-achieving students	2.39*	3.46*	1.00	0.48*	0.31*	0.83
Restructuring the school day to teach core content areas in greater depth (e.g., establishing a literacy block)	1.85*	1.29	2.84*	1.66*	0.55*	1.18
Increasing instructional time for all students (e.g., by lengthening the school day or year, shortening recess)	1.86*	1.22	2.48*	1.77*	0.53	0.99
Providing extended-time instructional programs (e.g., before-school, after-school or weekend instructional programs)	3.54*	2.11*	2.51*	2.49*	0.46*	1.12
Implementing strategies for increasing parents' involvement in their children's education	1.86*	2.19*	2.33*	1.33	0.76	0.98
Increasing the intensity, focus, and effectiveness of professional development	1.61	1.39	2.38*	1.3	0.54*	1.00

* = Statistically significant at the 95% confidence level.
Source: GAO analysis of NLS-NCLB data.

APPENDIX III. LIST OF EDUCATION RESEARCHERS

Name	Affiliation
Dr. David K. Cohen	John Dewey Collegiate Professor of Education Walter H. Annenberg Professor of Education Policy University of Michigan
Dr. Linda Darling-Hammond	Charles Ducommon Professor of Education Stanford University
Dr. Richard Elmore	Gregory R. Anrig Professor of Educational Leadership Director, Consortium for Policy Research in Education Harvard University
Dr. David Figlio	Institute for Policy Research Northwestern University National Bureau of Economic Research
Dr. William A. Firestone	Director, Center for Educational Policy Analysis; Principal Investigator, New Jersey Math Science Partnership; Professor Rutgers University
Dr. Susan Fuhrman	President, Teachers College Columbia University
Dr. Margaret Goertz	Professor Co-Director, Consortium for Policy Research in Education University of Pennsylvania
Dr. Laura Hamilton	Senior Behavioral/Social Scientist RAND
Dr. Jane Hannaway	Director of Education Policy Urban Institute
Dr. Richard Murnane	Juliana W. and William Foss Thompson Professor of Education and Society Harvard University
Dr. William Sanders	Senior Research Fellow University of North Carolina
Dr. Brian Stecher	Senior Social Scientist RAND

Source: GAO.

APPENDIX IV. STUDIES MEETING GAO'S CRITERIA FOR METHODOLOGICAL QUALITY

Title	Author	Source	Method
Accountability and Teaching Practices: School Level Actions and Teacher Responses	Laura. S Hamilton; Brian M Stecher; Jennifer Linn Russell; Julie A. Marsh; Jeremy Miles	"Strong States, Weak Schools: The Benefits and Dilemmas of Centralized Accountability" *Research in Sociology of Education.* vol. 16, 2008	Case studies of three states; representative surveys for these states
Catching Up Impact of the Talent Development Ninth Grade Instructional Interventions in Reading and Mathematics in High-Poverty High Schools	Robert Belfanz; Nettie Legters; Will Jordan	Report 69 April 2004 The Johns Hopkins University Center for Research on the Education of Students Placed at Risk	Quasi-experimental design with matched groups; multiple regressions used with data. Limitations: Two school districts (around Baltimore); small percentage of all those enrolled in the 9th grade
Differentiated Curriculum Enhancement in Inclusive Middle School Science: Effects on Classroom and High-Stakes Tests	Margo A. Mastropieri; Thomas E. Scruggs; Jennifer J. Norland; Sheri Berkeley; Kimberly McDuffie; Elizabeth Halloran Tornquist; Nicole Connors	*The Journal of Special Education* vol. 40, no. 3. 2006, 130-137	Quasi-experimental design; 13 classes matched by teacher, and randomly assigned to treatment or control group. Limitations: some external validity issues
Effective Programs in Elementary Mathematics: A Best-Evidence Synthesis	Robert E. Slavin; Cynthia Lake	Review of Educational Research. Washington: September 2008. vol. 78, issue 3. 427	Literature review using a best-evidence synthesis (related to a meta-analysis)
Feeling the Florida Heat? How Low-Performing Schools Respond to Voucher and Accountability Pressure	Cecilia Elena Rouse; Jane Hannaway; Dan Goldhaber; David Figlio	Calder/Urban Institute National Center for Analysis of Longitudinal Data in Education Research Working Paper November 2007	Administrative data used to develop comparison groups of schools; regression discontinuity design; results apply to Florida schools only
Formulating Secondary-Level Reading Interventions	Debra M. Kamps; Charles R. Greenwood	Journal of Learning Disabilities, vol. 38, no. 6. November/December 200, 500-509	Quasi-experimental; random assignment of schools, but not students; Limitations: cannot be generalized beyond the 8 schools involved in the study
Helping At-Risk Students Meet Standards A Synthesis of Evidence-Based Classroom Practices	Zoe Barley; Patricia A. Lauer; Sheila A. Arens; Helen S. Apthorp; Kelly S. Englert; David Snow; Motoko Akiba	Regional Education Laboratory Office of Educational Research and Improvement U.S. Department of Education Mid-continent Research for Education and Learning October 2002 corrected 12/02	Literature review; in some cases a meta-analysis was conducted; effect sizes were computed for meta-analysis when available; some studies were outside the time frames of our search criteria

(Continued)

Title	Author	Source	Method
High Poverty Schools and the Distribution of Teachers and Principals	Charles Clotfelter; Helen F. Ladd; Jacob Vigdor; Justin Wheeler	Sanford Working Paper Series SAN06-08 December 2006	Time series analysis using administrative data for all schools in North Carolina. Limitation: applies to North Carolina only
High Stakes Testing and Curricular Control: A Qualitative Metasynthesis	Wayne Au	Educational Researcher; vol. 36, no. 5, June/Jul 2007; 258-267	Meta-synthesis of qualitative studies Limitations: Results for Chicago only; some coding issues
Instructional Policy and Classroom Performance: The Mathematics Reform in CA	David K. Cohen; Heather C. Hill	Teachers College Record, vol. 102, no. 2. February 2000, 294-343	Regression analysis of data from teacher surveys and administrative data. Limitations: results based on a 1994 survey; response rate was 61 percent
Instructional Time in Elementary Schools A Closer Look at Changes for Specific Subjects	Center on Education Policy	From the Capital to the Classroom: Year of the No Child Left Behind Act Center on Education Policy February 2008	Survey of school districts and states, qualitative interviews Limitation: high non-response rate from school districts in large urban areas
Standards in Classroom Practice: Research Synthesis	Helen S. Apthorp; Ceri B. Dean; Judy E. Florian; Patricia A. Lauder; Robert Reichardt; Nancy M. Sanders; Ravay Snow-Renner	Regional Education Laboratory Office of Educational Research and Improvement U.S. Department of Education Mid-continent Research for Education and Learning October 31, 2001	Literature review; no meta-analysis conducted; some studies outside our time frame
Standards-Based Reform in Practice: Evidence on State Policy and Classroom Instruction from the NAEP State Assessments	Christopher B. Swanson; David Lee Stevenson	*Educational Evaluation and Policy Analysis*, vol. 24, no. 1. Spring 2002, 1-27	Hierarchical linear modeling on survey data from the National Assessment of Educational Progress (NAEP); limitation is that only30 of the original 40 states are included, with some of the largest of the states missing

Title	Author	Source	Method
Studying Large-Scale Reforms of Instructional Practice: An Example from Mathematics and Science	Laura S. Hamilton; Daniel F. McCaffrey; Brian Stecher; Stephen P. Klein; Abby Robyn; Delia Bugliari	*Educational Evaluation and Policy Analysis*, vol. 25, no. 1. Spring 2003, 1-29	Regression analysis; Limited to 11 sites; results small and positive, but not statistically significant
Supporting Literacy Across the Sunshine State: A Study of Florida Middle School Reading Coaches	Julie A. Marsh; Jennifer Sloan McCombs; J.R. Lockwood; Francisco Martorell; Daniel Gershwin; Scott Naftel; Vi-Nhuan Le; Molly Shea; Heather Barney; Al Crego	RAND Corporation 2008	Case study of Florida; longitudinal data analysis of data from 1997-1998 to 2006-2007 based on a survey of teachers, principals, and students in 8 middle schools
Teaching Methods for Secondary Algebra: A Meta-Analysis of Findings	Matthew Haas	*National Association of Secondary School Principals. NASSP Bulletin*, March 2005, 89, 642; Research Library 24	Meta-analysis of 35 studies
Test Preparation in New Jersey: inquiry-oriented and didactic responses	William A. Firestone; Lora Monfils; Roberta Y. Schorr	*Assessment in Education: Principles, Policy & Practice*, vol. 11, no.1. March 2004, 67-88	Survey, exploratory factor analysis, and hierarchical linear modeling time series; results limited to New Jersey
The Influence of Standards on K-12 Teaching and Student Learning: A Research Synthesis	Patricia A. Lauer; David Snow; Mya Martin-Glenn; Rebecca J. Van Buhler; Kristen Stoutemyer; Ravay Snow-Renner	Regional Education Laboratory, August 19, 2005	Literature review; no meta-analysis; both quantitative and qualitative studies used; comprehensive selection process
The New Accountability, Student Failure, and Teachers' Work in Urban High Schools	Dorothea Anagnostopoulous	*Educational Policy*, vol. 17, no. 3. July 2003, 291-316	Case study of two high schools; findings are suggestive
Value-Added Assessment in Practice: Lessons from Pennsylvania Value-Added Assessment System Pilot Project	Daniel F. McCaffrey; Laura S. Hamilton	RAND Corporation 2007	Quasi-experimental design for 93 non-random study districts in Pennsylvania; not generalizable to the nation or the state

Source: GAO analysis.

APPENDIX V. COMMENTS FROM THE DEPARTMENT OF EDUCATION

UNITED STATES DEPARTMENT OF EDUCATION

OFFICE OF PLANNING, EVALUATION AND POLICY DEVELOPMENT

October 2, 2009

Ms. Cornelia M. Ashby
Director
Education, Workforce, and
  Income Security Issues
U.S. Government Accountability Office
Washington, DC 20548

Dear Ms. Ashby:

Thank you for the opportunity to comment on the draft GAO report, *Student Achievement: Schools Use Multiple Strategies to Help Students Meet Academic Standards, Especially Schools with Higher Proportions of Low Income and Minority Students*.

GAO's report asks important questions about the effects of standards-based accountability on instructional practices and the effectiveness of specific instructional practices in improving student achievement, and seeks to answer these questions through a literature review and interviews with prominent education researchers. The report also examines data on the types of instructional practices that schools and teachers are using to help students achieve to state academic standards, in part based on surveys conducted for the Department's National Longitudinal Study of No Child Left Behind. While the report addresses important policy questions, there are some issues pertaining to the study's approach that we recommend be taken into consideration.

First, the draft report does not clearly explain how GAO selected the 20 studies included in its literature review or the methods used in the studies that were selected. Moreover, in discussing specific findings from the literature review, the report frequently does not indicate which studies are being relied on as evidence for each finding.

Second, the report mixes findings that may be based on rigorous research with findings that appear to be based on conjecture and on what "some researchers believe," and does not always present a complete and balanced summary of the relevant research. For example, the report states that "difficulties in aligning practice with standards were attributed, in part, to current accountability requirements," but appears to rely only on expert opinion for this causal conclusion. Similarly, the report states that "a few researchers as well as some of the literature we reviewed report some unintended negative consequences on instruction as a result of assessment practices," including the reported consequences of "multiple choice tests that do not encourage more challenging teacher practices" and "instructional practices that narrow the curriculum." These statements may accurately report the opinions of the individuals interviewed, but the report provides weak empirical evidence to support these conclusions and does not include all of the available evidence.

With respect to the assertion that the assessment provisions in the Elementary and Secondary Education Act, as amended by the No Child Left Behind Act (NCLB), have resulted in multiple choice tests that do not encourage more challenging teaching practices, the report does not present any data on the extent to which test formats have changed or on the relationship between test format and teaching practices. Instead the report notes that some researchers believe that states are increasingly using multiple-choice testing formats, and hypothesizes that teachers "may be influenced" to change their teaching approaches because of the tests. Any conclusions about what the "research shows" should be supported by specific references to rigorous research that used appropriate methods for measuring impacts.

In the discussion of whether there has been narrowing of the curriculum, the report notes that a Department survey found that 18 to 22 percent of elementary teachers reported increasing instructional time for mathematics and reading, respectively, and concludes that this is occurring "at the expense of other non-tested subjects." However, the report does not mention the finding from the same survey that most elementary teachers reported no change from 2004-05 to 2006-07 in the amount of instructional time that they spent on other subjects. The report also notes that some research has raised concern that teachers may be restricting the breadth of content covered within a particular subject, but does not acknowledge the converse concern, based on research conducted for the Third International Math and Science Study (TIMSS), that curricula in American schools may be "a mile wide and an inch deep" and thus some refocusing of curricula may be beneficial.

The Department recognizes that improvements in assessment and accountability systems could help enable schools to strengthen instructional practices and improve student achievement. As one step toward that goal, the American Recovery and Reinvestment Act included $250 million for Statewide Data Systems to help ensure that states and school districts have the robust data systems they need to provide information on individual student outcomes that educators and policymakers can use to drive educational improvement. More research is needed to better understand what instructional practices and policy changes could be most effective in closing achievement gaps and improving educational outcomes.

Attached are technical comments provided by Department staff on the text of the report. If you have any questions, we would be glad to discuss our comments with your research team.

Sincerely,

Alan Ginsburg
Director
Policy and Program Studies Service

Enclosure

End Notes

[1] Pub. L. No. 107-110.

[2] We use the phrase "instructional practices" to include tools for improving classroom teaching practices, such as providing additional professional development.

[3] State and Local Implementation of the No Child Left Behind Act Volume III— Accountability under NCLB: Interim Report. A report from the National Longitudinal Study of No Child Left Behind (NLS-NCLB) and the

160   United States Government Accountability Office

Study of State Implementation of Accountability and Teacher Quality under No Child Left Behind (SSI-NCLB) Kerstin Carlson Le Floch, AIR, Felipe Martinez, RAND, Jennifer O'Day, AIR, Brian Stecher, RAND, James Taylor, AIR, Andrea Cook, AIR. Prepared for: U.S. Department of Education Office of Planning, Evaluation and Policy Development Policy and Program Studies Service (2007).

[4] Laura S. Hamilton, Brian M. Stecher, Julie A. Marsh, Jennifer Sloan McCombs, Abby Robyn, Jennifer Lin Russell, Scott Naftel, and Heather Barney. "Standards-Based Accountability under No Child Left Behind: Experiences of Teachers and Administrators in Three States." Sponsored by the National Science Foundation. RAND 2007. The survey also asked about reported changes in strategies for science instruction as a result of the state science test, but we are only reporting on math instruction.

[5] Of the 20 studies we used that met our criteria for methodological quality, we relied heavily on two literature syntheses conducted by the Department of Education because of the large number of studies they included and the breadth of the topics they covered. For a list of these and the other studies meeting our criteria for methodological quality, see appendix IV. Additionally, a few other studies are cited in footnotes throughout the report but not included in the list of studies that we formally reviewed. Those cited in the footnotes were used because they provided more details or supplementary information about points that the experts made during our interviews.

[6] For a list of knowledgeable individuals with whom we spoke, see appendix III.

[7] Pub. L. No. 89-10.

[8] Pub. L. No. 103-382.

[9] Assessments in science, which were first required under NCLBA in school year 2007-2008, are required at least once in grades 3 to 5, grades 6 to 9, and grades 10 to 12. High school students are required only to be assessed once in math and reading or language arts. In addition to annual assessments, high schools must include students' graduation rate, and elementary and middle schools must include one other academic indicator determined by the state to assess whether they made AYP.

[10] GAO, *No Child Left Behind Act: Improvements Needed in Education's Process for Tracking States' Implementation of Key Provisions*, GAO-04-734 (Washington, D.C.: Sept. 30, 2004).

[11] For more information on teacher quality, see GAO, *Teacher Quality: Sustained Coordination among Key Federal Education Programs Could Enhance State Efforts to Improve Teacher Quality*, GAO-09-593 (Washington, D.C.: July 2009).

[12] For purposes of this report, we use the term "school improvement" to refer to the voluntary strategies used by school administrators and teachers to address various challenges within a school. By way of contrast, under NCLBA, schools that are identified for "school improvement" are those that have failed to make AYP for 2 or more consecutive years. These schools must implement certain activities identified in NCLBA that are meant to improve student academic achievement.

[13] Education classified schools as having "high—75 percent or more," "moderate—35 to less than 75," or "low—35 percent or less" percentages of low-income students using the number of students at the school that were eligible for the free and reduced-price lunch program. Schools were classified as having "high—75 percent or more," "moderate—25 to less than 75," or "low—25 percent or less" percentages of minority students, based on the school population that principals reported to be American Indian/Alaskan Native, Asian, Black or African-American, Hispanic or Latino, and Native Hawaiian or other Pacific Islander. Schools also were classified as central city (urban), urban fringe/large town (suburban), or small/fringe town (rural).

[14] See appendix II for additional information about how principals' responses differed across school characteristics.

[15] Core content areas include those subjects for which testing is required under NCLBA— specifically, reading, math, and science.

[16] For the last three of these five strategies and one other–providing additional instruction to low-achieving students—there were also significant differences between moderate-poverty and low-poverty schools.

[17] See appendix II for a table that indicates which six strategies differed by school minority level.

[18] Urban fringe or large town schools were no different from the central city schools with respect to making these strategies a major or moderate focus. In the 2003-2004 school year, about 30 percent of all U.S. elementary and secondary public schools were located in rural areas and approximately 20 percent of public school students were enrolled in rural schools. See S. Provasnik, A. KewalRamani, M. M. Coleman, L. Gilbertson, W. Herring, and Q. Xie, *Status of Education in Rural America* (NCES 2007-040). National Center for Education Statistics, Institute of Education Sciences, U.S. Department of Education (Washington, D.C.: 2007). See appendix II for a table that indicates which five strategies differed by school geographic type.

[19] When we compared moderate-poverty schools to high-poverty and low-poverty schools, we saw fewer statistically significant differences than in our high-poverty and low-poverty school comparison.

[20] For the three state data, we conducted a simple analysis that did not control for multiple factors, since we had access only to RAND's bi-variate analyses of the data rather than the data itself. Because of this, we could not perform a multivariate analysis, which would allow us to control for other factors.

[21] The National Governors' Association and the Council of Chief State School Officers are coordinating a committee of experts to develop common academic standards for math and language arts skills. As of June 2009, 46 states had signed onto this effort to adopt the common standards once they were completed.

[22] W. Firestone, R. Schorr, and L. Monfils, editors. *Ambiguity of Teaching to the Test: Standards, Assessments, and Educational Reform*, 160-161 (2004).

[23] Helen S. Apthorp, et al., "Standards in Classroom Practice Research Synthesis," Mid- Continent Research for Education and Learning (October 2001).

[24] NCLBA added to the assessment requirements included in IASA. For example, NCLBA requires states to implement annual assessments for all students in every grade for grades 3-8 in reading and math; IASA required assessments at least once in each of three grade spans: 3-5, 6-9, and 10-12. Additionally, unlike IASA, NCLBA sets a uniform timeline for when all students must meet state proficiency targets.

[25] P. A. Lauer, D. Snow, M. Martin-Glenn, R.J.Van Buhler, K. Stoutemyer, R. Snow-Renner, *The Influence of Standards on K-12 Teaching and Student Learning: A Research Synthesis*, Regional Education Laboratory, August 19, 2005, p. 91.

[26] GAO, *No Child Left Behind Act: Enhancements in the Department of Education's Review Process Could Improve State Academic Assessments*, GAO-09-911, (Washington, D.C.: September 2009).

[27] For example, according to data from Education's national survey, about 18 percent of elementary school teachers reported that instruction time for math increased from school years 2004-2005 to 2006-2007, and about 22 percent of elementary school teachers reported that instruction time for reading/language arts increased over the same period. However, approximately three-quarters of teachers reported no change in instructional time in these two subjects. GAO, *Access to Arts Education: Inclusion of Additional Questions in Education's Planned Research Would Help Explain Why Instruction Time Has Decreased for Some Students*, GAO-09-286 (Washington, D.C.: February 2009). In addition, a report by the Department of Education states that from 1987-1988 to 2003-2004, teacher survey results from the Schools and Staffing Survey conducted by the National Center for Education Statistics indicate that elementary teachers had increased instructional time on reading and mathematics and decreased the amount of time spent on science and social studies during this period. See U.S. Department of Education, Office of Planning, Evaluation, and Policy Development, Policy and Program Studies Service, *Title I Implementation—Update on Recent Evaluation Findings* (Washington, D.C.: 2009).

[28] The final report of the National Mathematics Advisory Panel takes a slightly different position regarding this practice stating that "All-encompassing recommendations that instruction should be entirely 'student centered' or 'teacher directed' are not supported by research . . . High-quality research does not support the exclusive use of either approach." National Mathematics Advisory Panel. *Foundations for Success: The Final Report of the National Mathematics Advisory Panel*, U.S. Department of Education (Washington, D.C.: 2008).

[29] L. Darling-Hammond, R. Wei, A. Andree, N. Richardson, and S. Orphanos, *Professional Learning in the Learning Profession: A Status Report on Teacher Development in the United States and Abroad, Technical Report* (National Staff Development Council and The School Redesign Network at Stanford University: February 2009) 18 and 22.

[30] GAO, *No Child Left Behind Act: Enhancements in the Department of Education's Review Process Could Improve State Academic Assessments*, GAO-09-911 (Washington, D.C.: September 2009).

[31] Several education experts we spoke to said the list of practices was fairly complete, but one expert noted that professional development is also an important instructional practice.

[32] Laura S. Hamilton, Brian M. Stecher, Julie A. Marsh, Jennifer Sloan McCombs, Abby Robyn, Jennifer Lin Russell, Scott Naftel, and Heather Barney, "Standards-Based Accountability under No Child Left Behind: Experiences of Teachers and Administrators in Three States" (Sponsored by the National Science Foundation. RAND 2007).

[33] Scott Naftel, Laura S. Hamilton, and Brian M. Stecher, "Working Paper Supplemental Analyses of ISBA Survey Responses" (WR-628-EDU. RAND. November 2008).

[34] Some research, including the syntheses that we reviewed, included some studies outside these date parameters. Additionally, the syntheses used to support some of the findings were not meta-analyses but literature reviews, although both qualitative and quantitative studies were included in the syntheses.

[35] Table 1 does not include AYP status, because we found that the demographic characteristics of poverty and minority explained the patterns of principals' responses more fully than AYP status.

In: Teacher Quality and Student Achievement
Editor: Katherine E. Westley

ISBN: 978-1-61728-274-4
© 2010 Nova Science Publishers, Inc.

Chapter 6

STATEMENT OF CHAIRMAN RUBEN HINOJOSA, CHAIRMAN OF THE HOUSE SUBCOMMITTEE ON HIGHER EDUCATION, LIFELONG LEARNING AND COMPETITIVENESS – "PREPARING TEACHERS FOR THE CLASSROOM: THE ROLE OF THE HIGHER EDUCATION ACT AND NO CHILD LEFT BEHIND"[*]

Rubén Hinojosa

WASHINGTON, D.C. – *Below are the prepared remarks of U.S. Rep. Rubén Hinojosa (D-TX), chairman of the House Subcommittee On Higher Education, Lifelong Learning, and Competitiveness, for a subcommittee hearing on "Preparing Teachers for the Classroom: The Role of the Higher Education Act and No Child Left Behind."*

Good Morning. Welcome to the Subcommittee on Higher Education. Lifelong Learning and Competitiveness hearing on "Preparing Teachers for the Classroom: The Role of the Higher Education Act and No Child Left Behind."

Reaching the goals of the No Child Let Behind Act will hinge on the quality of teaching in our classrooms. Unfortunately, too often, the number of poor and minority students in a school is also an indicator of the number of teachers who are not certified or who are teaching outside of their field of expertise in a school. The students who need the most experienced and skilled teachers are typically in schools that have the least experienced teachers. Our goal should be to change that.

Not only do we need to ensure that teachers are experts in the subjects that they are teaching. We also need to ensure that they are highly qualified to teach the students they have in their classrooms. The National Center for Education Statistics reported in its 1999-2000 Schools and Staffing Survey that 41.2 percent of teachers in the country had limited English

---

[*] This is an edited, reformatted and augmented version of a U. S. House of Representatives publication dated May 2007.

proficient students in their classroom. Yet, only 12.5 percent of teachers had more than 8 hours of training in how to teach these students. Clearly, there is room for improvement.

Our federal programs in the Higher Education Act and the No Child Left Behind Act are aimed toward improving the quality of teaching through better preparation and professional development. They are also aimed at improving the distribution of these teachers so that concentrations of poverty or minority populations are no longer coupled with a concentration of under-prepared teachers They also recognize that we need to do a better job of making sure that the teaching profession reflects the diversity of America's schools.

Title II of the Higher Education Act supports teacher quality by focusing on improving the quality of teacher preparation programs, rigor of teacher certification requirements and recruiting teachers to serve in high need districts and schools. It is funded at less than $60 million. Title II of the No Child Left Behind Act is a formula grant to states to improve teacher quality and reduce class size. It is funded at $2.9 billion - -significant federal investment. While similar in goals, it is not clear how complementary these two programs are.

This Congress, we will reauthorize both the Higher Education Act and the No Child Left Behind Act. This presents a unique opportunity to improve these laws so that they operate in a more integrated fashion and move us closer to our goal of a highly qualified teacher in every classroom.

I would like to thank our excellent panel of witnesses for joining us today. I am looking forward to your testimony on how the programs are currently working and on what steps we can take to better coordinate them.

I would like to yield to my good friend and ranking Member, Mr. Ric Keller of Florida, for his opening statement.

In: Teacher Quality and Student Achievement
Editor: Katherine E. Westley

ISBN: 978-1-61728-274-4
© 2010 Nova Science Publishers, Inc.

Chapter 7

TEACHER QUALITY: APPROACHES, IMPLEMENTATION, AND EVALUATION OF KEY FEDERAL EFFORTS[*]

George A. Scott

WHY GAO DID THIS STUDY

Teachers are the single largest resource in our nation's elementary and secondary education system. However, according to recent research, many teachers lack competency in the subjects they teach. In addition, research shows that most teacher training programs leave new teachers feeling unprepared for the classroom.

While the hiring and training of teachers is primarily the responsibility of state and local governments and institutions of higher education, the federal investment in enhancing teacher quality is substantial and growing. In 1998, the Congress amended the Higher Education Act (HEA) to enhance the quality of teaching in the classroom and in 2001 the Congress passed the No Child Left Behind Act (NCLBA), which established federal requirements that all teachers of core academic subjects be highly qualified.

This testimony focuses on (1) approaches used in teacher quality programs under HEA and NCLBA, (2) the allowable activities under these acts and how recipients are using the funds, and (3) how Education supports and evaluates these activities.

WHAT GAO FOUND

While the overall goal of Title II in both HEA and NCLBA is to improve teacher quality, some of their specific approaches differ. For example, a major focus of HEA provisions is on the training of prospective teachers while NCLBA provisions focus more on improving

---

[*] This is an edited, reformatted and augmented version of a U. S. Government Accountability Office publication dated May 2007.

teacher quality in the classroom and hiring highly qualified teachers. Both laws use reporting mechanisms to increase accountability; however, HEA focuses more on institutions of higher education while NCLBA focuses on schools and districts. In addition, HEA and NCLBA grants are funded differently, with HEA funds distributed through one-time competitive grants, while Title II under NCLBA provides funds annually to all states through a formula.

Both acts provide states, districts, or grantees with the flexibility to use funds for a broad range of activities to improve teacher quality, including many activities that are similar, such as professional development and recruitment. A difference is that NCLBA's Title II specifies that teachers can be hired to reduce class-size while HEA does not specifically mention class-size reduction. Districts chose to spend about one-half of their NCLBA Title II funds on class-size reduction in 2004-2005. On the other hand, professional development and recruitment efforts were the two broad areas where recipients used funds for similar activities, although the specific activities varied somewhat. Many HEA grantees we visited used their funds to fill teacher shortages in urban schools or recruit teachers from nontraditional sources, such as mid-career professionals. Districts we visited used NCLBA funds to provide bonuses, advertise open teaching positions, and attend recruitment events, among other activities.

Under both HEA and NCLBA, Education has provided assistance and guidance to recipients of these funds and is responsible for holding recipients accountable for the quality of their activities. GAO's previous work identified areas where Education could improve its assistance on teacher quality efforts and more effectively measure the results of these activities. Education has made progress in addressing GAO's concerns by disseminating more information to recipients, particularly on teacher quality requirements, and improving how the department measures the results of teacher quality activities by establishing definitions and performance targets under HEA.

While HEA and NCLBA share the goal of improving teacher quality, it is not clear the extent to which they complement each other. States, districts, schools, and grantees under both laws engage in similar activities. However, not much is known about how well, if at all, these two laws are aligned. Thus, there may be opportunities to better understand how the two laws are working together at the federal, state, and local level.

Mr. Chairman and Members of the Subcommittee:

I am pleased to be here this morning to discuss the federal government's efforts to improve teacher quality. Teachers are the single largest resource in our nation's elementary and secondary education system. Approximately 3 million teachers are responsible for educating over 48 million students and they account for over one half of public school expenditures ($215 billion) each year. Research has shown that teachers play a significant role in improving student performance. However, research has also shown that many teachers—especially those in high- poverty districts—lack competency in the subjects they teach and that most teacher training programs leave new teachers feeling unprepared for the classroom.

While the hiring and training of teachers is primarily the responsibility of state and local governments and institutions of higher education, the federal investment in enhancing teacher quality is substantial and growing. In 1998, the Congress amended the Higher Education Act (HEA) to enhance the quality of teaching in the classroom by improving training programs for prospective teachers and the qualifications of current teachers. In 2001, the Congress passed the No Child Left Behind Act (NCLBA)—the most recent reauthorization of the Elementary and Secondary Education Act—which established federal requirements that all teachers of core academic subjects be highly qualified. In 2006, about $3 billion of federal funds were appropriated for NCLBA Title II and HEA Title II to address teacher quality. Given that NCLBA and HEA are both slated for reauthorization in 2007, this hearing presents a timely opportunity to explore teacher quality provisions covered under those laws.

This statement focuses on the approaches, implementation, and evaluation of teacher quality programs under HEA and NCLBA. I will first provide information on the goals, approaches, and funding of these programs. Then I will discuss the allowable activities and how recipients are using the funds. Finally, I will summarize our findings related to Education's support and evaluation of these activities.

My remarks today are drawn from previous GAO reports covering HEA teacher quality programs and Title II under NCLBA,[1] supplemented with updated information. We updated information by interviewing state officials, officials from institutions of higher education, and Education officials. We also reviewed recent studies and Education documents. We conducted our work in accordance with generally accepted government auditing standards.

In summary:

- While the overall goal of Title II in both HEA and NCLBA is to improve teacher quality, some of the specific approaches differ. For example, HEA focuses more on training prospective teachers than NCLBA. In addition, HEA and NCLBA are funded differently, with HEA funds distributed through competitive grants, while Title II under NCLBA provides funds annually to all states through a formula.
- Both acts provide states, districts, and grantees with the flexibility to use funds for a broad range of activities to improve teacher quality, including many activities that are similar, such as professional development and recruitment. A difference is that NCLBA's Title II specifies that teachers can be hired to reduce class size, while HEA does not specifically mention class-size reduction. With the broad range of activities allowed, we found both similarities and differences in the activities undertaken.
- Under both HEA and NCLBA, Education has provided assistance and guidance to recipients of these funds and is responsible for holding recipients accountable for the quality of their activities. Our previous work identified areas in which Education could improve its assistance to states on their teacher quality efforts and more effectively measure the results of these activities. Education has made progress in addressing our concerns by disseminating more information to recipients particularly on teacher quality requirements and activities and improving how the department measures the results of teacher quality activities by, for example, establishing performance targets.

Teacher Quality Provisions under HEA and NCLBA Have Somewhat Different Approaches and Are Funded Differently

While the overall goal of Title II under both HEA and NCLBA is to improve student achievement by improving the teacher workforce, some of the specific approaches differ. For example, a major focus of HEA provisions is on the training of prospective teachers (preservice training) while NCLBA provisions focus more on improving teacher quality in the classroom (in service training) and hiring highly qualified teachers. Also, both laws use reporting mechanisms to increase accountability. However, HEA focuses more on institutions of higher education while NCLBA focuses on schools and school districts. Additionally, HEA focuses on expanding the teacher workforce by supporting recruitment from other professions.

In addition, HEA and NCLBA Title II funds are distributed differently. HEA teacher quality funds are disbursed through three distinct types of grants: state, partnership, and recruitment grants. State grants are available for states to implement activities to improve teacher quality in their states by enhancing teacher training efforts, while partnership grants support the collaborative efforts of teacher training programs and other eligible partners.[2] Recruitment grants are available to states or partnerships for teacher recruitment activities.

All three types of grants require a match from non-federal sources. For example, states receiving state grants must provide a matching amount in cash or in-kind support from non-federal sources equal to 50 percent of the amount of the federal grant.[3] All three grants are one-time competitive grants; however, state and recruitment grants are for 3 years while partnership grants are for 5 years.[4] HEA amendments in 1998 required that 45 percent of funds be distributed to state grants, 45 percent to partnership grants, and 10 percent to recruitment grants. As of April 2007, 52 of the 59 eligible entities (states, the District of Columbia, and 8 territories) had received state grants.[5] Because the authorizing legislation specifically required that entities could only receive a state grant once, only seven would be eligible to receive future state grants. In our 2002 report, we suggested that if Congress decides to continue funding teacher quality grants in the upcoming reauthorization of HEA, it might want to clarify whether all 59 entities would be eligible for state grant funding under the reauthorization, or whether eligibility would be limited to only those states that have not previously received a state grant. We also suggested that if Congress decides to limit eligibility to entities that have not previously received a state grant, it may want to consider changing the 45 percent funding allocation for state grants. In a 2005 appropriation act, Congress waived the allocation requirement. In 2006, about 9 percent of funds were awarded for state grants, 59 percent for partnership grants, and 33 percent for recruitment. When Congress reauthorizes HEA, it may want to further clarify eligibility and allocation requirements for this program.

NCLBA, funded at a much higher level than HEA, provides funds to states through annual formula grants. In 2006, Congress appropriated $2.89 billion through NCLBA and $59.9 million for HEA for teacher quality efforts.[6] While federal funding for teacher initiatives was provided through two other programs prior to NCLBA, the act increased the level of funding to help states and districts implement the teacher qualification requirements. States and districts generally receive NCLBA Title II funds based on the amount they received in 2001, the percentage of children residing in the state or district, and the number of those children in low- income families. After reserving up to 1 percent of the funds for administrative purposes, states pass 95 percent of the remaining funds to the districts and retain the rest to support state-level teacher initiatives and to support NCLBA partnerships between higher education institutions and high-need districts that work to provide professional development to teachers.

While there is no formula in NCLBA for how districts are to allocate funds to specific schools, the act requires states to ensure that districts target funds to those schools with the highest number of teachers who are not highly qualified, schools with the largest class sizes, or schools that have not met academic performance requirements for 2 or more consecutive years. In addition, districts applying for Title II funds from their states are required to conduct a districtwide needs assessment to identify their teacher quality needs. NCLBA also allows districts to transfer these funds to most other major NCLBA programs, such as those under Title I, to meet their educational priorities. [7]

SOME HEA AND NCLBA FUNDS WERE USED FOR SIMILAR ACTIVITIES AS ALLOWED UNDER BOTH ACTS

HEA provides grantees and NCLBA provides states and districts with the flexibility to use funds for a broad range of activities to improve teacher quality, including many activities that are similar under both acts. HEA funds can be used, among other activities, to reform teacher certification requirements, professional development activities, and recruitment efforts. In addition, HEA partnership grantees must use their funds to implement reforms to hold teacher preparation programs accountable for the quality of teachers leaving the program. Similarly, acceptable uses of NCLBA funds include teacher certification activities, professional development in a variety of core academic subjects, recruitment, and retention initiatives. In addition, activities carried out under NCLBA partnership grants are required to coordinate with any activities funded by HEA. Table 1 compares activities under HEA and NCLBA.

With the broad range of activities allowed under HEA and NCLBA, we found both similarities and differences in the activities undertaken. For example, districts chose to spend about one-half of their NCLBA Title II funds ($1.2 billion) in 2004-2005 on class-size reduction efforts, which is not an activity specified by HEA.[8] We found that some districts focused their class-size reduction efforts on specific grades, depending on their needs. One district we visited focused its NCLBA-funded class-size reduction efforts on the eighth grade because the state already provided funding for reducing class size in other grades. However, while class-size reduction may contribute to teacher retention, it also increases the number of classrooms that need to be staffed and we found that some districts had shifted funds away from class-size reduction to initiatives to improve teachers' subject matter knowledge and instructional skills. Similarly, Education's data showed that the percent of NCLBA district funds spent on class-size reduction had decreased since 2002-2003, when 57 percent of funds were used for this purpose.

Table 1. Examples of Activities under HEA Title II and NCLBA Title II

HEA	NCLBA
Reforming teacher certification or licensure requirements	Reforming teacher and principal certification or licensing requirements
Recruitment and retention	Recruitment and retention
Professional development	Professional development
Implement reforms within teacher preparation programs to hold the programs accountable for preparing highly competent teachers	Reforming tenure systems, implementing teacher testing for subject matter knowledge, and implementing teacher testing for State certification or licensing, consistent with Title II of HEA
Providing preservice clinical experience and mentoring	Hiring teachers to reduce class size
Disseminating information on effective practices	Developing systems to measure the effectiveness of specific professional development programs
Teacher education scholarships	Funding projects to promote reciprocity of teacher and principal certification or licensing between or among States
Follow-up services for new teachers	Support to teachers or principals

Source: GAO summary of HEA Title II and NCLBA Title II.

HEA and NCLBA both funded professional development and recruitment efforts, although the specific activities varied somewhat. For example, mentoring was the most common professional development activity among the HEA grantees we visited. Of the 33 HEA grant sites we visited, 23 were providing mentoring activities for teachers. In addition, some grantees used their funds to establish a mentor training program to ensure that mentors had consistent guidance. One state used the grant to develop mentoring standards and to build the capacity of trainers to train teacher mentors within each district. Some districts used NCLBA Title II funds for mentoring activities as well. We also found that states and districts used NCLBA Title II funds to support other types of professional development activities. For example, two districts we visited spent their funds on math coaches who perform tasks such as working with teachers to develop lessons that reflected state academic standards and assisting them in using students' test data to identify and address students' academic needs. Additionally, states used a portion of NCLBA Title II funds they retained to support professional development for teachers in core academic subjects. In two states that we visited, officials reported that state initiatives specifically targeted teachers who had not met the subject matter competency requirements of NCLBA. These initiatives either offered teachers professional development in core academic subjects or reimbursed them for taking college courses in the subjects taught.

Both HEA and NCLBA funds supported efforts to recruit teachers. Many HEA grantees we interviewed used their funds to fill teacher shortages in urban schools or to recruit new teachers from nontraditional sources— mid-career professionals, community college students, and middle- and high-school students. For example, one university recruited teacher candidates with undergraduate degrees to teach in a local school district with a critical need for teachers while they earn their masters in education. The program offered tuition assistance, and in some cases, the district paid a full teacher salary, with the stipulation that teachers continue teaching in the local school district for 3 years after completing the program. HEA initiatives also included efforts to recruit mid-career professionals by offering an accelerated teacher training program for prospective teachers already in the workforce. Some grantees also used their funds to recruit teacher candidates at community colleges. For example, one of the largest teacher training institutions in one state has partnered with six community colleges around the state to offer training that was not previously available. Finally, other grantees targeted middle and high school students. For example, one district used its grant to recruit interns from 14 high-school career academies that focused on training their students for careers as teachers. Districts we visited used NCLBA Title II funds to provide bonuses to attract successful administrators, advertise open teaching positions, and attend recruitment events to identify qualified candidates. In addition, one district also used funds to expand alternative certification programs, which allowed qualified candidates to teach while they worked to meet requirements for certification.

Finally, some states used HEA funds to reform certification requirements for teachers. Reforming certification or licensing requirements was included as an allowable activity under both HEA and NCLBA to ensure that teachers have the necessary teaching skills and academic content knowledge in the subject areas. HEA grantees also reported using their funds to allow teacher training programs and colleges to collaborate with local school districts to reform the requirements for teacher candidates. For example, one grantee partnered with institutions of higher education and a partner school district to expose teacher candidates to urban schools by providing teacher preparation courses in public schools.

EDUCATION IS WORKING TO PROVIDE BETTER ASSISTANCE AND IMPROVE ITS EVALUATION AND OVERSIGHT EFFORTS

Under both HEA and NCLBA, Education has provided assistance and guidance to recipients of these funds and is responsible for holding recipients accountable for the quality of their activities. In 1998, Education created a new office to administer HEA grants and provide assistance to grantees. While grantees told us that the technical assistance the office provided on application procedures was helpful, our previous work noted several areas in which Education could improve its assistance to HEA grantees, in part through better guidance. For example, we recommended that in order to effectively manage the grant program, Education further develop and maintain its system for regularly communicating program information, such as information on successful and unsuccessful practices. We noted that without knowledge of successful ways of enhancing the quality of teaching in the classroom, grantees might be wasting valuable resources by duplicating unsuccessful efforts. Since 2002, Education has made changes to improve communication with grantees and potential applicants. For example, the department presented workshops to potential applicants and updated and expanded its program Web site with information about program activities, grant abstracts, and other teacher quality resources. In addition, Education provided examples of projects undertaken to improve teacher quality and how some of these efforts indicate improved teacher quality in its 2005 annual report on teacher quality.[9]

Education also has provided assistance to states, districts and schools using NCLBA Title II funds. The department offers professional development workshops and related materials that teachers can access online through Education's website. In addition, Education assisted states and districts by providing updated guidance. In our 2005 report, officials from most states and districts we visited who use Education's Web site to access information on teacher programs or requirements told us that they were unaware of some of Education's teacher resources or had difficulty accessing those resources. We recommended that Education explore ways to make the Web-based information on teacher qualification requirements more accessible to users of its Web site. Education immediately took steps in response to the recommendation and reorganized information on its website related to the teacher qualification requirements.

In addition to providing assistance and guidance, Education is responsible for evaluating the efforts of HEA and NCLBA recipients and for overseeing program implementation. Under HEA, Education is required to annually report on the quality of teacher training programs and the qualifications of current teachers. In 2002, we found that the information collected for this requirement did not allow Education to accurately report on the quality of HEA's teacher training programs and the qualifications of current teachers in each state. In order to improve the data that states are collecting from institutions that receive HEA teacher quality grants, and all those that enroll students who receive federal student financial assistance and train teachers, we recommended that Education should more clearly define key data terms so that states provide uniform information. Further, in 2004, the Office of Management and Budget (OMB) completed a Program Assessment Rating Tool (PART) assessment[10] of this program and gave it a rating of "results not demonstrated," due to a lack of performance information and program management deficiencies. Education officials told us that they had aligned HEA's data collection system with NCLBA definitions of terms such as "highly qualified teacher." However, based on the PART assessment, the Administration proposed eliminating funding for HEA teacher quality grants in its proposed budgets for fiscal years 2006-2008, and redirecting the funds to other programs. Congress has continued to fund this program in fiscal years 2006 and 2007.

Education has responded to our recommendations and issues raised in the PART assessment related to evaluating grantee activities and providing more guidance to grantees on the types of information needed to determine effectiveness. When the Congress amended HEA in 1998 to provide grants to states and partnerships, it required that Education evaluate the activities funded by the grants. In 2005, Education established performance measures for two of the teacher quality enhancement programs—state grants and partnership grants—and required grantees to provide these data in their annual performance plans submitted to Education. [11] The performance measure for state grants is the percentage of prospective teachers who pass subject matter tests, while the measure for partnership grants is the percentage of participants who complete the program and meet the definition of being "highly qualified." In addition, in 2006, Education included information in letters to grantees on the types of information that it requires to assess the effectiveness of its teacher quality programs. For example, in its letters to state grantees, Education noted that when reporting on quantitative performance measures, grantees must show how their actual performance compared to the targets (e.g., benchmarks or goals) that were established in the approved grant application for each budget period.

In addition, in May 2006, Education issued its final report on HEA's partnership grants, focusing on the 25 grantees of the 1999 cohort.[12] The goal of the study was to learn about the collaborative activities taking place in partnerships. It was designed to examine approaches for preparing new and veteran teachers and to assess the sustainability of project activities after the grant ends. Among its findings, Education reported that partnerships encouraged and supported collaboration between institutions of higher education and schools to address teacher preparation needs.

Under NCLBA, Education holds districts and schools accountable for improvements in student academic achievement, and holds states accountable for reporting on the qualifications of teachers. NCLBA set the end of the 2005-2006 school year as the deadline for teachers of core academic subjects, such as math and science, to be highly qualified.[13] Teachers meeting these requirements must (1) have at least a bachelor's degree, (2) be certified to teach by their state, and (3) demonstrate subject matter competency in each core academic subject they teach.[14] Education collects state data on the percent of classes taught by highly qualified teachers and conducts site visits in part to determine whether states appropriately implemented highly qualified teacher provisions.[15]

In state reviews conducted as part of its oversight of NCLBA, Education identified several areas of concern related to states' implementation of teacher qualification requirements and provided states feedback.[16] For example, some states did not include the percentage of core academic classes taught by teachers who are not highly qualified in their annual state report cards,[17] as required. In addition, because some states inappropriately defined teachers as highly qualified, the data that these states reported to Education were inaccurate according to a department official. In many states, the requirements for teachers were not sufficient to demonstrate subject matter competency. Since subject matter competency is a key part of the definition of a highly qualified teacher, such states' data on the extent to which teachers have met these requirements could be misleading. Education also found that a number of states were incorrectly defining districts as high-need, in order to make more districts eligible for partnerships with higher education institutions. According to Education, each of these states corrected their data and the department will continue to monitor states to ensure they are using the appropriate data.

In addition to Education's oversight efforts, OMB completed a PART assessment of NCLBA Title II in 2005 and rated the program as "moderately effective." While OMB noted that the program is well-managed, it also noted that the program has not demonstrated cost-effectiveness and that an independent evaluation has not been completed to assess program effectiveness. In response to OMB's assessment, Education took steps to more efficiently monitor states and conducted two program studies related to teacher quality. An Education official told us that the program studies had been conducted but the department has not yet released the findings.

CONCLUDING OBSERVATIONS

In conclusion, the nation's public school teachers play a key role in educating 48 million students, the majority of our future workforce. Recognizing the importance of teachers in improving student performance, the federal government, through HEA and NCLBA, has committed significant resources and put in place a series of reforms aimed at improving the quality of teachers in the nation's classrooms. With both acts up for reauthorization, an opportunity exists for the Congress to explore potential interrelationships in the goals and initiatives under each act.

174 George A. Scott

While HEA and NCLBA share the goal of improving teacher quality, it is not clear the extent to which they complement each other. Our separate studies of teacher quality programs under each of the laws have found common areas for improvement, such as data quality and assistance from Education. We have also found that states, districts, schools, and grantees under both laws engage in similar activities. However, not much is known about how well, if at all, these two laws are aligned. Thus, there may be opportunities to better understand how the two laws are working together at the federal, state, and local level. For example, exploring links between efforts aimed at improving teacher preparation at institutions of higher education and efforts to improve teacher quality at the school or district level could identify approaches to teacher preparation that help schools the most.

Mr. Chairman, this concludes my prepared statement. I welcome any questions you or other Members of this Subcommittee may have at this time.

End Notes

[1] GAO, *Higher Education: Activities Underway to Improve Teacher Training but Reporting on These Activities Could Be Enhanced*, GAO-03-6 (Washington, D.C.: Dec. 11, 2002) and GAO, *No Child Left Behind Act: Improved Accessibility to Education's Information Could Help States Further Implement Teacher Qualification Requirements*, GAO-06-25 (Washington, D.C.: Nov. 21, 2005).

[2] Eligible partnerships must include at least three partners, consisting of teacher training programs, colleges of Arts and Sciences, and eligible local school districts. Partnerships may include other groups such as state educational agencies, businesses, and nonprofit educational organizations.

[3] Partnerships must match from non-federal sources 25 percent of the partnership grant in the first year, 35 percent in the second, and 50 percent in each succeeding year. States and partnerships that receive recruitment grants have the same matching requirements for these grants as they have under their separate grant programs.

[4] According to Education, an institution of higher education can have more than one grant (simultaneously or sequentially) as long as the members of the partnership are not identical (i.e. a new partnership is formed).

[5] Since 1999, 63 partnership grants have been made to various entities, and 68 recruitment grants were made.

[6] The funding authorizations for Title II, along with the rest of HEA, were extended through June 30, 2007, under the Third Higher Education Extension Act of 2006 (Pub. L. No. 109- 292).

[7] Specifically, districts are allowed to transfer up to 50 percent of the funds allocated to them under most major NCLBA programs, including Title II, into other programs under NCLBA. For example, districts may transfer a portion of their Title II funds into Title I for initiatives designed to improve student achievement.

[8] Education surveyed approximately 800 districts and found that they spent $1.2 billion, about half of their NCLBA Title II funds in 2004-2005, to hire more teachers in order to reduce class size. According to an Education official, no comparable HEA expenditure data is available.

[9] *The Secretary's Fourth Annual Report on Teacher Quality,* U.S. Department of Education (Washington, D.C.) August 2005.

[10] OMB uses the PART as a diagnostic tool meant to provide a consistent approach to evaluating federal programs as part of the executive budget formulation process and as a central component of its overall governmentwide management efforts.

[11] Grantees are required to submit data on how well they meet their project performance measures that they negotiate with their Education grant managers.

[12] See *Partnerships for Reform: Changing Teacher Preparation through the Title II HEA Partnership Program*: Final Report, May 2006. Department of Education, 2006.

[13] Although 2005-2006 was the original deadline, on October 15, 2005 Education sent a policy letter to the Chief State School Officers saying that states that do not quite reach the 100 percent goal by the end of the 2005-2006 school year will not lose federal funds if they are implementing the law.

[14] Veteran teachers may demonstrate subject matter competency through a state-developed High Objective Uniform State Standard of Evaluation, whereby subject matter competency is established through teaching experience, professional development, coursework, and other activities.

[15] In 2003, Education aligned HEA's definition of highly qualified teacher" to that in NCLBA.

[16] As of April 2006, Education officials had completed reviews of all states.

[17] States must prepare and disseminate an annual report card that includes information on student achievement and the professional qualifications of teachers in the state, the percentage of teachers teaching with emergency or

provisional credentials, and the percentage of classes in the state not taught by highly qualified teachers. These data are presented in the aggregate and are also disaggregated by high-poverty compared to low- poverty schools.

In: Teacher Quality and Student Achievement
Editor: Katherine E. Westley

ISBN: 978-1-61728-274-4
© 2010 Nova Science Publishers, Inc.

Chapter 8

TESTIMONY OF SHARON P. ROBINSON, EdD., PRESIDENT AND CEO, BEFORE THE SUBCOMMITTEE ON HIGHER EDUCATION, LIFELONG LEARNING, AND COMPETITIVENESS, "PREPARING TEACHERS FOR THE CLASSROOM: THE ROLE OF THE HIGH EDUCATION ACT AND THE NO CHILD LEFT BEHIND ACT"

Sharon P. Robinson

Good morning, Chairman Hinojosa and members of the Subcommittee. Thank you for the opportunity to testify before you today.

I represent the American Association of Colleges for Teacher Education. Our members are 800 schools and colleges of education in all states of the nation. Schools of education produce over 90% of the new teachers who enter our classrooms every year.

Colleges of education have changed dramatically over the last decade. Major reforms of programs since the late 1980s have created a curriculum much stronger in content and how to teach it, in how to serve diverse learners well, and in how to apply what is learned in courses to the classroom through tightly connected clinical training. Gone from most universities are the education majors that ducked serious subject matter and provided abstract theory divorced from practice. Our teacher candidates have also changed. A major share are mid-career professionals moving into teaching as a second career. Many are instructional aides who have returned to school to become highly qualified teachers. Others go to classes from their own living rooms via the Internet. And a growing number attend their university classes in the public schools where they are teaching, which function like teaching hospitals do in medicine.

Indeed, we are not your grandmothers' schools of education!

Although there are still some weak programs of teacher education that are a matter of significant concern to us, most of the enterprise has changed dramatically as a result of reforms launched by states, universities, and the federal government.

I would like to dispel three myths about schools of education that often masquerade as facts.

Myth #1 holds that teacher candidates leaving the academy are weak in content knowledge. While that once was often true, nothing could be further from the truth today. In every state, beginning teachers demonstrate significant content knowledge in their area of concentration either by completing a major or by passing a rigorous content test or both. The most recent MetLife survey reported that 98% of principals reported that first-time teachers are well prepared to teach subject matter. Nearly 60% of principals found the quality of new teachers entering the profession today to be noticeably better than the quality of new teachers in the past. And in states like Kentucky and California where major reforms of preparation were undertaken, studies have found that at least 85% of teachers and employers report that new teachers from public colleges are entering teaching well prepared for their work. Preliminary findings from a forthcoming report from the Education Testing Service indicate that the academic quality of teacher candidates is improving – in terms of SAT scores, grade point averages, and Praxis scores. Indeed, an earlier ETS study found that newly prepared high school teachers have higher SAT scores than their peers and equivalent or higher grade point averages in their subject matter majors. The practice of majoring in education without strong subject matter preparation and then entering teaching as a mathematics or chemistry teacher is a thing of the past.

Myth #2 holds that schools of education are ivory towers, divorced from the realities of the K-12 classroom, producing teachers who are unprepared for today's schools. This, too, has changed dramatically. Schools of education are integrally involved with K-12 schools. Professional development schools, which are schools modeled after teaching hospitals in the medical profession, are increasingly the norm. In the last decade, universities have launched more than 1,000 such school partnerships across the country, which provide state-of-the-art sites for preparing teachers, pursuing reforms, and conducting research. Studies have found that teachers trained in these sites—many of which are in hard-to-staff urban communities—feel better prepared and are rated as more effective. In addition, veteran teachers report improvements in their own practice, and curriculum reforms stimulated by these university partnerships have produced student achievement gains. Candidates in these sites often complete a full year of student teaching or residency under the wing of an expert veteran teacher. Research tells us that such sustained clinical experiences are a predictor of effectiveness and retention.

Myth #3, my personal favorite, suggests that schools of education reject accountability. In fact, we may be the only portion of the higher education community that fully *embraces* accountability. We want to know if our graduates are effective; if they remain in the profession; if they generate high achievement from their students. Higher education systems in Texas, Louisiana, California, Florida, and Ohio, to name a few, are actively developing the capacity to follow education graduates and make determinations about program effectiveness. These efforts are underway based on the initiative of the colleges of education supported by external funding.

Even though national professional accreditation is voluntary in most states, most teacher education institutions volunteer to undertake national accreditation, even though about 1/4 of institutions do not receive full approval on their first attempt. NCATE accreditation now requires solid evidence of teacher education outcomes, including how candidates perform on licensing examinations, how they succeed in classrooms, how many enter and stay in teaching, and, increasingly, how they influence student learning. Teacher educators are committed to evaluating preparation programs based on the success of graduates

I am not asserting that there is no room for improvement in schools of education— for there certainly is considerable work yet to be done. But I think it is important to acknowledge that we are not standing still. It is also important to acknowledge that schools of education alone cannot solve the nation's teacher supply and distribution problems. Federal incentives are needed to support able candidates in becoming well-prepared and to distribute these well-prepared teachers to the schools where they are most needed.

Teachers in the U.S. are paid considerably less than their peers who go into other lines of work, and many must go into debt to complete their preparation, as there is very little governmental support to help them gain the skills they need to do their extraordinarily complex jobs well. If they go to teach in high-need communities, they will generally earn considerably less than if they teach in wealthy districts. Meanwhile, our competitor nations that are higher achieving (such as Finland, Sweden, Norway, Netherlands, Germany, France, Australia, New Zealand, Japan, Taiwan, and Singapore) have made substantial investments in teacher training and equitable teacher distribution in the last two decades. These nations recruit their best and brightest into high-quality graduate-level teacher education (which includes a year of practice teaching in a clinical school connected to the university), completely subsidized for all candidates at government expense. They provide mentoring for all beginners in their first year of teaching, and their funding mechanisms ensure equitable salaries, often with additional stipends for hard-to-staff locations, which are competitive with other professions.

In order to make headway on the issue of recruiting, preparing, and retaining teachers where they are needed most, we need a much more systemic approach.

I would like to submit for the record a copy of the "Marshall Plan for Teaching" that was written recently by AACTE Board member and internationally renowned teacher educator Dr. Linda Darling-Hammond. This bold plan points out that in order for our nation to ensure that every student has a teacher who knows how to teach challenging content to diverse learners, we need to invest $3 billion annually. Chairman Miller's TEACH ACT that he recently introduced includes some features of this plan. The simple fact is that the federal government has not made the kind of investment in either higher education or pre-K-12 education that is needed to get the result we want.

The two Title IIs—of the Higher Education Act and of the No Child Left Behind Act—are lynchpins in the federal investment in teacher quality. Yet neither is currently robust enough to produce the transformation that is needed.

Title II of the Higher Education Act was first authorized in 1998, four years before the enactment of No Child Left Behind. This will be the first time Congress has had an opportunity to look at the Higher Education Act in relation to the requirements of NCLB.

The purpose of Title II of HEA is to transform teacher preparation—so that it is rigorous and accountable. I am pleased to report to you that transformation is under way. Schools of education are deeply involved with other components of the university -- including schools of arts and sciences -- and with local school districts. The successes of some of these new models of preparation have been documented in a number of recent reports, including a major volume by the National Academy of Education. When the "highly qualified" mandate was enacted in NCLB, Title II HEA funds were increasingly used to prepare teachers to meet those requirements.

Schools of education are at the beginning of developing more meaningful and robust capacity for accountability – through collection of rich assessment data regarding their candidates and their programs. The development of valid and reliable performance assessments is an essential element of those activities. For example, a consortium of universities in California has developed the PACT assessment (Performance Assessment for California Teachers) that, like the National Board's assessments, measures the actual teaching skills and outcomes of prospective teachers. This assessment and similar efforts in Wisconsin, Washington, Oregon, North Carolina, and elsewhere demonstrate the possibilities for improving preparation by measuring whether new teachers can actually teach before they enter the profession. Such measures build on earlier work -- such as the teacher work sample assessment -- and could provide much stronger accountability than the current requirements for teachers to pass paper-and-pencil tests of basic skills and subject matter knowledge that, though important, fall short of looking at whether teachers can actually succeed in teaching diverse students.

We believe that state certification requirements should include this type of performance assessment so that parents and students are assured that a beginning teacher is skilled in instructing all students. A modest investment by the federal government could facilitate the continued development of valid and reliable teacher performance assessments so that states may adopt them. Such an investment is called for in the TEACH Act recently re-introduced by Chairman Miller.

The Higher Education Act has also put a premium on partnerships among K-12 schools, colleges of education, and schools of arts and sciences. Such partnerships are no longer novel, but are increasingly routine.

But the transformation envisioned by the law—systemic and comprehensive—has not occurred. The transformation remains spotty and unsustained given the minimal $60 million federal investment. Title II of the Higher Education Act was envisioned in 1998 as a $300 million program. This amount is a bare minimum for starting on the critical agenda of ensuring that every beginning teacher is adequately prepared to teach the challenging content standards required under NCLB and to do so successfully with students with a wide array of learning needs. Yet every year the funds dwindle.

I would like to submit our reauthorization recommendations for Title II of the Higher Education Act for the record. In summary, we propose

- A targeted investment in the development of data systems so that schools of education can follow their graduates and assess their impact on student learning, track teacher movement, and measure retention.
- An investment in partnerships among schools of education, schools of arts and sciences, and K-12 schools that targets sustained clinical experience, teaching diverse learners (including ELL and special education students), addressing the critical shortage areas (including, math, science, special education, and ELL) and addressing teacher turnover in high-need schools – with a significant increase in funding. This would include support for partnerships that provide high-quality internships and residencies in communities where teachers are most needed.
- A new Teaching Fellowship program that would provide service scholarships to cover the cost of preparation in exchange for teaching in high-need fields and high-need schools for at least four years.
- A revision of the Pass Rate requirements so that pass rates are reported for candidates who have completed 100% of their coursework. (This will ensure that candidates taking certification exams have completed all content and pedagogical curricula courses.)

Title II of the No Child Left Behind Act is the federal government's $2.9 billion investment in professional development. Yet, according to the Department of Education, only 28% of the funds are actually spent on professional development. About half of the funds go to class-size-reduction initiatives in states.

Title II NCLB funds should be targeted to produce systemic and sustainable change in states—working through partnership involving higher education and local school districts. The funds should support developing and carrying out statewide initiatives to address the following challenges:

- Persistent and critical shortages in fields such as math, science, special education, and ELL.
- The maldistribution of teachers so that the neediest students are most likely to have the least qualified teachers.
- Ensuring that rural and urban schools have effective teachers and high retention rates.
- Ensuring that all teachers can provide instruction in a rigorous curriculum to diverse learners.

I submit for the record our recommendations for improving the No Child Left Behind Act, which include:

- Partnerships to reduce teacher shortages in urban and rural areas;
- Preparation that will ensure that all new teachers are prepared to teach diverse populations, including English language learners and special education students;
- Preparation and professional development to help teachers learn to use data and assessments to improve teaching and learning; and
- State-of-the-art mentoring programs for beginning teachers so that they become increasingly competent and stay in teaching.
- Support for the development of teacher performance assessments that enhance teacher preparation and teacher accountability.

I would also like to submit our publication "Teacher Education Reform: The Impact of Federal Investments," which profiles grants funded by Title II of the Higher Education Act. Next month, I will be pleased to submit to the Subcommittee our upcoming publication, "Preparing STEM Teachers: The Key to Global Competitiveness."

The relationship between higher education and K-12 schools has changed dramatically in the last decade. There is no longer a clear line between the role of higher education and the role of public schools. Rather, there are ongoing innovative relationships that promote the improvement of instructional practice in both the academy and the classroom. Both Title IIs need to support and fund these rich partnerships to yield maximum benefit for our nation's learners.

Thank you, Mr. Chairman.

In: Teacher Quality and Student Achievement
Editor: Katherine E. Westley

ISBN: 978-1-61728-274-4
© 2010 Nova Science Publishers, Inc.

Chapter 9

TESTIMONY OF JANICE WILEY, DEPUTY DIRECTOR FOR INSTRUCTIONAL SUPPORT SERVICES OF THE REGION ONE EDUCATION SERVICE CENTER, BEFORE THE SUBCOMMITTEE ON HIGHER EDUCATION, LIFELONG LEARNING, AND COMPETITIVENESS – "PREPARING TEACHERS FOR THE CLASSROOM: THE ROLE OF THE HIGHER EDUCATION ACT AND NO CHILD LEFT BEHIND ACT"

Janice Wiley

Mr. Chairman and members of the Subcommittee, I thank you for the opportunity to testify today. I am Dr. Janice Wiley, Deputy Director for Instructional Support Services of the Region One Education Service Center located in Edinburg, Texas. The Region One Service Center serves a student population of over 373,000 located along the south Texas-Mexico border, of which approximately 144,000 students are limited English proficient. Ninety-seven percent of the student population is of Hispanic descent with 85% qualifying as Economically Disadvantaged. To serve these students, there are over 23,256 teachers in the Region One area, with over 18,000 teachers in the academic core subject areas. Of those, only 12.6% hold a master's degree and approximately 40% have less than 10 years experience.

Imagine a first-year teacher entering his/her first day of teaching at local high school. There are 25-30 students in each class period; the class made up of many of the demographic characteristics that I just mentioned. There are also many diverse learners including students that are Limited English Proficient, migrant students, as well as special needs students. For many of them, at least half will be the first in their family to earn a high school diploma and the first to attend college, much less have an advanced degree. Not only is the novice teacher faced with the challenge of helping all of these students meet state and federal standards, but the school is rated based on the passing rates of his/her students. Can you feel the immense pressure this teacher must be facing? What can we do to support this teacher so that after a few years he/she does not feel burned out or worse yet, feel like they are facing a losing battle all by themselves? We can continue to provide quality professional development and mentoring programs to assist the teacher so that their students are successful in not only meeting, but surpassing state and federal academic standards. The Region One Education Service Center believes vehemently that a key factor in increasing student achievement lies in improving the quality of teachers in our classrooms. Title II funds make it possible to provide these learning opportunities for our teaching force.

It is impossible for teachers to learn everything they need to know for a lifetime of teaching during their college preparation work; therefore professional development and mentor programs are crucial for beginning teachers. Research clearly shows that a well-trained teacher is the greatest factor in predicting student achievement and that, dollar for dollar, monies that are spent on professional development produce far greater gains in student learning than do investments in tests, materials, or programs.

Even our most experienced teachers have professional development needs. Many graduated from teacher preparation programs before state content standards were developed and well before technology played such an important role in our profession. Additionally, due to brain research we know more about how students learn cognitively than ever before. Experienced teachers must be knowledgeable about new scientifically researched-based strategies in order to reach all students.

Through Title II funds we have been able to fulfill many of our teachers' professional development needs. Many efforts are being coordinated locally with the service center facilitating many of the activities. We have formed a local P-16 council to align instruction from high school to our colleges and universities and to create a seamless transition for our students.

Title II funds have been used to serve identified needs and have been used by the Region One Education Service Center to form the numerous initiatives:

- Texas Regional Science and Math Collaborative – A network of statewide universities, education service centers, and school districts that provide professional development in math and science. Teacher mentors are developed and participating teachers may earn college credit and pursue graduate degrees in the math and science content fields.
- Texas Science, Math, Engineering, and Technology (TSTEM) Center – Region One ESC is one of only 5 centers in Texas created to develop professional development opportunities in the STEM content areas. Project-based learning will be emphasized in which teachers will learn how to engage students in more relevant real-world problem solving activities. This is a collaboration of local school districts, Region One ESC, universities, community colleges, and the Workforce of South Texas.
- CSCOPE Curriculum – Region One Esc has formed a collaborative to produce a curriculum based on the state content standards. Districts use Title II funds to pay for the professional development needed to implement the standards-based curriculum. Key participants in the training are campus administrators who also learn how to support the curriculum, monitor the implementation, and provide feedback to teachers through analysis of data from six weeks tests and walk- through observations.

- Teaching American History Grant - This program is designed to raise student achievement by improving teachers' knowledge and understanding of and appreciation for traditional U.S. history. This is a partnership between local school districts, Region One ESC, University of Texas Pan American, and local museums.

Title II monies have also been used in recruitment and retention in the following manner:

- Stipends to recruit highly qualified teachers in shortage areas;
- Mentor programs for beginning teachers and principals;
- Hiring of additional teachers to reduce class size, particularly in the early grades

Since the 2004 school year, Region One has shown significant gains in student achievement for all students on state assessments. Reading increased from 71% to 81% passing rate, a gain of 10%. Mathematics increased from 58% to 69%, a gain of 11%. Social Studies increased from 77% to 81%, a gain of 4%. Science has seen the largest increase, from 43% to 61%, a gain of 18%. We firmly believe that these gains are due to the professional development that we provide to our teachers through Title II funds. We are hopeful that these funds will continue to be available to meet the needs of the children in south Texas.

Thank you for the opportunity to be here today to present this information. I will be happy to answer any questions that the committee may have.

In: Teacher Quality and Student Achievement
Editor: Katherine E. Westley

ISBN: 978-1-61728-274-4
© 2010 Nova Science Publishers, Inc.

Chapter 10

TESTIMONY OF DANIEL FALLON, DIRECTOR, PROGRAM IN HIGHER EDUCATION, CARNEGIE CORPORATION OF NEW YORK, BEFORE THE SUBCOMMITTEE ON HIGHER EDUCATION, LIFELONG LEARNING AND COMPETITIVENESS – "PREPARING TEACHERS FOR THE CLASSROOM: THE ROLE OF THE HIGHER EDUCATION ACT AND NO CHILD LEFT BEHIND"

Daniel Fallon

INTRODUCTION

My name is Daniel Fallon. I serve as Director of the Program in Higher Education at Carnegie Corporation of New York, which is the philanthropic organization established in 1911 by Andrew Carnegie to maintain the benefaction he intended to pursue with the wealth he had accrued in his lifetime. In Mr. Carnegie's words, our mission is to promote "...the advancement and diffusion of knowledge and understanding to benefit the citizens of the United States."

Over the course of the twentieth century Carnegie Corporation of New York has provided support for many worthwhile American activities, with a particular focus on education. For example, resources from the philanthropy helped establish the first nationally available pension fund for college teachers, the Teachers Insurance Annuity Association, known by its initials TIAA. Research supported by the Corporation provided the basis for establishing national need-based financial aid, now known more commonly as Pell Grants. Other investments were instrumental in establishing the College Board, the Educational Testing Service, and more recently the National Board for Professional Teaching Standards.

Since the early 1980's the Corporation has increased its efforts to improve the quality of teaching in the nation's schools. Under its current president, Vartan Gregorian, it undertook a major initiative beginning in 2001 to reform teacher education. The initiative is called *Teachers for a New Era* and I am its principal designer and have directed its development since its inception. The Annenberg Foundation and the Ford Foundation have joined Carnegie Corporation in this effort, contributing significant resources to extend the reach of *Teachers for a New Era* and to disseminate positive findings arising from its work.

PURPOSE OF THIS TESTIMONY

I have accepted your invitation to describe today the work we are doing in teacher education reform. Some of our findings thus far may be helpful to you if you begin to consider ways to facilitate the production of high quality teachers. For example, in my testimony I will discuss three areas you may find useful: (1) the value for states of recording educational data, releasing such data to higher education institutions for purposes of improvement of teacher education programs, and placing responsibility for educational data with research institutions; (2) how academy-based induction functioning as a complement to district-based induction increases efficiency, reduces costs, and improves pupil learning; and (3) why it may be worthwhile to provide incentives for teacher-education programs to adopt evidence-based continuous-improvement designs focused on facilitating pupil learning.

I speak on behalf of the eleven institutions of higher education that are participating in *Teachers for a New Era*, and with their consent. I should add that the presidents of the *Teachers for a New Era* institutions, led by President Simon of Michigan State University and President Hennessy of Stanford University, are preparing a letter to the National Research Council. You will be receiving a copy of this letter, which addresses the congressional charge to the Council to prepare a report on teacher education. It echoes some of the themes I raise today, but also places a particular emphasis on the value of teacher education reform to improve the nation's competitiveness in the areas of science, technology, engineering, and mathematics.

As an officer of Carnegie Corporation of New York I hope my testimony may serve one of our basic purposes: to increase the life chances of citizens of the United States.

WHY TRY TO REFORM TEACHER EDUCATION?

We decided to undertake this work seven years ago with no illusions. There was a well-justified consensus within the policy community about teacher education. It was judged in general to be intellectually incoherent. Its value in providing certified teachers was of unproven effectiveness. Finally, numerous well-organized efforts at reform of teacher education had not led to any fundamental change in the enterprise. In short, most informed observers did not think that teacher education was a worthy target of philanthropic attention. Nonetheless, we decided to make a big bet on it.

We undertook our initiative on teacher education for two principal reasons. The first is the much-discussed emergence in the U.S. of a knowledge-based economy. Our nation is today and for the foreseeable future generating wealth principally through knowledge, information, and services. If the nation is to preserve its standard of living and protect the quality of life of its citizens, it must place priority on producing a highly educated work force. We understand the reauthorizations of the Elementary and Secondary Education Act and the Higher Education Act in recent years as a rational political response to the challenge of a new economy.

The second reason for our investment is a fundamental paradigm shift in our conception of how well children learn in schools. For more than a generation our knowledge was based on the excellent pioneering work of sociologist James Coleman sponsored by the U.S. government in the late 1960's. These analyses led to a prevailing conclusion that pupil achievement was largely controlled by economic inequality mediated in large part by family circumstances. The science on which this idea was based depended for the most part on cross-sectional analyses of average test scores of some groups of pupils compared with others. Longitudinal data permitting the analysis of the change in test scores by individual pupils over time were largely nonexistent and thus not available to Coleman. That circumstance changed with the broad introduction in several states during the decade of the 1980's of mandatory state-wide testing in the public schools. As the accumulation of these data made further analysis possible, researchers began to look at the performance of individual pupils in successive years with different teachers. They discovered that some teachers demonstrated an ability to raise pupil achievement reliably, in some cases quite dramatically, even in the face of severe economic hardship experienced by the pupil. In other words, our knowledge shifted from thinking that wealth, families, and neighborhoods were the principal source of pupil achievement to understanding that high quality teaching made a very significant contribution.

The two new developments, a new knowledge-based economy and an understanding that the quality of the teacher was likely the single most important school-based factor influencing the achievement of pupils, were foremost in giving Carnegie Corporation of New York confidence that an investment in improving the quality of teacher education would be worthwhile. To these we added other considerations. We believe, on principle, that higher education institutions are the best place to educate teachers. Further, we are convinced that a new generation of faculty at colleges and universities are more prepared than ever before to accept the challenge of designing strong programs of teacher education.

EVIDENCE-BASED GUIDELINES FOR REFORM

The U.S. has not on the whole invested heavily in rigorous research on education. Primarily for that reason we do not know with high confidence what an ideal teacher education program might look like. We began with a straightforward presumption that observable pupil learning is the only way to make high quality teaching visible. Therefore, if we want to see evidence of high quality teaching, we must look for pupil learning. We studied the limited amount of relevant research literature carefully and could find no reason based on evidence to recommend a specific structure or curriculum for teacher education. Instead, we asked higher education institutions to respond to challenges for teacher education around three large design principles that were justified to the best of our ability on sound evidence.

The first design principle is cultivating a respect for evidence. Within this general framework we embedded a radical idea, that the higher education institution must find a way to measure the quality of the teacher education program by demonstrable pupil learning occurring in classrooms of teachers who were graduates of the program.

The second design principle is effectively engaging faculty from the disciplines of the arts and sciences. This includes acquiring knowledge of the content that the teacher will teach, of course, but also speaks to the importance of general education for the teacher. Also important is the idea that faculty from the disciplines of the arts and sciences will learn from their contact with teacher candidates and with their colleagues in colleges of education more effective ways of representing content so that it is readily learned by students.

Finally, the third design principle calls for understanding the act of teaching as skilled clinical practice. Thus, it considers pupils as clients, the classroom as a clinic, and the teacher as a clinician who assists each child in learning to high standards. Taking this idea seriously requires that teacher education programs work closely with representative school districts, that teacher candidates be exposed early and often to working classrooms, that some highly effective teachers from schools be appointed to positions as "professors of practice" in the teacher education program, and that higher education faculty from the disciplines of the arts and sciences also observe teaching in classrooms and assist in instructing teacher candidates about the teaching of the content. The third design principle embeds a second radical idea within the teacher education program, namely, that the teacher education program should offer to each of its graduates a program of intensive mentoring and support during the first two full years of professional clinical practice. Through this device the novice teacher who was once a teacher candidate in the teacher education program continues to receive education to become an effective teacher. We call this idea academy-based induction, or residency.

By tightly coupling the teacher education program to working classrooms in schools, requiring an ongoing professional relationship with recent graduates who are working as novice teachers, and using pupil learning in the classrooms of graduates as the primary means of measuring quality, *Teachers for a New Era* is explicitly a design for continuous improvement. We believe this is an evidence-based program that will enable a teacher education program to gather the data it needs to improve continuously over time. The functional nature of the reform challenge ensures that any teacher education program anywhere in the United States today could meet it by applying the design principles.

A CAPSULE DESCRIPTION OF HOW TEACHERS FOR A NEW ERA IS BEING IMPLEMENTED

Instead of requesting proposals to participate, Carnegie Corporation of New York engaged policy analysts from the RAND Corporation, and appointed a National Advisory Panel of distinguished figures from the world of policy, practice and research. With assistance from these two groups, we went through an iterative process of investigation of teacher education programs, culminating in site visits to numerous institutions, and ultimately in the identification of eleven institutions of higher education that we believed were capable of meeting the challenges we posed in our general prospectus, which is attached to this document. We then invited proposals from just these eleven, and went through multiple revisions of the proposals until each proposal was judged to have produced a work plan capable of meeting our requirements.

In addition to the prospectus describing *Teachers for a New Era*, I have separately provided each member of the Subcommittee with a laminated 4x6 card containing a list of the eleven participating institutions on one side, and a schematic summary of the design principles on the other side. We designed the initiative so as to provide strong support for fundamental reform. Each of the eleven institutions of higher education was awarded $5 million over a five to seven year period, and was then asked to raise another $5 million independently, with at least 30% of the matching money dedicated to a permanent endowment to support the reconfigured program of teacher education. In addition, each institution received $500,000 to be shared with "partners," such as school districts or other cooperating institutions, to facilitate relationships necessary for preparing effective teachers. Thus, each institution received $10.5 million in direct support. Carnegie Corporation of New York also contracted with outside partners, primarily the Academy for Educational Development, to provide direct technical assistance for the life of the project that included assistance for each institution with budget development, monitoring of benchmarks, consultation services, and several meetings of teams from all institutions each year to discuss progress on the design principles. All in all, the philanthropic investment in this unusual national initiative has exceeded $125 million.

EARLY FINDINGS AND IMPLICATIONS

Although it is too early to draw many confident conclusions about the long-term success of this initiative, a few patterns are becoming clear. First, in a few pilot studies several of the institutions have been able to link pupil learning gains in public school classrooms with teachers who have pursued distinct teacher education programs before being appointed as teachers. These investigations have been very helpful in pointing to areas within the teacher education curriculum that require strengthening. The promise of this approach seems clear. Nonetheless, we have found in many instances that there are severe obstacles to retrieving data for legitimate program improvement purposes, even when the data are available, there are no objections from union representatives, and proper safeguards have been taken to protect the identities of particular teachers and particular students. In other cases, state or local data are not collected in ways that make comparisons for research purposes useful.

We thus find ourselves faced with the dilemma that (a) we cannot mount an evidence-based system for program improvement without data from the schools; and (b) the authorities responsible for school data are often unable to provide data for program improvement. Therefore, if your legislative deliberations include data systems, and you wish to improve the education of future teachers, you may wish to consider incentives to states and local school districts to construct comprehensive data systems that collect measures that can be compared directly from school to school within a district, and from district to district within a state. It would be helpful if such data systems included unique identifiers that permitted the linking of performance of individual pupils with the teachers that taught them, in ways that protect the identity of the pupils and the teachers, and also included provisions that require such data to be made available to institutions of higher education with teacher education programs for the purpose of program improvement. There may also be distinct advantages in ensuring that school data repositories be entrusted to research institutions in the state rather than to state regulatory agencies.

A second finding of importance has been the remarkable success of the implementation of academy-based induction as a supplement to district-based induction programs. For example, one of our grantees, the University of Virginia, has shown that its academy-based induction achieved a 33% reduction in attrition of novice teachers over and above the existing district-based induction program by itself. Innovations of this kind result in enormous cost savings to districts and lead to more effective instruction for pupils. To offset the cost of design and introduction of academy-based induction nationally, you may want to consider offering incentives to partnerships between teacher-education programs and school districts to propose them.

Finally, a third finding is that the introduction of an evidence-based continuous-improvement program built around the *Teachers for a New Era* design principles has resulted in substantial long-term administrative and organizational changes within these higher education institutions. The effect of new management has been to promote greater institution-wide responsibility for teacher education and to improve the application of the considerable knowledge resources throughout these institutions to the enterprise of teacher education. Therefore, you may want to consider some form of incentive grants to higher education institutions that propose to restructure teacher education by agreeing to design principles similar to *Teachers for a New Era*.

SUMMARY AND CONCLUSION

As we review the fifth year of implementation since the first group of institutions received awards under *Teachers for a New Era*, a wide variety of very encouraging developments are beginning to emerge. The comprehensive application of the design principles appears to be shaping a coherent vision of effective teaching as academically-taught skilled clinical practice. Therefore, we have reason to hope that a foundation is being laid for an evidence-based program of teacher education driven by attention to pupil learning in working classrooms in a form that enables continuous improvement of teacher education.

Ours is a vision for reliable means of preparing effective teachers who can teach all children, from all walks of life, to learn to high standards. It is a vision of higher education in the nation's service.

Thank you for your attention this morning.

In: Teacher Quality and Student Achievement
Editor: Katherine E. Westley

ISBN: 978-1-61728-274-4
© 2010 Nova Science Publishers, Inc.

Chapter 11

TESTIMONY OF EMILY FEISTRITZER, PRESIDENT, NATIONAL CENTER FOR ALTERNATIVE CERTIFICATION AND THE NATIONAL CENTER FOR EDUCATION INFORMATION, BEFORE THE SUBCOMMITTEE ON HIGHER EDUCATION, LIFELONG LEARNING AND COMPETITIVENESS – "PREPARING TEACHERS FOR THE CLASSROOM: THE ROLE OF THE HIGHER EDUCATION ACT AND NO CHILD LEFT BEHIND"

Emily Feistritzer

Mr. Chairman and members of the Committee, thank you for the opportunity to speak before you today on the critical topic of preparing teachers for the classroom. My name is Emily Feistritzer and I am the president of the National Center for Alternative Certification which was created in 2003 with a discretionary grant awarded to the National Center for Education Information to serve as a comprehensive clearinghouse for information about alternative routes to teacher certification.

The Center's web site, www.teach-now.org, is used by tens of thousands of individuals *per day*, including policy makers and individuals seeking to become teachers.

In addition to collecting, analyzing and disseminating information about teacher preparation and certification since 1979, the National Center for Education Information has been documenting what is going on in the development of alternatives to college-based undergraduate teacher education program routes to certification since 1983 and publishing descriptions of alternative routes in an annual publication, *ALTERNATIVE TEACHER CERTIFICATION: A State-by-State Analysis*. I have made the 2007 edition of this 346-page document available to you, as well as *Alternate Routes to Teaching*, a book I co-authored with Charlene K. Haar which was published by Pearson Education, Inc. in April of this year.

I would like to discuss with you data and information about these alternative routes to teaching and their impact on the preparation of all teachers going forward.

Alternate routes to teacher certification are having a profound impact on the who, what, when, where and how of K-12 teaching. What began in the early 1980s as a way to ward off projected shortages of teachers and replace emergency certification has evolved into a sophisticated model for recruiting, training and certifying people who already have at least a bachelor's degree and want to become teachers.

When the National Center for Education Information (NCEI) first began in 1983 asking state certification officials the question, "What is your state's status regarding alternatives to the traditional college teacher education program route for certifying teachers?" eight states said they were implementing some type of alternative route to teacher certification.

Now, in 2007, all 50 states and the District of Columbia report they have at least some type of alternate route to teacher certification. All toll, 130 alternate routes to teacher certification now exist in these 50 states and the District of Columbia. In addition, these states report that approximately 485 alternate routes programs are implementing the alternative routes to teacher certification they established.

Based on data submitted by the states, NCEI estimates that approximately 59,000 individuals were issued teaching certificates through alternative routes in 2005-06, up from approximately 50,000 in 2004-05 and 39,000 in 2003-04. As shown in the figure below, the numbers of teachers obtaining certification through alternative routes have increased substantially since the late 1990s. Nationally, approximately one-third of new teachers being hired are coming through alternative routes to teacher certification.

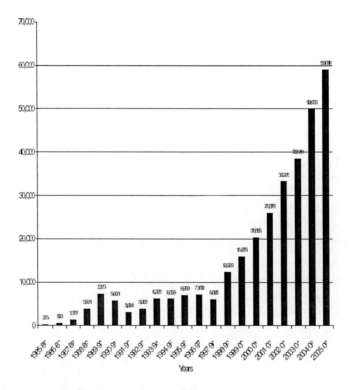

Number of Individuals Issued Certificates to Teach Through Alternate Routes by Year

Furthermore, an analysis of the NCLB Title II reports the states re-submitted to the U.S. Department of Education last summer after none of the original reports showed that any state had met the highly qualified teacher requirement, revealed that 38 states specifically stated they intend to utilize alternate routes to ensure that all of their teachers meet the highly qualified teacher requirements. This illustrates, further, the market-driven, solution-oriented role these effective programs are having in meeting the demand for qualified teachers.

A hallmark of alternative routes is that they are market-driven. Alternate routes to teaching are created for the explicit purpose of filling a demand for teachers in specific subject areas in specific schools in specific geographic regions. They are designed for individuals who already have at least a bachelor's degree – many of whom have experience in other careers – who want to teach the subjects in areas where there is a demand for teachers.

WHY ALTERNATE ROUTES?

Since the mid 1960s, reforming teacher education and certification was the focus of solving teacher quantity *and* quality issues. Having enough qualified teachers has been at the root of most reform efforts concerning teachers.

For decades, teacher education and certification have been identified as both the cause and solution of many of the problems regarding teachers. The 1,300 or so Colleges of Education have taken the brunt of criticism for not adequately preparing qualified teachers. Additionally, state agencies responsible for licensing (certifying) teachers have been targets for an array of attacks - from the complicated certification processes to weak assessments that fail to measure competencies for teaching.

In 1983, the state of New Jersey grabbed national headlines with its out-of-the-box solution. New Jersey created an alternative route to teacher certification specifically to attract a new market for teaching - liberal arts graduates – and transition them into elementary and secondary teaching without going through a traditional college teacher education program.

This solution to teacher quantity and quality began the alternative teacher certification movement and the nation took notice. Significant changes in alternative routes to teacher certification have occurred since the mid-1990s. In addition to the development of alternative routes at the state level, an evolving consensus of essential characteristics shows that most alternate routes:

- are specifically designed to recruit, prepare and license individuals who already have at least a bachelor's degree – and often other careers.
- require rigorous screening processes, such as passing tests, interviews, and demonstrated mastery of subject matter content.
- provide on-the-job training.
- include coursework or equivalent experiences in professional education studies before and while teaching.
- involve work with mentor teachers and/or other support personnel.
- set high performance standards for completion of the programs.

WHAT DO WE KNOW ABOUT PREPARING TEACHERS THROUGH ALTERNATE ROUTES?

1. There is wide variation in preparation programs – from about a third that require 31 or more college credit hours of education courses to a third that require none for which a candidate pays college tuition.
2. About half of alternate route programs now are being administered by higher education institutions, a fourth by school districts and a fourth by collaborations, states, or private entities.
3. Nearly all alternate route programs are field-based teacher preparation programs that include mentoring and learning experiences directly related to classroom teaching.
4. More than half of alternate route teachers came into the profession with experience from a professional career outside of education.
5. Only one-fourth a teachers who have entered teaching through alternate routes say they would have become a teacher if the program had not been available.

WHAT DOES THE RESEARCH SAY ABOUT THE EFFECTIVENESS OF VARIOUS TEACHER PREPARATION ROUTES?

Most of the research conducted concerning alternative routes to teacher certification shows that alternate routes do what they are designed to do: bring people into teaching who would not otherwise have become teachers. The research also indicates that the route one goes through does not seem to matter all that much as far as effective teaching goes. Experience and effective mentoring seem to be the most important variables for becoming a competent teacher.

A growing body of research shows that after a couple of years' experience, differences in teacher performance measures and/or student achievement disappear regardless of what kind of route a teacher comes into teaching through.

A scientifically designed study still underway shows similar results. *How Changes in Entry Requirements Alter the Teacher Workforce and Affect Student Achievement* reported findings from this study being conducted by Donald Boyd, Pamela Grossman, Hamilton Lankford, Susanna Loeb, and James Wyckoff. The researchers focused their study on pathways into teaching in New York City and the "effects of such programs on the teacher workforce and on student achievement" (1). The study's basic findings indicate that, after two years, the small differences among the groups at the beginning of teaching disappear (Boyd, *et al*, 2005).

In 2005, the American Educational Research Association (AERA) released *Studying Teacher Education: The Report of the AERA Panel on Research and Teacher Education* (2005).

The compendium's findings regarding alternate routes included:

- The studies provided some evidence that alternatively certified teachers may be "more willing than traditionally certified teachers to teach in low-SES urban schools, but these data may reflect more where teachers can get jobs than actual teacher preferences" (663).

- "there were no differences between alternatively and traditionally certified teachers in terms of teacher efficacy or in teaching competence as measured by classroom observations" (663).
- The research showed "very little difference between alternatively and traditionally certified teachers" (670).
- "The studies of the alternative certification programs in Houston, Dallas, and Milwaukee school districts indicate inconclusive results" (674). Anticipated retention was higher in Milwaukee in alternative programs. In Houston there were no significant differences between traditionally certified and alternatively certified teachers' "perception of the problems they faced in the classroom," at the end of the first academic year (674).
- The studies that "compared the impact of multiple teacher education programs on various dimensions of teacher quality have suggested that alternatively certified teachers may in some circumstances have higher expectations for the learning of students of color living in poverty than teachers who have been traditionally certified" (689).

More targeted research needs to be done to find out what it is that makes for effective teachers. The research conducted thus far seems to indicate that preparation route does not matter.

I would like to conclude my statement with some statistics from the U.S. Department of Education that shed light on who actually is being prepared to teach and who actually become teachers, as well as the structure of K-12 education which illustrates the realities of teacher demand.

A. Are Bachelor Degree Recipients a Reliable Market for Teachers?

Getting clarity about college graduates who are qualified to teach upon receiving their bachelor's degree and who go into teaching, as well as those who do not, is not easy. The U.S. Department of Education's *Baccalaureate and Beyond Longitudinal Studies* are often cited for these data which are based on samples, so NCES does not report these findings in numbers of individuals, but rather in percentages.

The latest published *Baccalaureate and Beyond Longitudinal Studies* show that 12.2 percent of baccalaureate degree recipients in 1999-2000 had taught as regular teachers "in a K- 12 school at some point between receiving the 1999-2000 bachelor's degree and the 2001 interview" (USDoE, 2000/01, 5).

Given that NCES data show that 1,237,875 bachelor's degrees were awarded by degree-granting institutions in 1999-2000, one could estimate that 151,000 new graduates were teaching *at some point* within a year of receiving their baccalaureate degree.

The data indicate that, of those 151,000 who received a bachelor's degree in 1999-2000 and were teaching in 2001, 21 percent were neither certified nor had prepared to teach as part of their undergraduate program. It is conceivable that some of these individuals were becoming certified to teach through alternate route programs.

NCES data also show that more than one-third (35 percent) of Education Bachelor's Degree recipients in 1999-2000 were not teaching the following year. Furthermore, the data indicate that one-fourth (25 percent) of education bachelors' degree recipients in 1999-2000 had not even prepared to teach and/or were not certified to teach.

Fewer than half (47.5 percent) of graduates with education degrees in 1992-93 were teaching in 1994.

Furthermore, of the B.A. recipients who *were* certified and/or had prepared to teach as part of their undergraduate program, 23 percent were not teaching within a year of graduating.

A follow-up survey in 1997 of 1992-93 baccalaureate degree recipients indicated that 13 percent of those graduates had taught by 1997. However, the B&B follow-up report also stated that "8 percent expected to teach full-time in three years and 7 percent expected to teach in the longer term. Thus, it appears that many graduates who teach soon after college do not expect to spend much time teaching, let alone make it a career" (USDoE, 2000-152, x).

These statistics lead one to question the efficiency of the model for teacher production. The problem is further compounded by NCES data that show that about one-third of these new teachers leave within the first three years of teaching, and about half of them have left teaching after five years.

Alternative routes to teacher certification programs, on the other hand, accept only individuals who not only already have a bachelor's degree, but come into a program because *they want to teach.* In most alternate route programs, the participants fill particular existing teacher vacancies. Alternative routes exist to recruit, train and certify baccalaureate degree holders to meet the demand for specific teachers to teach specific subjects at specific grade levels in specific schools.

The retention rate for alternate route teachers in California and other large teacher-production states is 85-90 percent after five years.

B. School District Size and Student Enrollment.

The sizes of school districts and where students are enrolled vary greatly and bear directly on teacher demand.

National Center for Education Statistics (NCES) data indicate there were 14,383 regular public school districts in 2003-04. *Fewer than 2 percent of these school districts enrolled one- third of all the students enrolled in the United States.* These are the 256 school districts that enroll 25,000 or more students. When the next category of school districts by size is added – those that enroll between 10,000 and 24,999 – 587 additional school districts enter the count, taking the number of school districts that enroll 10,000 or more students to 843; these school districts represent just *6 percent of all school districts that enroll more than half (52.1 percent) of all the public elementary and secondary students.*

At the other end of the spectrum, more than one-fifth (2,994) of all school districts enroll between 1 and 299 students each and account for less than 1 percent of all students enrolled. *Nearly half of all school districts (6,703 or 46.6 percent) enroll fewer than 1,000 students each, and collectively account for only 5.5 percent of total public elementary and secondary school enrollment across the nation.*

Since these local school districts are responsible for hiring and placing teachers, it is obvious that the needs and demands for teachers in a metropolitan school district with a diverse population that includes several hundred schools, each of which likely enrolls anywhere from fewer than 100 students to more than 3,000 are different from a school district that has a handful of small schools in a rural predominantly white community.

Alternate routes, again, by their very nature, address such disparities. Alternate routes are created to meet specific needs for specific teachers in specific areas.

C. Public School Size and Student Enrollment

NCES data indicate that *more than one in 10 (11.02 percent) of all schools and nearly 17 percent of secondary schools enroll fewer than 100 students each.*

Furthermore, *more than one-third (35.89 percent) of public secondary schools enroll fewer than 300 students each.* These statistics are crucial in any discussion about out-of-field teaching or having a teacher with a major or minor teaching every class in ever school in the country. In these small schools, generally there is no more than one physics class, one chemistry class and one biology class per day. The chances that a teacher with a major or minor in each of these sciences will be teaching each of those three classes per day in each of these schools are slim to none.

Many alternative routes to teacher certification meet the needs for highly qualified teachers in these and other high demand subjects, such as special education, in small schools by targeting programs that ensure that teachers have – or obtain – content and pedagogical mastery in the subjects they are teaching. Alternate routes that utilize technology and distance learning opportunities are likely to appeal to the needs of small schools

D. Teacher Vacancies (Demand)

The 2003-04 SASS data (2006-3 13) also show that the demand for teachers, as indicated by vacancies in schools and subjects, is greatest:
In schools

- at the secondary level,
- in central cities and urban fringe/large towns,
- that enroll 750 or more students;

In subjects of

- Special education,
- English/language arts,
- Mathematics,
- Sciences, and

- Foreign languages.

All of these statistics are important in understanding the context in which teachers are recruited, prepared and hired.

Alternate route programs, by their very nature, are established to meet specific needs for specific teachers in specific subject areas in specific schools.

The targeted nature of alternate routes is the reason they are proliferating at a rapid rate, why thousands of people who would not otherwise have done so are choosing to become teachers.

RECOMMENDATIONS

I urge the Congress in its reauthorization of Title II of the Higher Education Act (HEA) and of Title II of No child Left Behind (NCLB) to make changes that reflect the significant and growing role alternate routes have in bringing high quality individuals into the teaching profession who – without them – would not otherwise become teachers. As I have documented earlier in this statement, these competent teachers make a commitment to teach in classrooms where teachers are most needed. They now constitute one-third of all new teachers being hired.

The Federal government needs to target the nation's resources so that the most qualified individuals who intend to teach can do so in high-quality efficient programs that meet the need for specific teachers in specific subjects in specific schools across this nation. Both HEA and NCLB are the very vehicles to ensure that programs of preparation are created and/or enhanced to attract highly qualified, experienced adults who know their subject matter and are eager to use their life experiences and practical knowledge to – as they report themselves – "help young people learn and develop."

Specific recommendations in the reauthorization of the Higher Education Act and No Child Left Behind are:

1. Shift the focus in the preparation of teachers from institutions of higher education exclusively to a wide variety of providers of recruitment and preparation programs that are targeted to actually producing effective teachers in the classrooms where they are needed.
2. Encourage school districts and state departments to collect and disseminate data about their teachers, including their preparation to teach and their effectiveness.
3. Encourage research that could be utilized by the public as well as researchers and policymakers that would yield answers to such critical questions as, "What makes for truly effective teachers and how do they come by those qualities?"
4. Funding should be more market-driven and flow to programs that are proving their effectiveness in recruiting and preparing competent teachers where they are needed.
5. One of the chief contributions of alternate routes to teaching has been infusing the teacher workforce with experienced adults that have earned valuable life skill equity. The federal government should encourage initiatives that help transition more of these people into teaching, particularly in high schools, where there is a need for their

applied knowledge. With their real world experience base and maturity, alternate route teachers can do much to accelerate the development of skills high school students need to excel in college and the workforce.

6. The federal government should create incentives for states and school districts to expand alternate routes to solve particular shortfalls in highly qualified areas. Alternate routes have been a wonderful incubator for innovation in addressing niche teaching shortages with highly qualified teachers. A market driven environment needs to be encouraged not stifled by attempts to standardize or develop regulations constricting experimentation with alternate routes.

Thank you for this opportunity to speak before you today.

CHAPTER SOURCES

The following chapters have been previously published:

Chapter 1 – This is an edited, reformatted and augmented version of a Congressional Research Service, Report R40514, dated January 26, 2010.

Chapter 2 – This is an edited, reformatted and augmented version of a Congressional Research Service, Report RL33333, dated April 2, 2009.

Chapter 3 – This is an edited, reformatted and augmented version of a Congressional Research Service, Report R41051, dated January 26, 2010.

Chapter 4 – This is an edited reformatted and augmented version of United States Government Accountability Office, Report GAO-09-593, dated July 2009.

Chapter 5 – This is an edited reformatted and augmented version of United States Government Accountability Office, Report GAO-10-18, dated November 2009.

Chapter 6 – These remarks were delivered as testimony given on May 17, 2007. Rubén Hinojosa, United States Representative, before the United States House of Representatives, Subcommittee on Higher Education, Lifelong Learning, and Competitiveness, Committee on Education and Labor.

Chapter 7 – These remarks were delivered as a testimony given on May 17, 2007. George A. Scott, Director, Education, Workforce, and Income Security Issues, before the United States House of Representatives, Subcommittee on Higher Education, Lifelong Learning, and Competitiveness, Committee on Education and Labor.

Chapter 8 – These remarks were delivered as a testimony given on May 17, 2007. Sharon P. Robinson, American Association of Colleges for Teacher Education, President and CEO, before the United States House of Representatives, Subcommittee on Higher Education, Lifelong Learning, and Competitiveness, Committee on Education and Labor.

Chapter 9 – These remarks were delivered as a testimony given on May 17, 2007. Janice Wiley, Deputy Director, Instructional Support Services of the Region One Education Service Center, before the United States House of Representatives, Subcommittee on Higher Education, Lifelong Learning, and Competitiveness, Committee on Education and Labor.

Chapter 10 – These remarks were delivered as a testimony given on May 17, 2007. Daniel Fallon, Director, Program in Higher Education at Carnegie Corporation of New York, before the United States House of Representatives, Subcommittee on Higher Education, Lifelong Learning, and Competitiveness, Committee on Education and Labor.

Chapter 11 – These remarks were delivered as a testimony given on May 17, 2007. Emily Feistritzer, President, National Center for Alternative Certification and the National Center for Education Information, before the United States House of Representatives, Subcommittee on Higher Education, Lifelong Learning, and Competitiveness, Committee on Education and Labor.

INDEX

A

AAS, 27, 28, 37, 40
academic growth, 81, 100
academic performance, ix, 64, 122, 135, 137, 169
academic success, 65
accessibility, 27
accreditation, 179
accuracy, 109, 152
achievement test, 2, 8
adjustment, 74
administration, 8, 10, 12, 14, 16, 24, 30, 39, 74, 92, 118
administrators, 5, 7, 15, 16, 17, 24, 32, 44, 67, 68, 69, 113, 114, 120, 160, 171, 184
adult, 119, 121
adult education, 121
adult literacy, 119, 121
advocacy, 118
AEP, vii, 1, 2, 12, 156
African-American, 160
after-*school*, 118, 140, 153
age, 5, 8, 36, 111, 112, 119, 121
agent, 112
aid, 77
air, 40
Alaskan Native, 160
alternative, viii, 5, 33, 47, 48, 51, 57, 58, 59, 61, 73, 81, 83, 85, 95, 111, 132, 171, 193, 194, 195, 196, 197, 199
amendments, 53, 54, 168
American Educational Research Association, 196
American History, 87, 91, 92, 95, 96, 117, 185
American Indian, 118, 160
American Recovery and Reinvestment Act, ix, 57, 59, 78, 79, 89, 117, 132, 148
analysts, 68, 70, 71, 72, 108, 190
APA, 39

appendix, 80, 104, 148, 149, 153, 160
application, 10, 46, 54, 68, 112, 147, 149, 171, 172, 192
applied research, 38
appropriations, 89, 110, 111, 112, 113, 114, 115, 116
arithmetic, 36, 38
armed forces, 113
Armed Forces, 113
Asian, 160
assessment requirements, 161
assessment tools, 13
assignment, 55, 73
assumptions, 25
attacks, 195
attitudes, 16
auditing, 80, 106, 167
authority, 47, 52, 53, 54, 82, 83, 106, 108, 123, 131, 133
authors, 5, 15, 143
autism, 13

B

baby boom, 81
barrier, 105, 146
battery, 13
beginning teachers, 178, 182, 184, 185
behavior, 4, 13, 16, 97, 149
beliefs, 101, 145
benchmark, 3, 5, 6, 7, 10, 15, 24, 34, 39
benefits, 122, 145
bias, 21, 22, 25, 26, 29, 30, 34, 36, 65, 67, 74
bilingual, 118
bipartisan, 12
blindness, 13
bonus, 68
borrowing, 18

206 Index

brain, 13, 184
brain injury, 13
budget cuts, 100

C

candidates, 44, 81, 95, 170, 171, 177, 178, 179, 180, 181, 190
capacity building, 29, 73
category a, 25
cation, 113
cell, 152
census, 54, 55
Census Bureau, 54, 55
central city, 54, 141, 152, 153, 160
CEO, vi, 177, 203
certification, viii, 43, 44, 45, 46, 47, 48, 50, 51, 53, 54, 81, 82, 83, 87, 95, 96, 101, 106, 111, 113, 114, 116, 132, 164, 169, 170, 171, 180, 181, 193, 194, 195, 196, 197, 198, 199
cheating, 33, 36, 67
childhood, 115, 118, 119, 121
children, 31, 33, 81, 89, 94, 95, 103, 111, 115, 116, 117, 118, 119, 120, 121, 122, 123, 124, 140, 153, 169, 185, 189, 192
citizens, 81, 187, 188, 189
city, 127, 196
clarity, 197
class period, 183
class size, 164, 167, 169, 170, 174, 185
classes, 50, 51, 52, 83, 155, 173, 175, 177, 199
classical, 37
classification, 19, 21
classroom management, 147
classroom practice, 6, 81, 97, 145
classroom settings, 53
classroom teacher, 23, 60, 62, 63, 97, 110
clients, 190
clinician, 190
clusters, 28
coaches, 170
codes, 54
coding, 156
cognitive ability, 8
cognitive function, 4, 13
cohort, 172
collaboration, ix, 27, 29, 77, 78, 80, 89, 90, 100, 101, 103, 104, 106, 108, 120, 131, 173, 184
college students, 170

colleges, 94, 95, 171, 174, 177, 178, 179, 180, 184, 189, 190
Committee on Appropriations, 150
communication, 102, 171
community, 65, 71, 111, 112, 115, 121, 123, 148, 170, 178, 184, 188, 199
compensation, viii, 57, 58, 67, 70, 71, 73, 89, 111
competency, viii, x, 13, 14, 43, 44, 46, 47, 48, 121, 165, 166, 170, 173, 174
competition, 60, 75, 88, 115, 117, 133
competitive process, 83
competitiveness, 188
competitor, 179
compilation, 54
complement, 166, 174, 188
complexity, 27, 28, 71
compliance, 92, 93
components, ix, 14, 45, 58, 59, 64, 180
comprehension, 8, 28
computation, 23
concentration, 164, 178
conception, 189
confidence, 20, 26, 34, 37, 39, 153, 189
confidence interval, 20, 26, 34, 37, 39
confidentiality, 70, 72
configuration, 80, 90
conflict, 66
confusion, 5, 68
congress, iv, v, viii, ix, x, 1, 21, 30, 39, 43, 44, 45, 52, 57, 58, 60, 73, 102, 132, 138, 164, 165, 166, 168, 172, 173, 180, 200
conjecture, 149
consensus, 9, 10, 22, 81, 188, 195
consent, 188
Consolidated Appropriations Act, ix, 135, 137
constraints, 54
construction, 30
content analysis, 108
contractors, 12
contracts, 94
control, 6, 10, 60, 62, 68, 74, 82, 146, 152, 155, 160
control group, 152, 155
conversion, 74
cooperative learning, 147
correlation, 19, 35, 69, 141
cost saving, 192
cost-effective, 8, 9, 173
costs, 78, 95, 102, 119, 188
counseling, 113, 118, 122
coupling, 190

Index

course work, 46
covariate, 61, 62, 64, 74
covering, 167
creativity, 29, 147
credentials, 44, 175
credit, 33, 184, 196
critical thinking, 8, 17, 29, 145
critical thinking skills, 17, 145
criticism, 9, 22, 31, 32, 195
cross-program, 78, 104
cross-sectional, 189
CRS, 1, 38, 40, 41, 43, 51, 54, 55, 57, 73, 74
CRT, 8, 9, 12, 24, 37
cultural factors, 65
culture, 65
current account, 73, 136, 145, 150
curricula, 15, 122, 123, 152, 153, 181
curriculum change, 150
curriculum development, 106, 110, 115, 120
customers, 90

D

data analysis, 71, 99, 157
data collection, 70, 72, 99, 138, 151, 152, 172
data set, 133
database, 62, 63, 70, 151
deafness, 13
debt, 179
decision making, 4, 29
decisions, 6, 10, 17, 19, 21, 22, 26, 33, 35, 62, 63, 64, 66, 67, 69, 70, 71, 75, 145
declassification, 21
deficits, 5, 15
definition, viii, ix, 5, 9, 13, 14, 36, 39, 44, 45, 46, 52, 53, 55, 58, 59, 61, 73, 85, 90, 119, 172, 173, 174
delivery, 5, 87
demographic characteristics, 8, 36, 141, 161, 183
Demonstration Project, 127
Department of the Interior, 113, 114
deviation, 8, 36, 37, 38, 39
diffusion, 187
digital technologies, 40
diplomas, 15, 21
direct measure, 44
directors, 99
disability, 13, 21, 22, 30, 36, 40, 60, 61, 62, 63, 64, 72, 74
disadvantaged students, 18, 22, 23, 31, 32, 33, 45
discontinuity, 155

discourse, 147
discretionary, 26, 59, 85, 107, 193
dispersion, 36, 37, 38
disseminate, 103, 174, 188, 200
distance learning, 199
distribution, 36, 45, 83, 99, 164, 179
diversity, 65, 80, 109, 122, 138, 151, 164
division, 18, 19, 110
draft, 89, 104, 108, 148
duplication, 99
duties, 53

E

ears, 161
economically disadvantaged, 32
economics, 46, 47, 53, 55, 73, 124, 132
editors, 161
education reform, 60, 133, 188
educational assessment, vii, 1, 2, 4, 7, 10, 17, 19, 20, 21, 22, 23, 30, 34, 37
educational experience, 60
educational practices, 85
educational programs, 121, 123
educational services, 115
educational settings, 46, 69, 72
educators, 8, 9, 12, 16, 78, 79, 94, 97, 98, 115, 124, 133, 179
electronic systems, 93
Elementary and Secondary Education Act, vii, viii, 1, 2, 37, 44, 57, 58, 78, 79, 110, 112, 124, 137, 138, 167, 189
elementary school, viii, 43, 44, 45, 46, 52, 62, 161
elementary students, 21
elementary teachers, 53, 149, 161
eligibility criteria, 14
ELL, 61, 63, 64, 72, 74, 181
e-mail, 108, 109
emotional, 13
employers, 178
employment, 113
engagement, 138
English Language, 84, 91, 96, 107, 111, 120, 127
English Language Learner, 127
English language proficiency, 68
enrollment, 15, 83, 199
enterprise, 178, 188, 192
environment, 22, 23, 64, 65, 201
equality, 21, 22
equating, 25

208 Index

equity, 22, 27, 30, 32, 33, 122, 200
ERA, 190, 196
estimating, 60, 63, 69, 71
ethnic groups, 32
ethnic minority, 36
ethnicity, 8, 63, 67, 68
Even Start, 119, 121, 124
evidence-based program, 190, 192
examinations, 5, 179
exclusion, 100
expenditures, 89, 119, 166
experimental condition, 73
experimental design, 155, 157
expertise, 44, 48, 53, 70, 90, 99, 104, 108, 112, 117, 133, 163
exposure, 23
external validity, 155

F

factor analysis, 157
failure, 23
fairness, vii, 1, 2, 17, 21, 22, 23, 25, 30, 34, 35, 39
faith, 49, 112, 115
family, 62, 63, 72, 119, 121, 124, 183, 189
family literacy, 119, 121, 124
federal funds, 49, 83, 93, 94, 167, 174
federal government, ix, 72, 83, 85, 135, 137, 166, 173, 178, 179, 180, 181, 200, 201
federal law, vii, 1, 2, 10, 14, 80, 85, 106, 107, 138, 152
Federal Register, 46, 73
feedback, 5, 32, 100, 101, 108, 173, 184
finance, 124
financial aid, 187
financial support, 78, 100
first-time, 178
flexibility, 13, 46, 47, 48, 49, 52, 54, 55, 95, 166, 167, 169
flow, 200
fluctuations, 21, 36
focusing, 4, 31, 79, 80, 94, 106, 136, 138, 140, 142, 146, 151, 164, 172
foreign language, 32, 46, 53, 73, 116, 123, 132
funding, vii, 1, 2, 12, 45, 49, 52, 59, 72, 73, 78, 79, 80, 83, 85, 86, 87, 89, 94, 99, 102, 103, 104, 109, 115, 117, 132, 133, 167, 168, 169, 172, 174, 179, 181
futures, 81

G

gauge, 62, 65
gender, 8, 12, 68, 122
gender equity, 122
general education, 190
General Education Provisions Act, 55
general knowledge, 23
generalizability, 35
generation, 81, 189
geography, 12, 46, 53, 55, 66, 73, 132
gifted, 123
girls, 97, 122
global economy, 59
goals, vii, viii, 1, 2, 3, 5, 7, 15, 33, 43, 44, 57, 58, 74, 84, 86, 90, 92, 93, 95, 98, 102, 104, 105, 106, 132, 139, 147, 163, 164, 167, 172, 173
governance, 82, 99, 100, 106, 108, 131, 133
government, iv, ix, x, 46, 53, 72, 73, 77, 80, 83, 85, 106, 132, 135, 137, 165, 166, 167, 173, 178, 179, 180, 181, 189, 200, 201
Government Performance and Results Act, 78, 90, 132
governors, 12
grades, vii, 1, 2, 8, 11, 12, 16, 28, 48, 62, 66, 89, 112, 139, 160, 161, 169, 185
grants, viii, 27, 39, 57, 58, 73, 78, 83, 85, 86, 89, 91, 92, 93, 97, 103, 107, 113, 114, 115, 117, 119, 120, 121, 122, 123, 129, 166, 167, 168, 169, 171, 172, 174, 182, 192
group work, 144
groups, 8, 12, 18, 32, 39, 53, 67, 71, 83, 89, 102, 106, 139, 145, 152, 155, 174, 189, 190, 196
growth, ix, 9, 19, 24, 25, 28, 33, 58, 59, 60, 63, 70, 73, 81, 83, 100
guidance, 23, 27, 45, 46, 47, 48, 49, 51, 53, 54, 67, 80, 92, 102, 107, 122, 133, 147, 166, 167, 170, 171, 172
guidelines, 12, 13, 23, 29, 136, 144

H

Head Start, 121, 124, 125, 127
health, 13, 65, 118
Health and Human Services, 150
health problems, 65
health services, 118
hearing, 13, 65, 163, 167
hearing impairment, 13

high school, vii, 1, 2, 6, 10, 11, 14, 15, 17, 18, 21, 22, 26, 66, 103, 117, 133, 157, 160, 171, 178, 183, 184, 200

Higher Education Act, v, vi, x, 79, 85, 115, 163, 164, 165, 166, 180, 181, 182, 183, 187, 189, 193, 200

higher-order thinking, 29, 144, 147

hiring, x, 44, 48, 132, 165, 166, 168, 199

hispanic, 160, 183

homework, 137

hospitals, 177, 178

House, v, x, 41, 79, 137, 150, 163, 203, 204

House Appropriations Committee, 137

human, 70, 72

human capital, 71

human resources, 70

I

ideal, 74, 189

identification, 3, 72, 190

identity, 191

IES, 75, 79, 97, 129, 133

IHEs, 110, 111, 112, 113, 114, 117, 123

illusions, 188

images, 82, 141, 143

Impact Aid, 84

impairments, 13

implementation, vii, viii, ix, 6, 43, 44, 45, 46, 48, 49, 52, 57, 58, 59, 60, 70, 71, 89, 92, 94, 95, 96, 105, 115, 121, 122, 124, 167, 172, 173, 184, 192

Improving America's Schools Act (IASA), 137, 138, 139, 161

incentive, 59, 192

incidence, 116

income, 111, 115, 119, 120, 137, 139, 160, 169

increased access, 33, 120

Indian, 84, 88, 91, 96, 113, 114, 118, 119, 120, 121, 122, 123

indication, 140

indicators, vii, 1, 2, 24, 31, 68, 81, 92

indices, 68

individual students, 5, 6, 12, 14, 15, 16, 24, 62, 83, 133

Individuals with Disabilities Education Act (IDEA), vii, 1, 2, 13, 30, 37, 39, 40, 54, 85, 116

induction, 81, 82, 87, 95, 96, 101, 188, 190, 192

industry, 5

inequality, 74, 189

inferences, 17, 22, 23, 26, 31, 34

inflation, 31, 33, 34, 36, 67, 74

information sharing, 103

Information System, 41

innovation, vii, 1, 2, 3, 26, 27, 29, 133, 201

insight, 92

Inspector General, 79, 89, 107, 132

institutions of higher education, x, 78, 79, 81, 82, 83, 85, 86, 89, 90, 103, 104, 106, 112, 118, 121, 132, 165, 166, 167, 168, 171, 173, 174, 188, 190, 191, 200

instruction time, 161

instructional activities, 142

instructional materials, 115

instructional methods, 110

instructional practice, ix, 79, 135, 136, 137, 138, 139, 142, 143, 145, 146, 147, 148, 150, 151, 159, 161, 182

instructional skills, 169

instructional time, 32, 33, 140, 148, 149, 153, 161

instruments, 27, 99

integration, 110, 122, 131

intentions, 33

interactions, 146

internal consistency, 19, 35

Internet, 78, 80, 87, 93, 97, 107, 129, 177

internship, 95

interrelationships, 173

interval, 20, 34

intervention, 116, 133

interview, 99, 197

investment, x, 29, 70, 164, 165, 166, 179, 180, 181, 189, 191

ions, 114

isolation, 121

ivory, 178

J

job training, 195

jobs, 179, 197

judgment, 7, 8, 9, 10

K

key indicators, vii, 1, 2, 31

kindergarten, 78, 79, 106, 108, 121, 124, 131, 133

knowledge-based economy, 81, 188, 189

L

labor, 15
laminated, 191
language, 4, 10, 13, 14, 28, 32, 46, 53, 61, 63, 65, 68, 73, 95, 111, 116, 121, 122, 123, 132, 152, 153, 160, 161, 182, 199
language barrier, 65
language development, 95
language impairment, 13
language proficiency, 68
language skills, 14, 121
large-scale, ix, 5, 29, 30, 58, 60, 63, 67, 70, 71
Latino, 128, 160
law, vii, viii, 1, 2, 10, 13, 14, 39, 43, 44, 48, 49, 50, 52, 85, 141, 174, 180
LEA, 11, 13, 27, 37, 48
leadership, 115, 118
learners, 111, 177, 179, 181, 182, 183
learning disabilities, 13
learning process, 4, 35, 136, 145, 147
legislation, vii, 1, 2, 90, 168
lesson plan, 3, 148
liberal, 103, 195
licenses, 71, 113
licensing, viii, 43, 44, 46, 170, 171, 179, 195
life experiences, 200
lifetime, 184, 187
likelihood, 3, 5, 6, 15, 17, 19, 20, 25, 34, 72, 151
limitation, 149, 156
line, 4, 182
linear, 75, 156, 157
linear model, 75, 156, 157
linguistic, 22
linkage, 31, 84
links, 31, 73, 102, 147, 174
listening, 14, 94, 147
literacy, 16, 24, 95, 111, 112, 119, 121, 124, 152, 153
local government, x, 165, 166
location, 80, 109, 138, 140, 142, 143, 151, 152
low-income, 111, 115, 119, 120, 137, 139, 160

M

magnet, 121, 122
malnutrition, 65
management, 83, 92, 93, 94, 103, 147, 172, 174, 192
mandates, 94

market, 15, 71, 81, 195, 200, 201
MAS, 27, 28, 37
mastery, 8, 9, 195, 199
mathematics, vii, ix, 1, 2, 6, 11, 12, 14, 15, 16, 19, 23, 24, 30, 31, 32, 46, 53, 63, 66, 69, 73, 77, 79, 96, 97, 110, 116, 121, 123, 132, 133, 142, 148, 150, 153, 161, 178, 188
measures, vii, ix, 1, 2, 18, 27, 29, 34, 35, 36, 37, 44, 47, 58, 59, 67, 68, 70, 72, 73, 75, 83, 92, 139, 151, 166, 167, 172, 174, 180, 191, 196
media, 6, 87, 115, 120, 124
median, 39
medicine, 177
membership, 22
mental retardation, 13
mentor, 88, 112, 170, 184, 195
mentor program, 184
mentoring, 81, 87, 88, 95, 101, 170, 179, 182, 184, 190, 196
meta-analysis, 155, 156, 157
metric, 9, 12, 30, 133
mid-career, 111, 166, 170, 177
middle schools, 151, 157, 160
migrant, 118, 121, 183
military, 113
minority, 33, 36, 67, 68, 79, 81, 121, 136, 137, 138, 139, 140, 141, 142, 143, 151, 152, 153, 160, 161, 163, 164
minority students, 33, 137, 139, 140, 160, 163
misleading, 31, 173
missions, 101
misunderstanding, 7
mobility, 65, 68
model, 60, 61, 62, 63, 64, 66, 67, 68, 72, 73, 74, 83, 100, 115, 122, 124, 194, 198
model specification, 68
money, 148, 191
mothers, 81
motivation, 64, 147
motor skills, 13
movement, 14, 25, 181, 195
multicultural, 118
multiple factors, 60, 160
multiple regression, 155
multiplication, 18, 19
multivariate, 74, 152, 160
music, 66, 87, 115

N

nation, ix, x, 12, 50, 72, 77, 79, 83, 115, 157, 165, 166, 173, 177, 179, 182, 188, 192, 195, 199, 200

National Academy of Sciences, 96

National Assessment of Educational Progress, vii, 1, 2, 12, 37, 156

National Center for Education Statistics, 39, 50, 51, 84, 133, 160, 161, 163, 198

National Research Council, 30, 133, 188

National Science Foundation, 137, 138, 151, 160, 161

Native American, 120, 122

Native Hawaiian, 120, 122, 123, 160

NCES, 39, 55, 160, 197, 198, 199

NCL, 160

NCLB, vii, viii, 1, 2, 4, 6, 9, 11, 12, 14, 15, 20, 27, 29, 30, 31, 32, 33, 38, 41, 43, 44, 45, 46, 47, 49, 50, 51, 52, 53, 54, 55, 57, 58, 66, 73, 131, 137, 138, 139, 140, 141, 150, 152, 153, 159, 180, 181, 195, 200

need-based, 187

negative consequences, 7, 136

negative influences, 149

network, 38, 99, 103, 184

non-random, 157

Northeast, 38

NRTs, 7, 8, 9, 11, 14, 24

O

objectives, ix, 6, 26, 48, 72, 77, 80, 83, 85, 92, 100, 105, 132, 138, 149, 150, 151

observations, 184, 197

odds ratio, 152

Office of Management and Budget, 132, 172, 173, 174

Office of Vocational and Adult Education, 84

Omnibus Appropriations Act,, 133

online, 54, 171

on-the-job training, 195

order, 4, 5, 6, 7, 11, 14, 29, 35, 71, 116, 131, 136, 139, 146, 147, 149, 152, 171, 172, 173, 174, 179, 184

Organization for Economic Cooperation and Development, 16

orientation, 81, 88

outcome of interest, 18, 64

oversight, 139, 173

P

PACE, 41

Pacific Islander, 122, 160

Pacific Region, 115

paradigm shift, 189

parameters, 161

parenting, 121

parents, 8, 9, 71, 140, 153, 180

partnership, 92, 95, 103, 111, 112, 113, 114, 115, 168, 169, 172, 174, 181, 185

pass/fail, 8, 21

pathways, 95, 196

PCT, 41

pedagogical, 44, 181, 199

peer, 108

peer review, 108

Pell Grants, 187

penalties, 49

pension, 187

percentile, 39

perception, 197

personally identifiable information, 70, 71

philanthropic, 187, 188, 191

physical education, 121

physics, 199

pilot studies, 191

PISA, 16, 24, 38, 39

planning, 9, 68, 90, 92, 105, 148

platforms, 87

play, ix, 77, 80, 83, 166, 173

policy community, 188

policy makers, viii, 57, 58, 61, 62, 67, 68, 69, 70, 73, 193

poor, 26, 52, 54, 163

population, 18, 21, 30, 35, 36, 54, 74, 80, 109, 136, 160, 183, 199

portfolio, 26, 28, 145

portfolio assessment, 28

positive influences, 150

postsecondary education, 15, 78, 85, 89, 100, 117, 124

poverty, 52, 54, 79, 81, 84, 85, 115, 119, 120, 121, 131, 136, 138, 139, 140, 141, 142, 143, 151, 152, 153, 160, 161, 164, 166, 175, 197

poverty line, 119, 120

poverty rate, 85

practical knowledge, 200

predictive validity, 7

premium, 180

preschool, 21, 111, 118, 121
preschool children, 118
president, 188, 193
pressure, 32, 183
prevention, 118, 121, 124
privacy, 71, 72, 100, 103
private, 22, 111, 112, 115, 117, 123, 196
probability, 26
problem solving, 8, 23, 29, 144, 145, 147, 148, 184
production, 146, 188, 198
professional qualifications, 174
professional teacher, 113, 114
professions, 113, 168, 179
profit, 111, 117
Program Assessment Rating Too (PART), 172, 173, 174
program outcomes, 94, 132
programming, 113, 114
property, iv, 17
protection, 71, 72
protocols, 99
psychometric properties, 62
public, 10, 12, 33, 44, 45, 48, 50, 68, 79, 82, 85, 111, 112, 115, 117, 118, 119, 121, 122, 123, 133, 160, 166, 171, 173, 177, 178, 182, 189, 191, 198, 199, 200
public education, 33, 119, 122
public schools, 50, 121, 160, 171, 177, 182, 189
publishers, 5
pupil, 188, 189, 190, 191, 192
pupil achievement, 189

Q

qualifications, viii, 43, 50, 57, 58, 79, 81, 85, 95, 96, 132, 166, 172, 173, 174
quality improvement, 78, 92, 101, 104, 105, 106
quality of life, 189
quality research, 129, 161
quality standards, 45
quartile, 39
Quasi-experimental design, 155, 157
questioning, 3, 5
questionnaire, 108

R

race, 63
random, 10, 64, 73, 74, 155

random assignment, 73, 155
range, vii, 1, 2, 5, 8, 10, 18, 19, 20, 21, 34, 36, 80, 87, 101, 108, 138, 140, 151, 166, 167, 169
rating scale, 9
reading assessment, 13, 22, 63
reading comprehension, 28
reading skills, 63
reality, 4, 9, 63, 65
reasoning, 8, 25, 29, 144
reasoning skills, 29
reciprocity, 170
recruiting, 59, 87, 95, 164, 179, 194, 200
reflection, 147
Reform Act, 79, 85
reforms, 44, 121, 131, 133, 169, 170, 173, 177, 178
region, 99, 103, 133
regional, 49, 78, 80, 93, 97, 98, 103, 106, 111, 115
regression, 74, 155
regular, 63, 89, 99, 104, 118, 197, 198
regulation, 45, 46, 49, 51, 83
regulatory requirements, 83, 132
relationship, 7, 15, 38, 95, 97, 148, 182, 190
reliability, vii, 1, 2, 17, 18, 19, 20, 21, 23, 25, 26, 34, 35, 36, 37, 62, 74, 145, 151
relief, 54
reparation, 81, 84
requirements, 38, 62, 70, 74, 132, 174, 196
research and development, 26, 71
research design, 99
resistance, 100
resources, 33, 41, 55, 65, 70, 78, 90, 92, 99, 100, 102, 104, 105, 148, 171, 172, 173, 187, 188, 192, 200
response format, 145
responsibilities, 82, 83, 90, 102, 105
restructuring, 137, 141
retardation, 13
retention, 87, 95, 96, 101, 106, 111, 169, 170, 178, 181, 185, 197, 198
rewards, 6
risk, 92, 93, 142, 143
risk management, 92
rubrics, 9, 10
rural, 48, 52, 53, 54, 119, 132, 138, 140, 151, 152, 160, 181, 182, 199
rural areas, 54, 160, 182
rust, 109

S

safeguards, 191

salary, 68, 170

sample, 8, 9, 12, 16, 22, 23, 24, 28, 35, 38, 55, 108, 180

sample survey, 108

sampling error, 108

SAS, 75

SAT scores, 178

savings, 192

scaling, 66

scholarships, 170, 181

school activities, 65

school climate, 72

school enrollment, 199

Schools and Staffing Survey, 50, 51, 133, 149, 161, 163

science department, 110

science literacy, 16

scores, 7, 8, 9, 12, 13, 14, 15, 16, 18, 19, 20, 21, 22, 23, 24, 25, 26, 27, 28, 30, 31, 33, 34, 35, 36, 37, 38, 39, 62, 63, 66, 67, 68, 72, 74, 83, 100, 145, 149, 178, 189

SEA, 11, 30, 38, 45, 47, 48, 79, 83, 97, 98, 101, 106, 108, 109, 110, 111, 112, 113, 114, 115, 116, 123

search, 155

secondary education, x, 115, 117, 123, 165, 166

secondary school students, vii, 1, 2, 117, 121, 123

secondary schools, vii, 1, 2, 3, 10, 52, 72, 84, 106, 110, 121, 199

secondary students, 95, 198

security, 70

selecting, 12

self-contained classrooms, 53

self-report, 32

SEM, 20

Senate, 137, 150

series, ii, 12, 49, 55, 83, 156, 157, 173

service provider, 98

services, iv, 3, 4, 10, 13, 14, 21, 22, 39, 93, 96, 97, 98, 115, 116, 118, 119, 121, 122, 124, 133, 148, 170, 189, 191

SES, 196

shaping, 192

shares, 32

sharing, 77, 93, 103, 104, 105

short period, 20, 21

shortage, 45, 113, 132, 181, 185

short-term, 6, 54, 72, 78, 104

sites, 107, 151, 157, 170, 178

skills, 8, 13, 14, 17, 18, 19, 21, 28, 29, 35, 40, 45, 47, 63, 71, 85, 94, 110, 112, 113, 114, 118, 120, 121, 122, 132, 136, 144, 145, 147, 160, 169, 171, 179, 180, 201

social competence, 4

social work, 113, 114

social workers, 113, 114

socioeconomic, 36, 60, 61, 62, 63, 64, 65, 67, 68, 72, 74

socioeconomic status, 36, 60, 61, 62, 63, 64, 65, 67, 68, 72, 74

sociologist, 189

software, 71, 72, 75, 96

sounds, 94

special education, 4, 10, 13, 21, 39, 46, 54, 63, 79, 85, 113, 116, 119, 181, 182, 199

spectrum, 198

speech, 13, 119

sporadic, 81

SSI, 160

stability, 19, 20, 37, 69

staffing, 100

stakeholder, 102

stakeholder groups, 102

standard deviation, 8, 36, 37, 38, 39

standard error, 20, 36, 39, 151

standard of living, 189

standardized testing, 33

standards-based assessments, 11, 137

State Grants, 48, 91, 92, 94, 96, 97, 110, 120

statistics, 85, 197, 198, 199, 200

statutes, 79, 88

statutory, 55, 72, 90, 132

STEM, 79, 91, 96, 116, 182, 184

STEM fields, 116

strategies, ix, 3, 5, 13, 33, 78, 81, 97, 104, 111, 112, 122, 123, 135, 136, 137, 138, 139, 140, 141, 142, 143, 146, 151, 152, 153, 160, 184

strategy use, 146

strength, 38, 44, 151

student characteristics, 68

student group, 67, 83

student motivation, 64

student populations, 132, 136, 140

student proficiency, 137

subgroups, 11, 12, 18, 22, 25, 31, 32, 33, 34, 52, 137

subjectivity, 20, 25

subtraction, 18

suburban, 151, 152, 160

214 Index

supervision, 47
supplemental, 13, 14, 123
supply, 45, 83, 179
support services, 118, 119, 121
support staff, 121
sustainability, 71, 172
synthesis, 5, 138, 145, 147, 152, 155, 156

T

targets, 137, 139, 161, 166, 167, 172, 181, 195
teach to the test, 32
teacher assessment, 101
teacher effectiveness, ix, 58, 59, 60, 61, 62, 63, 64, 65, 66, 67, 68, 69, 70, 71, 73, 74, 75, 89, 90, 100, 104, 133
teacher instruction, 59
teacher performance, viii, 57, 58, 59, 66, 73, 133, 180, 182, 196
teacher preparation, 63, 81, 85, 86, 87, 88, 94, 95, 96, 100, 101, 103, 106, 115, 116, 132, 164, 169, 170, 171, 173, 174, 180, 182, 184, 193, 196
teacher training, x, 82, 106, 110, 115, 121, 165, 166, 168, 171, 172, 174, 179
teaching experience, 45, 47, 174
teaching process, 35
teaching strategies, 138, 151
technical assistance, 38, 92, 98, 103, 108, 115, 124, 133, 171, 191
technology, 27, 79, 95, 110, 116, 124, 184, 188, 199
telecommunication, 113, 114
telephone, 92, 108
TEM, 116
temperature, 30
tenure, 66, 67, 69, 70, 71, 170
test data, 170
test items, 18, 22, 28, 33, 35
test scores, 7, 17, 22, 26, 33, 34, 35, 36, 37, 62, 72, 83, 100, 145, 189
testimony, x, 164, 165, 188, 203, 204
test-retest reliability, 19, 20, 37
therapists, 119
thinking, 8, 17, 29, 103, 136, 144, 145, 147, 189
thoughts, 108
threshold, 118
tics, 116
time consuming, 101
time frame, 35, 145, 155, 156
time series, 157
timing, 6, 34, 66

title, 13
Title I-A, vii, 1, 2, 11, 12, 14, 38, 44, 74
Title II, 54, 85, 90, 92, 94, 132, 133, 164, 165, 166, 167, 168, 169, 170, 171, 173, 174, 180, 181, 182, 184, 185, 195, 200
Title V, 51, 55
tracking, 12, 83
training programs, x, 87, 115, 165, 166, 168, 171, 172, 174
transfer, 169, 174
transformation, 180
transition, 116, 122, 184, 195, 200
transparent, 71, 133
traumatic brain injury, 13
tribal, 119, 120
tribes, 113, 114, 118, 119, 120, 121, 122
tuition, 170, 196
turnover, 54, 181
tutoring, 118

U

U.S. history, 111, 185
uncertainty, 19, 20, 67, 73
undergraduate, 81, 170, 193, 198
uniform, 46, 161, 172
units of analysis, 50
universities, 80, 95, 103, 109, 177, 178, 180, 184, 189
urban areas, 156

V

vacancies, 198, 199
validation, 8, 17, 18, 37
validity, vii, 1, 2, 3, 7, 17, 18, 22, 23, 25, 26, 31, 33, 34, 37, 39, 62, 74, 155
values, 34
variables, 38, 62, 65, 68, 74, 138, 141, 146, 151, 196
variance, 37
vehicles, 93, 97, 200
veteran teachers, 51, 81, 94, 95, 101, 172, 178
video programming, 113, 114
violence, 72
visible, 189
vision, 65, 192
vocabulary, 3
vocational, 46
vocational education, 46

Index

W

war, 97
wealth, 187, 189
web, 193
Wechsler Intelligence Scale, 8
witnesses, 164
women, 119, 122
workers, 81, 113
workforce, 168, 171, 173, 196, 200
working class, 190, 192
working conditions, 45
workplace, 59
World Wide Web, 108
writing, 12, 14, 45, 46, 115, 145

Y

yield, 146, 164, 182, 200